GREAT TRUE ESCAPE STORIES

GREAT TRUE
ESCAPE STORIES

Edited by
FRED URQUHART

ARCO PUBLICATIONS
LONDON

First published 1958
Reprinted 1960

CONTENTS

		PAGE
I.	ESCAPE FROM THE BOERS	7
II.	TRAIN JUMP	21
III.	ESCAPE INTO VICHY FRANCE	32
IV.	ESCAPE FROM ST. HIPPOLYTE DU FORT	43
V.	ESCAPE ACROSS THE U.S. BORDER	52
VI.	ESCAPE FROM TOST BEI GLEIWITZ	67
VII.	ESCAPE FROM SHAMSUIPO	77
VIII.	ESCAPE FROM DEVIL'S ISLAND	87
IX.	ESCAPE FROM INDIA	101
X.	ESCAPE TO SPAIN	108
XI.	THE COFFIN PLAN	116
XII.	ESCAPE FROM THE WULZBURG	123
XIII.	THE GREAT ESCAPE FROM NEWGATE	130
XIV.	THIRD ESCAPE	139
XV.	ESCAPE FROM A CANADIAN GAOL	161
XVI.	ESCAPE INTO LITHUANIA	170
XVII.	ESCAPE FROM THE JAPANESE	183
XVIII.	ATTEMPTED RESCUE FROM MOUNTJOY	199
XIX.	ESCAPE FROM HOSPITAL	204
XX.	ESCAPE INTO RUSSIA	213

I

ESCAPE FROM THE BOERS

from

My Early Life

By WINSTON S. CHURCHILL

Sir Winston Churchill's escape during the South African War, an escape which caused the Boers to put a price on his head and which first made him a national figure, is only one of the many remarkable events in a remarkable career.

At the end of October 1899, Mr. Churchill, as he was at that time, was captured when the Boers ambushed an armoured train, "Wilson's Death Trap", on which he was travelling in his capacity as a war correspondent for the Morning Post. He was incarcerated with military prisoners in the State Model Schools, Pretoria, and, after unsuccessfully trying to persuade his captors that he should be repatriated as a non-combatant, he made up his mind to escape. In the company of Captain Aylmer Haldane and Sergeant-Major A. Brockie, he planned to elude the patrolling sentries, climb the wall surrounding the schools, and make a dash for it. Their attempt to do this on 11 December ended in failure because of the sentries' vigilance. The next day, however, Mr. Churchill managed to get away, the others being unable to follow.

The story of Captain Haldane's eventual escape with Sergeant-Major Brockie and Lieutenant Le Mesurier is told in How We Escaped From Pretoria.

Now or never! I stood on a ledge, seized the top of the wall with my hands, and drew myself up. Twice I let myself down again in sickly hesitation, and then with a third resolve scrambled up and over. My waistcoat got entangled with the ornamental metal-work on the top. I had to pause for an appreciable moment to extricate myself. In this posture I had one parting glimpse of the sentries still talking with their backs turned fifteen yards away. One of them was lighting his cigarette, and I remember the glow on the inside of his hands as a distinct impression which my mind recorded. Then I lowered myself lightly down into the adjoining garden and crouched among the shrubs. I was free! The first step had been taken, and it was irrevocable. It now remained to await the arrival of my comrades. The bushes in the garden gave a good deal of cover, and in the moonlight their shadows fell dark on the ground. I lay here for an hour in great impatience and anxiety. People were continually moving about in the garden, and once a man came and apparently looked straight at me only a few yards away. Where were the others? Why did they not make the attempt?

Suddenly I heard a voice from within the quadrangle say, quite loud, "All up." I crawled back to the wall. Two officers were walking up and down inside, jabbering Latin words, laughing and talking all manner of nonsense—amid which I caught my name. I risked a cough. One of the officers immediately began to chatter alone. The other said, slowly and clearly, "They cannot get out. The sentry suspects. It's all up. Can you get back again?" But now all my fears fell from me at once. To go back was impossible. I could not hope to climb the wall unnoticed. There was no helpful ledge on the outside. Fate pointed onwards. Besides, I said to myself, 'Of course, I shall be recaptured, but I will at least have a run for my money.' I said to the officers, "I shall go on alone."

Now I was in the right mood for these undertakings— failure being almost certain, no odds against success affected me. All risks were less than the certainty. The gate which led into the road was only a few yards from another sentry. I said to myself, *"Toujours de l'audace,"* put my hat on my head, strode into the middle of the garden, walked past the windows of the house without any attempt at concealment, and so went through the gate and turned to the left. I passed the sentry at less than five yards. Most of them knew me by sight. Whether he looked at me or not I do not know, for I never turned my head. I restrained with the utmost difficulty an impulse to run. But after walking a hundred yards and hearing no challenge, I knew that the second obstacle had been surmounted. I was at large in Pretoria.

I walked on leisurely through the night, humming a tune

and choosing the middle of the road. The streets were full
of burghers, but they paid no attention to me. Gradually I
reached the suburbs, and on a little bridge I sat down to
reflect and consider. I was in the heart of the enemy's
country. I knew no one to whom I could apply for succour.
Nearly three hundred miles stretched between me and
Delagoa Bay. My escape must be known at dawn. Pursuit
would be immediate. Yet all exits were barred. The town was
picketed, the country was patrolled, the trains were searched,
the line was guarded. I wore a civilian brown flannel suit.
I had seventy-five pounds in my pocket and four slabs of
chocolate, but the compass and the map which might have
guided me, the opium tablets and meat lozenges which
should have sustained me, were in my friends' pockets in
the State Model Schools. Worst of all, I could not speak a
word of Dutch or Kaffir, and how was I to get food or
direction?

But when hope had departed, fear had gone as well. I
formed a plan. I would find the Delagoa Bay Railway. Without map or compass, I must follow that in spite of the pickets.
I looked at the stars. Orion shone brightly. Scarcely a year
before he had guided me when lost in the desert to the banks
of the Nile. He had given me water. Now he should lead to
freedom. I could not endure the want of either.

After walking south for half a mile I struck the railway.
Was it the line to Delagoa Bay or the Pietersburg branch?
If it were the former, it should run east. But, so far as I could
see, this line ran northwards. Still, it might be only winding
its way out among the hills. I resolved to follow it. The night
was delicious. A cool breeze fanned my face, and a wild feeling of exhilaration took hold of me. At any rate, I was free,
if only for an hour. That was something. The fascination of
the adventure grew. Unless the stars in their courses fought
for me, I could not escape. Where, then, was the need of
caution? I marched briskly along the line. Here and there
the lights of a picket fire gleamed. Every bridge had its
watchers. But I passed them all, making very short détours
at the dangerous places, and really taking scarcely any precautions. Perhaps that was the reason I succeeded.

As I walked I extended my plan. I could not march three
hundred miles to the frontier. I would board a train in

motion and hide under the seats, on the roof, on the couplings—anywhere. I thought of Paul Bultitude's escape from school in *Vice Versa*. I saw myself emerging from under the seat, and bribing or persuading some fat first-class passenger to help me. What train should I take? The first, of course. After walking for two hours I perceived the signal lights of a station. I left the line, and circling round it, hid in the ditch by the track about two hundred yards beyond the platform. I argued that the train would stop at the station and that it would not have got up too much speed by the time it reached me. An hour passed. I began to grow impatient. Suddenly I heard the whistle and the approaching rattle. Then the great yellow head-lights of the engine flashed into view. The train waited five minutes at the station, and started again with much noise and steaming. I crouched by the track. I rehearsed the act in my mind. I must wait until the engine had passed, otherwise I should be seen. Then I must make a dash for the carriages.

The train started slowly, but gathered speed sooner than I had expected. The flaring lights drew swiftly near. The rattle became a roar. The dark mass hung for a second above me. The engine-driver silhouetted against his furnace glow, the black profile of the engine, the clouds of steam rushed past. Then I hurled myself on the trucks, clutched at something, missed, clutched again, missed again, grasped some sort of hand-hold, was swung off my feet—my toes bumping on the line, and with a struggle seated myself on the couplings of the fifth truck from the front of the train. It was a goods train, and the trucks were full of sacks, soft sacks covered with coal-dust. They were in fact bags filled with empty coal-bags going back to their colliery. I crawled on top and burrowed in among them. In five minutes I was completely buried. The sacks were warm and comfortable. Perhaps the engine-driver had seen me rush up to the train and would give the alarm at the next station; on the other hand, perhaps not. Where was the train going to? Where would it be unloaded? Would it be searched? Was it on the Delagoa Bay line? What should I do in the morning? Ah, never mind that. Sufficient for the night was the luck thereof. Fresh plans for fresh contingencies. I resolved to sleep, nor can I imagine a more pleasing lullaby than the clatter of the train that carries an escaping prisoner at twenty miles an hour away from the enemy's capital.

How long I slept I do not know, but I woke up suddenly with all feelings of exhilaration gone, and only the consciousness of oppressive difficulties heavy on me. I must leave the train before daybreak, so that I could drink at a pool and find some hiding-place while it was still dark. I would not run the risk of being unloaded with the coal-bags. Another night I would board another train. I crawled from my cosy hiding-place among the sacks and sat again on the couplings. The train was running at a fair speed, but I felt it was time to leave it. I took hold of the iron handle at the back of the truck, pulled strongly with my left hand, and sprang. My feet struck the ground in two gigantic strides, and the next instant I was sprawling in the ditch considerably shaken but unhurt. The train, my faithful ally of the night, hurried on its journey.

It was still dark. I was in the middle of a wide valley, surrounded by low hills, and carpeted with high grass drenched in dew. I searched for water in the nearest gully, and soon found a clear pool. I was very thirsty, but long after I had drenched my thirst I continued to drink, that I might have sufficient for the whole day.

Presently the dawn began to break, and the sky to the east grew yellow and red, slashed across with heavy black clouds. I saw with relief that the railway line ran steadily towards the sunrise. I had taken the right line, after all.

Having drunk my fill, I set out for the hills, among which I hoped to find some hiding-place, and as it became broad daylight I entered a small grove of trees which grew on the side of a deep ravine. Here I resolved to wait till dusk. I had one consolation: no one in the world knew where I was —I did not know myself. It was now four o'clock. Fourteen hours lay between me and the night. My impatience to proceed while I was still strong doubled their length. At first it was terribly cold, but by degrees the sun gained power, and by ten o'clock the heat was oppressive. My sole companion was a gigantic vulture, who manifested an extravagant interest in my condition, and made hideous and ominous gurglings from time to time. From my lofty position I commanded a view of the whole valley. A little tin-roofed town

lay three miles to the westward. Scattered farmsteads, each
with a clump of trees, relieved the monotony of the undula-
ting ground. At the foot of the hill stood a Kaffir kraal, and
the figures of its inhabitants dotted the patches of cultiva-
tion or surrounded the droves of goats and cows which fed
on the pasture. . . . During the day I ate one slab of chocolate,
which, with the heat, produced a violent thirst. The pool was
hardly half a mile away, but I dared not leave the shelter of
the little wood, for I could see the figures of white men riding
or walking occasionally across the valley, and once a Boer
came and fired two shots at birds close to my hiding-place. But
no one discovered me.

The elation and the excitement of the previous night had
burnt away, and a chilling reaction followed. I was very
hungry, for I had had no dinner before starting, and chocolate, though it sustains, does not satisfy. I had scarcely slept,
but yet my heart beat so fiercely and I was so nervous and
perplexed about the future that I could not rest. I thought
of all the chances that lay against me; I dreaded and detested
more than words can express the prospect of being caught
and dragged back to Pretoria. I found no comfort in any of
the philosophical ideas which some men parade in their
hours of ease and strength and safety. They seemed only
fair-weather friends. I realized with awful force that no
exercise of my own feeble wit and strength could save me
from my enemies, and that without the assistance of that
High Power which interferes in the eternal sequence of
causes and effects more often than we are always prone to
admit, I could never succeed. I prayed long and earnestly for
help and guidance. My prayer, as it seems to me, was swiftly
and wonderfully answered.

During the day I watched the railway with attention. I
saw two or three trains pass along it each way. I argued that
the same number would pass at night. I resolved to board
one of these. I thought I could improve on my procedure of
the previous evening. I had observed how slowly the trains,
particularly long goods-trains, climbed some of the steep
gradients. Sometimes they were hardly going at a foot's pace.
It would probably be easy to choose a point where the line
was not only on an up grade but also on a curve. Thus I could

board some truck on the convex side of the train when both
the engine and the guard's van were bent away, and when
consequently neither the engine-driver nor the guard would
see me. This plan seemed to me in every respect sound. I saw
myself leaving the train again before dawn, having been
carried forward another sixty or seventy miles during the
night. That would be scarcely one hundred and fifty miles
from the frontier. And why should not the process be
repeated? Where was the flaw? I could not see it. With three
long bounds on three successive nights I could be in Portu-
guese territory. Meanwhile I still had two or three slabs of
chocolate and a pocketful of crumbled biscuit—enough,
that is to say, to keep body and soul together at a pinch without running the awful risk of recapture entailed by accosting
a single human being. In this mood I watched with increasing
impatience the arrival of darkness.

The long day reached its close at last. The western clouds
flushed into fire; the shadows of the hills stretched out across
the valley; a ponderous Boer wagon with its long team
crawled slowly along the track towards the township, the
Kaffirs collected their herds and drew them round their kraal;
the daylight died, and soon it was quite dark. Then, and not
until then, I set forth. I hurried to the railway line, scrambling along through the boulders and high grass and pausing
on my way to drink at a stream of sweet cold water. I made
my way to the place where I had seen the trains crawling so
slowly up the slope, and soon found a point where the curve
of the track fulfilled all the conditions of my plan. Here,
behind a little bush, I sat down and waited hopefully. An
hour passed; two hours passed; three hours—and yet no train.
Six hours had now elapsed since the last, whose time I had
carefully noted, had gone by. Surely one was due. Another
hour slipped away. Still no train! My plan began to crumble
and my hopes to ooze. After all, was it not quite possible that
no trains ran on this part of the line during the dark hours?
This was in fact the case, and I might well have continued
to wait in vain till daylight. However, between twelve and
one in the morning I lost patience and started along the track,
resolved to cover at any rate ten or fifteen miles of my
journey. I did not make much progress. Every bridge was
guarded by armed men; every few miles were huts. At

intervals there were stations with tin-roofed villages clustering around them. All the veldt was bathed in the bright rays of the full moon, and to avoid these dangerous places I had to make wide circuits and even to creep along the ground. Leaving the railroad I fell into bogs and swamps, brushed through high grass dripping with dew, and waded across the streams over which the bridges carried the railway. I was soon drenched to the waist. I had been able to take very little exercise during my month's imprisonment, and I was quickly tired with walking and with want of food and sleep. Presently I approached a station. It was a mere platform in the veldt, with two or three buildings and huts around it. But laid up on the sidings, obviously for the night, were three long goods-trains. Evidently the flow of traffic over the railway was uneven. These three trains, motionless in the moonlight, confirmed my fears that traffic was not maintained by night on this part of the line. Where, then, was my plan which in the afternoon had looked so fine and sure?

It now occurred to me that I might board one of these stationary trains immediately, and hiding amid its freight be carried forward during the next day—and night too if all were well. On the other hand, where were they going to? Where would they stop? Where would they be unloaded? Once I entered a wagon my lot would be cast. I might find myself ignominiously unloaded and recaptured at Witbank or Middelburg, or at any station in the long two hundred miles which separated me from the frontier. It was necessary at all costs before taking such a step to find out where these trains were going. To do this I must penetrate the station, examine the labels on the trucks or on the merchandise, and see if I could extract any certain guidance from them. I crept up to the platform and got between two of the long trains on the siding. I was proceeding to examine the markings on the trucks when loud voices rapidly approaching on the outside of the trains filled me with fear. Several Kaffirs were laughing and shouting in their unmodulated tones, and I heard, as I thought, a European voice arguing or ordering. At any rate, it was enough for me. I retreated between the two trains to the extreme end of the siding, and slipped stealthily but rapidly into the grass of the illimitable plain.

There was nothing for it but to plod on—but in an

increasingly purposeless and hopeless manner. I felt very miserable when I looked around and saw here and there the lights of houses and thought of the warmth and comfort within them, but knew that they meant only danger to me. Far off on the moonlit horizon there presently began to shine the row of six or eight big lights which marked either Witbank or Middelburg station. Out in the darkness to my left gleamed two or three fires. I was sure they were not the lights of houses, but how far off they were or what they were I could not be certain. The idea formed in my mind that they were the fires of a Kaffir kraal. Then I began to think that the best use I could make of my remaining strength would be to go to these Kaffirs. I had heard that they hated the Boers and were friendly to the British. At any rate, they would probably not arrest me. They might give me food and a dry corner to sleep in. Although I could not speak a word of their language, yet I thought perhaps they might understand the value of a British banknote. They might even be induced to help me. A guide, a pony—but above all, rest, warmth, and food—such were the promptings which dominated my mind. So I set forth towards the fires.

I must have walked a mile or so in this resolve before a realization of its weakness and imprudence took possession of me. Then I turned back again to the railway line and retraced my steps perhaps half the distance. Then I stopped and sat down, completely baffled, destitute of any idea what to do or where to turn. Suddenly without the slightest reason all my doubts disappeared. It was certainly by no process of logic that they were dispelled. I just felt quite clear that I would go to the Kaffir kraal. I had sometimes in former years held a 'Planchette' pencil and written while others had touched my wrist or hand. I acted in exactly the same unconscious or subconscious manner now.

I walked on rapidly towards the fires, which I had in the first instance thought were not more than a couple of miles from the railway line. I soon found they were much farther away than that. After about an hour or an hour and a half, they still seemed almost as far off as ever. But I persevered, and presently between two and three o'clock in the morning I perceived that they were not the fires of a Kaffir kraal. The angular outline of buildings began to draw out against them, and soon I saw that I was approaching a group of houses around the mouth of a coal-mine. The wheel which worked the winding gear was plainly visible, and I could see that the fires which had led me so far were from the furnaces of the engines. Hard by, surrounded by one or two slighter structures, stood a small but substantial stone house two storeys high.

I halted in the wilderness to survey this scene and to revolve my action. It was still possible to turn back. But in that direction I saw nothing but the prospect of further futile wanderings terminated by hunger, fever, discovery, or surrender. On the other hand, here in front was a chance. I had heard it said before I escaped that in the mining district of Witbank and Middelburg there were a certain number of English residents who had been suffered to remain in the country in order to keep the mines working. Had I been led to one of these? What did this house which frowned dark and inscrutable upon me contain? A Briton or a Boer; a friend or a foe? Nor did this exhaust the possibilities. I had my seventy-five pounds in English notes in my pocket. If I revealed my identity, I thought that I could give reasonable assurance of a thousand. I might find some indifferent neutral-minded person who out of good-nature or for a large sum of money would aid me in my bitter and desperate need. Certainly I would try to make what bargain I could now— now while I still had the strength to plead my cause and perhaps extricate myself if the results were adverse. Still the odds were heavy against me, and it was with faltering and reluctant steps that I walked out of the shimmering gloom of the veldt into the light of the furnace fires, advanced towards the silent house, and struck with my fist upon the door.

There was a pause. Then I knocked again. And almost immediately a light sprang up above and an upper window opened.

"*Wer ist da?*" cried a man's voice.

I felt the shock of disappointment and consternation to my fingers.

"I want help; I have had an accident," I replied.

Some muttering followed. Then I heard steps descending the stairs, the bolt of the door was drawn, the lock was turned. It was opened abruptly, and in the darkness of the passage, a tall man hastily attired, with a pale face and dark moustache, stood before me.

"What do you want?" he said, this time in English.

I had now to think of something to say. I wanted above all to get into parley with this man, to get matters in such a state that instead of raising an alarm and summoning others he would discuss things quietly.

"I am a burgher," I began. "I have had an accident. I was going to join my commando at Komati Poort. I have fallen off the train. We were skylarking. I have been unconscious for hours. I think I have dislocated my shoulder."

It is astonishing how one thinks of these things. This story leapt out as if I had learned it by heart. Yet I had not the slightest idea what I was going to say or what the next sentence would be.

The stranger regarded me intently, and after some hesitation said at length, "Well, come in." He retreated a little into the darkness of the passage, threw open a door on one side of it, and pointed with his left hand into a dark room. I walked past him and entered, wondering if it was to be my prison. He followed, struck a light, lit a lamp, and set it on the table at the far side of which I stood. I was in a small room, evidently a dining-room and office in one. I noticed besides the large table, a roll desk, two or three chairs, and one of those machines for making soda-water, consisting of two glass globes set one above the other and encased in thin wire-netting. On his end of the table my host had laid a revolver, which he had hitherto presumably been holding in his right hand.

"I think I'd like to know a little more about this railway accident of yours," he said, after a considerable pause.

"I think," I replied, "I had better tell you the truth."

"I think you had," he said, slowly.

So I took the plunge and threw all I had upon the board.

"I am Winston Churchill, war-correspondent of the *Morning Post*. I escaped last night from Pretoria. I am making my way to the frontier." (Making my way!) "I have plenty of money. Will you help me?"

There was another long pause. My companion rose from the table slowly and locked the door. After this act, which struck me as unpromising, and was certainly ambiguous, he advanced upon me and suddenly held out his hand.

"Thank God you have come here! It is the only house for twenty miles where you would not have been handed over. But we are all British here, and we will see you through."

It is easier to recall across the gulf of years the spasm of relief which swept over me, than it is to describe it. A moment before I had thought myself trapped; and now friends, food, resources, aid were all at my disposal. I felt like a drowning man pulled out of the water and informed that he has won the Derby!

My host now introduced himself as Mr. John Howard, manager of the Transvaal Collieries. He had become a naturalized burgher of the Transvaal some years before the war. But out of consideration for his British race and some inducements which he had offered to the local Field Cornet, he had not been called up to fight against the British. Instead, he had been allowed to remain with one or two others on the mine, keeping it pumped out and in good order until coal-cutting could be resumed. He had with him at the mine-head, besides his secretary, who was British, an engineman from Lancashire and two Scottish miners. All these four were British subjects and had been allowed to remain only upon giving their parole to observe strict neutrality. He himself as burgher of the Transvaal Republic would be guilty of treason in harbouring me, and liable to be shot if caught at the time or found out later on.

"Never mind," he said, "we will fix it up somehow." And added, "The Field Cornet was around here this afternoon asking about you. They have got the hue and cry out all along the line and all over the district."

I said that I did not wish to compromise him.

Let him give me food, a pistol, a guide, and if possible a pony, and I would make my own way to the sea, marching by night across country far away from the railway line or any habitation.

He would not hear of it. He would fix up something. But he enjoined the utmost caution. Spies were everywhere. He had two Dutch servant-maids actually sleeping in the house. There were many Kaffirs employed about the mine premises and on the pumping machinery of the mine. Surveying these dangers, he became very thoughtful.

Then: "But you are famishing."

I did not contradict him. In a moment he had bustled off into the kitchen, telling me meanwhile to help myself from a whisky bottle and the soda-water machine which I had already mentioned. He returned after an interval with the best part of a cold leg of mutton and various other delectable commodities, and, leaving me to do full justice to these, quitted the room and let himself out of the house by a back door.

Nearly an hour passed before Mr. Howard returned. In this period my physical well-being had been brought into harmony with the improvement in my prospects. I felt confident of success and equal to anything.

"It's all right," said Mr. Howard. "I have seen the men, and they are all for it. We must put you down the pit tonight, and there you will have to stay till we can see how to get you out of the country. One difficulty," he said, "will be the *skoff* (food). The Dutch girl sees every mouthful I eat. The cook will want to know what has happened to her leg of mutton. I shall have to think it all out during the night. You must get down the pit at once. We'll make you comfortable enough."

Accordingly, just as the dawn was breaking, I followed my host across a little yard into the enclosure in which stood the winding-wheel of the mine. Here a stout man, introduced as Mr. Dewsnap, of Oldham, locked my hand in a grip of crushing vigour.

"They'll all vote for you next time," he whispered.

A door was opened and I entered the cage. Down we shot into the bowels of the earth. At the bottom of the mine were the two Scottish miners with lanterns and a big bundle which afterwards proved to be a mattress and blankets. We walked for some time through the pitchy labyrinth, with frequent turns, twists, and alterations of level, and finally stopped in a sort of chamber where the air was cool and fresh. Here my guide set down his bundle, and Mr. Howard handed me a couple of candles, a bottle of whisky, and a box of cigars.

"There's no difficulty about these," he said. "I keep them

under lock and key. Now we must plan how to feed you tomorrow."

"Don't you move from here, whatever happens," was the parting injunction. "There will be Kaffirs about the mine after daylight, but we shall be on the look-out that none of them wanders this way. None of them has seen anything so far."

My four friends trooped off with the lanterns, and I was left alone. Viewed from the velvety darkness of the pit, life seemed bathed in rosy light. After the perplexity and even despair through which I had passed I counted upon freedom as certain. Instead of a humiliating recapture and long months of monotonous imprisonment, probably in the common gaol, I saw myself once more rejoining the Army with a real exploit to my credit, and in that full enjoyment of freedom and keen pursuit of adventure dear to the heart of youth. In this comfortable mood, and speeded by intense fatigue. I soon slept the sleep of the weary—but of the triumphant.

II

TRAIN JUMP

from

Horned Pigeon

By GEORGE MILLAR

*Captured early in the war in North Africa, George
Millar, a lieutenant in a tank regiment, was imprisoned first
in Campo 66 in Italy, and then in an old monastery. After
making several unsuccessful attempts to escape, he was taken
to Stalag VIIA in Germany. On being transferred to another
Stalag, Millar and his friend, Wally Binns, made the successful escape told here.*

*They reached Munich, where they contacted sympathizers,
and later made a nightmare journey with eight escaping
Frenchmen in a railway wagon to Alsace. Jumping from
the train in a marshalling yard outside Strasbourg, they got
separated. Binns was recaptured, only to escape again.
Helped by members of the French Resistance, Millar
eventually reached England safely.*

*Afterwards he became a British Agent and was parachuted
into France to work with the Resistance, adventures which
he has written about in* Maquis.

THE compounds were separated by double fences of long-
pronged barbed wire stretched on oak saplings 14 ft. high.
Between each double fence was an 8-ft.-wide strip of criss-
cross low wire with loose barbed wire laid on the top. Almost
every evening a party of Russians, some of them officers,
climbed over this formidable obstacle to visit us. Twice when
I watched them climbing German sentries fired either at
them or in their direction. The Russians had no leather
gloves, and some of them were torn about the hands and
bodies. They cheerfully settled down in our hut to eat bully
beef and bread and jam, and drink tea. They were very pro-

fessionally-minded, with a great liking for discussions on the design and equipment of tanks and aircraft, or the weaknesses and strengths of their own and the German army. After tea they would ask us, as though to pay for the meal, whether we wanted lonely, sad songs, or joyous ones. The lonely, sad ones were the best.

These were exceptional men. Only the exceptional Russian prisoners had survived the journey from the Eastern front to Moosburg. They had been packed sixty-five to a cattle-truck. The doors had been shut in Russia and opened anything up to three weeks later at Moosburg. Many of them said that they had been obliged to eat their dead comrades. Their hatred and enmity for our common enemy were very terrible to see, particularly as hatred and enmity seemed to sit ill on these humorous men always ready to laugh at themselves or at us. Some of them had faces unimaginably scarred by wounds that had never been dressed or treated. They swaggered about, apparently unconscious of their man-made ugliness, or else supremely conscious of it, flaunting it like a banner.

The French spoke seriously of the Alsatian dogs that were led around by guards. They claimed that they had photographs secretly taken which showed that the dogs had been set on their comrades and had torn them about the throats and arms. But the Russians only laughed at the dogs; and indeed there was something excruciatingly funny about the strutting German with the ultra-fierce animal on a chain or a leather thong. Sometimes when you passed them the dogs would spring at you with bared fangs, only to be dragged back by his admiring jack-booted master.

The Russians told us that shortly before we arrived the Germans turned one dog loose in the Russian compound at night. The following day no trace of the dog could be found, not a tooth, not a hair from its coat. That night the Germans left a *Feldwebel* and two dogs in the compound. Next day one dog was found unharmed. "The other dog and the pig will never be found," said my informant.

I saw that George Sukas was working as I did at Moosburg, making friends with the French. Far from worrying me, this put me in good heart. George was a very intelligent customer, and I felt that I must be working on the right lines.

After three days of hard work, long talks about France, French guests for meals, I began to strike oil. I struck it in the person of one Robert Cahin, a Lorrain, a young and wealthy grain merchant from Metz. Cahin was an interpreter. He naturally spoke good German. He had been shut up at Moosburg since the fall of France, with two breaks when he had escaped. Each time he had been picked up near his home.

"It is very difficult at my home," he said sadly. "There are so many Boches in Lorraine, and some of our own people are bad too, though not many."

He and I took an instant liking to each other, which made things easy. Nevertheless, Cahin was most cautious. I saw from the first that he was not quite sure of me, and that gave me confidence in him. On the third day, when Wally had already completed our wardrobes of civilian clothes, Cahin began actively to help.

First he found me German money. It was forbidden in the Stalag to have anything but camp money, but the black market was so developed, and so many of the prisoners went outside each day on working parties, that there was no scarcity of ordinary marks. On the other hand, the civilian marks were highly prized, and it was difficult for two newcomers to get hold of them. We had sold a complete Red Cross parcel to some Poles for 100 marks (a ridiculously low price, but we did not know that then). Now I asked Cahin if he could dispose of my watch. That same evening he sold it for 250 marks to a German officer. Next day he sold two pairs of shoes and some clothing and food for us. I then had 500 marks and Wally had 300—quite enough money to get us out of the country, we hoped.

I discussed escape again and again with Cahin until finally he took pity on me and spoke of a party of French *sous-officers*, all friends of his, who had frequently refused to work on the land or in factories, but who, despite their protests, had been moved to work at a railway siding in Munich. From there they had sent a message to Cahin that if anyone in whom he had absolute confidence wanted to escape he might give that person their address.

Cahin gave me the following instructions:

"When you arrive in Munich, find the main station, the *Hauptbahnhof*. Face the front of the station, then take the

road on the left of the façade which follows the lines of the
railway. Shortly after crossing the first street crossing you will
see a railway yard in which French prisoners in uniform will
be working. Approach them most tactfully when no Boches
are watching and ask in French: 'Are you *Arbeitskommando
2903?*' If they answer: 'Yes, 2903 from Moosburg,' you must
tell them frankly that you are a British officer sent to them by
Robert Cahin."

He explained that the plan these *Arbeitskommando*
workers usually followed for getting people out of Germany
was to stow them secretly in railway wagons which were sealed
in the siding, and which then crossed the frontier
unexamined as far as Strasbourg, the main city of Alsace.
Although Strasbourg was apparently more German than
French, and since the battle of France Alsace and Lorraine
had been incorporated inside the frontiers of the Reich itself,
the population was mainly pro-French, Cahin believed (and
so did I).

Cahin also gave me excellent Michelin maps of Germany
from Munich to the Rhine and of Alsace and Lorraine
beyond that river. He would accept nothing in return for all
his precious gifts.

Not quite satisfied with Cahin's address, I moved about
continually among the French in the time that remained at
Stalag VIIA, and I succeeded in getting two other addresses.
Both belonged to Paris prostitutes imported by the Germans
originally to work in Munich factories. I decided that the
railway workers were the better bet, since the women would
not necessarily have any means of getting us away from
Munich.

We now set ourselves to finding a good way out of the
Stalag, but all the ways offered to us either by the French or
the Americans (the two richest groups of prisoners and therefore the ones who knew most about the venal German guards)
were uncertain, and necessitated a good deal of ground work
to build them into sound propositions. Neither of us was prepared to throw away all that we had gained in the Stalag on
some attempt that might be expected to fail. We had never
been so well equipped in Italy.

American prisoners, who at regular intervals bribed the
German sentries with an entire Red Cross parcel to let one of

their number out, told us that the recapture system at Moosburg was highly developed. The Stalag sat in the middle of an agricultural plain which offered few facilities for hiding, the peasants were unfriendly, and there existed a special pack of police dogs and human sleuths for trailing escaped prisoners.

On our fifth day there John de Jago, who was living in the hospital, went out of the front gate with a party of French prisoners who were going for their fortnightly walk. The Frenchmen hid him among them until they sat down in a wood to rest. Jago was able to crawl unobserved to the other side of the wood, whence he struck the main Munich road. He was dressed in civilian clothes, but in the first town he came to, Freising, some twelve miles from the Stalag, he was stopped by a plain-clothes policeman and brought back to the Stalag. He was courteously treated by the German commandant, and was given only ten days' cells as a punishment.

I had swung more and more to the theory that jumping from a train presented the best method of escape. If you got out of a camp there was an immediate hunt, and the camp had full facilities such as ready constituted and equipped search-parties, telephones, and so on. If you jumped from a train there was bound to be a delay in beginning the hunt, and they might be uncertain at which point you had begun your escape. Wally and I decided that we would jump from the train as soon as possible after leaving Moosburg station. We had been told that we should be going north, so we presumed that we should have to walk some distance to get back to Munich. George Sukas and Buck Palm, I observed (although of course we never discussed the matter with them), had also succeeded with their new French friends. George and Buck were living in hiding in the camp. They wore French uniforms, and they lived in the French compound. They never attended roll-calls. Among the remainder of our group I saw no signs of serious preparation or competition.

Early in the morning of Tuesday, 28 September, our party was told it must move at once to be searched and then to take the train. Carrying our luggage, we marched in column of threes to the big searching hut just inside the gates of the Stalag.

Our Italian rucksacks were innocent enough on the

surface, but underneath they contained all our escaping
equipment and clothing.

The searching-shed looked efficient, a long bare room
with a line of tables down one side, and German N.C.O.s,
stiff and smart, standing like *douaniers* behind the tables.

This was a crucial moment for Wally Binns and for me.
The first person to be searched, Tony Hay, had a saw and
some civilian marks taken out of his socks. But we had a plan.

Accustomed by this time to bribing German sentries at
Stalag VIIA, I intended to bribe one more German to get my
escaping gear out of the camp. Binns, who had led a more
sheltered life inside the Stalag, and who had more nerve, disliked the idea of bribing, and determined to slip the search.
Neither of us could have begun to take such liberties in an
Italian camp.

There was a general air of polished efficiency about the
searching-shed. An officer swaggered up and down the centre
of the floor. Poor officer! Although he shouted and stamped
and was absolutely unafraid of his men, he was quite incom-
petent. His mind was sliding about among the surface do's
and dont's. God bless him!

I was careful to get to the front of the second batch of
officers to be searched. From that position I was able to
examine the faces of the Germans doing the searching, and
I soon picked out the one who looked the most dishonest and
perfunctory. As soon as this *Feldwebel* had finished with his
first officer I seized my greatcoat and rucksack and hurried
across the concrete floor to him.

The German undid the lacing at the mouth of my rucksack. A few handkerchiefs were neatly packed on the top.
Delicately moving the handkerchiefs, he found a new
packet of Camel cigarettes. As soon as he found them I knew
that I was all right.

He shot a quick glance round the searching-shed, then his
blue eyes came back to flicker into mine. I nodded very, very
slightly. His hand flickered as quickly as his eyes, and the
packet of Camels was gone. For the next five minutes his
hands, buried in my rucksack, turned my camel-hair blanket
over and over, pretending to probe the secrets of my wardrobe.

When I joined the group of prisoners who had been

searched I found that several, like Tony Hay, had lost
escaping equipment. But Wally had managed, unobserved
by the cloddish Germans, to change himself over from the
group about to be searched to the group of those who had
been searched. The searching took a long time. When we
were finally marched out I found that I was sweating and
shaking with nerves. So very much had depended on the last
hour, and all had gone well.

We were halted in column of threes by the main gates.
Wally and I occasionally grinned at each other, like small
boys about to get into mischief. Jago came past to say good-
bye, on his way to the prison gaol-house to do time for his
escape. Alasdair (Baron) Cram stood in the file ahead of us,
his head swathed in bandages. He had managed to escape
from the hospital on the way to the Brenner, but he really
had been ill. His illness had got worse in the cold and the
wet. Then he had been caught by Austrian volunteers with
the letters S.O.D. on their arms. These men belonged to one
of the angry sections of the Tyrolean population. With the
Italian Armistice they had come raiding across the frontier
behind the waves of German troops. They had beaten the
Baron shamefully, and had nearly murdered him. The
greatest thing about Cram (and he was a very exceptional
man) was the philosophic way in which he took his failures.
He was smiling and enjoying a conversation with one of the
German guards who handed us out our travelling rations,
sour bread and a kind of sausage.

Far down the central roadway of the camp I could see an
enormous man in extremely tight American overalls. That
was Richard Carr, who had changed places with a sergeant in
the American Army Air Corps. The sergeant, whose name,
funnily enough, was Millar, wanted to see what prison life
was like as a British officer. They had completely exchanged
identities. The Americans had promised to buy Richard his
way out of the camp once our party was well away.

Wally and I ate our bread and *würst* immediately, at the
gate and on the way to the station, all of it. We were carrying
plenty of food. I saw at once that our time in the Stalag,
thanks to Wally's insistence on regular exercise and pressure
feeding, had given me back all the feeble strength with which
sparing nature endowed me. Wally also felt good. He said

that if necessary he would tear the train apart with his hands. But we had all the necessary tools.

When we neared the siding we saw to our disgust that we were to travel in third-class carriages instead of cattle-trucks. Carriages were usually the more difficult proposition for escape, since they always put guards inside them. There were two carriages. The first was divided into small compartments, each capable of holding eight people. The second was divided into two large compartments with a lavatory between them, in the centre of the carriage.

We climbed into one of the smaller compartments, then, seeing that the brigadier and the more senior officers were doing the same thing, and fearing that the enemy would put a sentry in each eight-seater, we struggled out with our baggage and went to the other carriage. In our compartment there we found three sentries and about eight other officers, all close friends of ours. We immediately saw that the central lavatory might offer good possibilities for a jump.

Before the train started we got down to relieve ourselves on the wheels and to say good-bye to Brigadier Clifton.

"George and I have been trying on and off for about twenty months," Wally said. "And this time we'll manage it."

The brigadier gave us a glint from his savage little eye.

"It may not be so easy," he said. "It seldom is."

"The brig. is going to jump for it too," Wally said to me as we climbed back into the train.

"Yes," I answered. "Obviously."

(And he did try, we learned later, but he was shot, wounded, and recaptured.)

This trip went well for us from the beginning.

Our three German guards, instead of distributing their persons about the compartment so that they could control everything that went on, sat together at the end farthest from the lavatory. They were a sleepy trio, and one of them was a weak-chinned Austrian who said that he was very tired indeed of the war and everything else.

Wally and I established immediately with Nugent Cairns, the senior officer in that coach, that we should be allowed to make the first jump. We next examined the window of the lavatory, and found that while it would not willingly open enough to let a man out, Binns, with his great strength, could easily force it when the occasion arose.

Last, and most wonderful of all, the train did not go north, but chugged south towards Munich. We had never expected such a piece of luck. Perhaps we owed it to R.A.F. bombing. It was obvious now that we were going south until we could be shunted on to the main Munich-Kassell line. Our destination, the guards told Wally, was an ancient fortress at Kassel.

"Oh, no it's not," Wally replied in English. Neither he nor I could keep still. All the way to Munich we were on tenterhooks. The train ran slowly, at a speed that would have invited jumping had it not been a bright day with good visibility. And there was scarcely a vestige of cover beside the line. At some points, when we ran through beautiful, but thin, pine-woods, the temptation to jump was almost overwhelming. But common sense prevailed, and we made up our minds to wait for darkness.

A strapping German Red Cross nurse gave us scientific cardboard cups holding sweet ersatz coffee and barley broth in the marshalling yard south of Munich, where we finally halted. Binns and I drank as much as we could hold, hoping that hot stomachs would make us feel sleepy. The German guards, to their disgust, were taken out of the warm carriages and placed in a ring around them. We were told that any officer who so much as put his head out of the window would be shot, and that we would move on, attached to a goods train, at eight o'clock that evening.

We composed ourselves to try to sleep, but we had little chance of doing so. Other people now approached Cairns for permission to escape whenever we left the marshalling yard. Cairns was firm with all of them when I had told him that we were extremely well equipped, and that, as well as having money and maps, we had an address to go to. It began to rain hard, and a brisk south-west wind drove the raindrops fiercely against our windows.

Many of the occupants of the carriage had influenza or bad colds, results of the long and draughty journey from Italy. None of them had stuffed themselves with food as we had both done at the Stalag, and it seemed that only two of them were really serious about facing the elements. They were South Africans,

Karl Koelges and Alec Wuth. The former, who had in a former attempt actually reached the frontier wire at Chiasso, was a friend of mine; and after fighting hard with my selfish nature, I gave him our address in Munich, pass-word and all. Koelges and Wuth very decently agreed that they had less chance than our pair of getting clear away, and we promised not to lock the lavatory door so that they could follow us whenever we had jumped.

We said good-bye to all the others while the train was still in the siding, and bequeathed our rucksacks and the big food suitcase to Tony Hay and his partner Dudley Schofield. Both of them were fevered and ill. Cairns, generous soul, disposed the others about the compartment to mask as much as possible our entry to the lavatory. No sooner had these pre-cautions been completed than the guards climbed in to take their old seat at the end. The train moved out, gathering speed all too quickly, it seemed to me. The time was 8.52.

Binns walked into the lavatory. I crawled between his feet, so that the guards if they were bothering to look would only see one man go in. I shut the door and locked it while Binns, without apparent effort, tore down part of the wooden window-frame and forced the sliding window wide enough to let even his broad body through. In an instant he had placed his two hands on a ledge above the window and had shot his legs through into the night. When I had unlocked the door no part of Binns was visible. I climbed through more gingerly. It was damnably cold, wet, and noisy outside. When I let myself down to the full extent of my arms my feet found a step. Feeling round with my hands I caught hold of a door-handle, and crouched on the step beside Wally. The train was going too fast to make jumping at all pleasant. At intervals telegraph-poles whisked past our noses with a blowing noise, like seals coming up to breathe on a pitch-dark night. I was shuddering with cold and fear, and was extremely glad that the powerful and strong-minded Wally was beside me. I reminded myself that the essential was to keep loose when I launched myself. Wally handed me the haversack which was our total baggage for that trip.

"Right! Jump!" he shouted. The crash of his landing sounded like tons of coals going down a chute at London Docks. I threw the haversack after him. Then I jumped.

Instead of hitting something very solid, as I had anticipated, I found myself doing neck rolls down a granite chip embankment. I came to rest in a little gully. The wheels of the train rolled past twelve feet above me. And on the other side a high embankment of loose stones mounted steeply. My eyes were getting used to the dark.

It was a long train. I lay still until the last wagon with its red light had rounded a bend, and suddenly the night was silent. Then I heard the crunch of stones and saw Wally's white raincoat approaching. He had found the haversack.

We climbed the embankment and saw on the other side a large area of allotments. Binns stood, a stocky figure peering out into the rain, his torso leaning slightly forward on his steady hips, his big feet making a wide angle.

"Well, damn your eyes," he said. "We made it."

It was stifling, suffocating, wonderful to be free.

III

ESCAPE INTO VICHY FRANCE

from

Wait for the Dawn

By Derrick Nabarro

*Shot down over the German coastline in June 1941,
Flight Lieutenant Derrick Nabarro, at that time a Sergeant
Pilot, escaped from a German prison camp and made his
way, dressed as a civilian, across France, his goal being
Gibraltar. He reached Paris, where he was helped by a girl
called Katrina, who put him on a train for Nevers.*

*After the incident related below, he was captured by
Vichy gendarmes and imprisoned, like so many other
escapees, in St. Hippolyte du Fort, from which he eventually
escaped and reached Gibraltar safely.*

*Wait For The Dawn is the story of his series of escapes,
for which he received the D.C.M., the first to be awarded to
the R.A.F.*

★

My thoughts sped faster than the train that was taking me to
Nevers, the base for crossing the demarcation line into Free
France. Once over that line and I would be out of German
Occupied Europe.

Earlier in the morning, Katrina had escorted me to the
station. There had been no farewell promises, just a smile,
a kiss, and a doubtful *au revoir*. I knew I should never forget
her, but I could not stay behind, nor could she leave Paris, so
we parted.

The train clattered on, over the long stretches of smooth
rails, over junctions, through stations. I wondered if Pierre
would be at Nevers in the first café on the way to the town
centre. I could not make up my mind about Pierre. There
were times when I despised him, when I thought he hated
me and all Englishmen. He had swallowed too much German
propaganda, he thought England would always fight to the
last drop of French blood. Reason warned me to be cautious,

32

not to trust him too much. Yet I could not believe he would
betray me.

There had been no check and, as I left the station, I saw
our rendezvous. I walked into the bar and ordered a coffee.
In the mirror behind the counter I saw Pierre's reflection.

"I expected you on this train," he said as I joined him;
"have you still the compass?"

I nodded.

"Good," he said, "we can start immediately."

"What's the plan?" I asked.

"While you've been enjoying yourself in Paris with some
woman or other I've been working," he laughed. There was
an undertone of bitterness in his voice.

"What do you mean with some woman or other?" I asked.

"Come off it," he said, "all you English are the same when
you get to Paris. You meet some prostitute no Frenchman
would touch and think you are the great Don Juan. How
those women must laugh when you are gone!"

"What's the plan?" I asked. He bent forward and looked
at the table. He only seemed to look me in the eye when he
was saying something derogatory about the English.

"South of here," he said, "is a wood which stretches across
the line. It's safe enough to pass through at certain times. On
the other side is Free France."

"How big is the wood?"

"Three or four kilometres where we cut through, that's
why we need the compass. You'd better let me have it so we
can start immediately." I handed it over. He had done all
the work, he knew the way, so he should lead. That was fair
enough.

We walked to a garage, climbed into a taxi and were
driven to a small village a few kilometres to the south. Pierre
had been busy, I thought. We had a drink in a café. We were
waiting for three o'clock.

The clouds were building up for rain as we left the café.
We cut round the back of the main street. A signpost at the
cross-roads pointed to Bourges, twenty-five kilometres away.
Ahead lay the promised wood.

"Now listen," said Pierre, "we go south-west from here.
A mile farther on we come to a path. We turn left by the path
and follow parallel to it out of the wood. There should be no

C

German patrols now. Nevertheless we must take no chances. I will lead the way. You follow behind, about twenty metres. You understand?"

"Yes," I said. "Let's start."

Pierre took the lead. I could hear a faint rustling as he brushed through the undergrowth. Occasionally I saw his head as he turned round to see where I was. I trod on a branch. The report echoed guiltily through the trees. Pierre turned round, his face red and angry as he waved me to hide and ducked down himself. I sank to my knees and waited. Nothing happened. Time passed, but there was no sign of Pierre. My eyes were focused on the spot where he had dropped. I moved slowly forward, to where I had seen him disappear but there was no sign of him. At last, after a long time, I realized that waiting any longer would be futile. He had the compass. Normally I could have found the direction but the sun was blotted out by clouds. I examined some tree-trunks. Moss was supposed to grow on the northern side, but French moss had no sense of direction, it grew all round the boles. I remembered which way the clouds had been blowing across the tree-tops, that was all I had to go by, and the wind might easily have changed. I moved forward slowly, looking for the path, listening for noises. A gloomy hush settled over the forest. A fine drizzle dampened the air. Not a bird sang. I could hear the silence. It beat on my ear-drums until I wanted to shout to reassure myself. Then in a clearing, I saw a solitary post bearing the words 'The Line' printed in French and German. For a brief moment my spirits rose. But there was no way of knowing which way the line ran. I could be walking along it or walking across it. This would not be the first time a fugitive had unwittingly re-crossed a frontier after being in safety.

The drizzle was thickening as I continued in the same direction, with the clouds, barely distinguishable, moving slowly across the sky from my right to my left hand. My mind was a receptive blank. I moved automatically, every sense alert for a sign that would end this vacuum of indecision. I saw a farmhouse in a clearing. As there were no curtains at the windows, it might be used as a German barracks. I slid back in among the trees. Tales about escapers crossing into Switzerland and then re-crossing back into the arms of waiting German guards came to my mind. I could understand now how easy was such a mistake.

Overhanging leaves emptied rivulets of water down my shoulders and neck as I brushed by. Suddenly the undergrowth crashed two yards away from me. Something on all fours with a tail like an Alsatian dog disappeared in the forest to my right. Was it a police dog? A few yards farther on I came to a barbed-wire fence. Beyond it was a road. Was this at last the line? What had been the significance of the first post? I climbed over the fence and jumped on to the road. There was nothing in sight either way. I crossed the road. From the far side I could see round a bend. Two hundred yards away, six Germans were standing around what seemed to be a police dog. I dived into the undergrowth hoping they had not seen me. I dare not re-cross that open road. They might not have seen me yet. All was quiet. Rain dripped heavily from the tree-tops. I froze by a trunk out of sight of the road. A shrill bird's cry in the distance warned the forest that it had been disturbed. They were coming. A twig broke behind me. I dropped to my knees and crawled forward. There was no undergrowth to hide in, for this part of the forest consisted only of tall trees and dead wood. Everywhere behind me there were rustlings. I jumped to my feet and raced through the trees. My only hope was speed. In front of me was a German. I veered away to my left. He fired at me. I zigzagged. If I were not surrounded, my speed would see me through. I was much faster than these jack-booted Germans. I dodged between the trees. Ten yards away was a small clearing. As I burst out of the forest I saw the German officer. He raised his revolver and fired. Involuntarily I threw myself flat on my face. I heard him walk up to me.

"Do not do anything stupid or you will catch a bullet with your stomach," he said in carefully pronounced French.

"You speak very good French, m'sieur," I said.

While he was running a hand over me to see if I carried a gun the other Germans came into the clearing, their rifles at the ready. When he was satisfied I was unarmed he asked if I was wounded. I shook my head. He still spoke in French. He thought I was a Frenchman.

"What are you doing here?" he asked.

"I am lost," I said.

"Where do you come from?"

I said nothing. If I said from Nevers he could check up on me. I knew no villages on the other side of the line.

"Where do you come from?" he said again.

"I was walking," I said, "and got lost."

"Where did you walk from?"

"You know," I said, "from the little village over there," and swept my arm around in a semi-circle that embraced half France.

"Which one?" he snapped. I could not have told him, even if I had wanted to.

"I do not know its name," I said.

"So you expect me to believe that you went for a walk and lost yourself? Do you think I'm a fool? With my own eyes I saw you trying to cross into Occupied France." At last he had said it. So I had been in Free France and had returned to the Germans, possibly to a firing squad. But they thought I had come from Free France. That was something. "Well?" he asked. I remained silent.

"Where is your friend?" he asked.

"I was alone," I said.

"We have him also," he jeered.

"But I am alone," I said. I knew that Pierre would not have been caught re-crossing the line. They were bluffing. Pierre had a compass, my compass, a German compass. If they had caught Pierre they would know we had come from Germany, not from Free France.

"How many times have you crossed the line already?" he asked.

"This is the first," I said, "but where are you taking me?"

"To headquarters," he replied.

"What will happen to me?" I asked.

"That depends," he replied.

We returned to the road. All but two of the guards cycled away. I walked with a guard on either side down the road.

"How far have we to go?" I asked.

Neither of them spoke French. They seeemed stupid. Folded in my pocket was an English-made safety-razor. There were English trade-marks on my underwear. I asked the guards in sign language if I could smoke. They nodded. I felt through my pockets for my tobacco. It had gone. On either side of the road was the forest, but there was no chance of escape. I stopped and pointed to the ditch and to myself. After a while they realized what I meant. Modestly they retired as I crouched in the ditch. I dropped the razor in the water and tore the label from my underpants but could not reach the one at the back of my neck on my vest. Then we continued our walk in silence. I had no identity papers and only about four hundred francs. My French was good, but not good enough to fool a Frenchman, a collaborator who might be acting as interpreter to the Hun. I had been caught crossing into Occupied France. That at least was in my favour, until they found I was English and treated me as a spy trying to gain entrance into German occupied territory.

Ahead stood a large château, half surrounded by an empty moat. We walked in single file past a sentry, through a side door and along a many-cornered corridor. We waited outside the Commandant's office. I thought about Pierre with the compass. He'd be safe now. I wondered how my capture would affect him. I thought about Katrina and M. Gaubert. If the Germans found out who I was, would they make me talk and give my helpers away? I had heard about their methods. How tough was I? How much could I take?

The door opened. The Commandant was a small, mild, middle-aged man. He looked kind and human. His office was large and primitive. A barrack-room stove burnt smokily on a polished oak-blocked floor. A bear rug sprawled by the side of a four-poster bed. Two battered filing cabinets ranged alongside a trestle table covered with papers. The Commandant was talking in German to my captor. The two guards stood at my back. The Commandant spoke to the Lieutenant in German. He was acting as interpreter. My luck was holding. Had he been a Frenchman my accent would have given me away.

"What is your name?"

"Henri Cartin," I said. I almost said 'Sidney'.

"Where do you live?"

"Lyons."

"Where do you live in Lyons?"

I said nothing. If I gave them an address they might have the organization to discover whether or not a family named Cartin lived there.

"Where do you live?"

"I don't know," I said.

"You don't know!" the interrogator barked with no prompting from the Commandant. "My young friend, I advise you to tell the truth or you will find yourself in real trouble."

I stared, suitably impressed, at the floor.

"Why did you try to enter Occupied France?"

Looking as dejected, miserable and spiritless as possible, I gave them a morsel to play with.

"I was trying to reach Paris."

The Germans looked at each other.

"What were you going to do in Paris?"

"My aunt lives there. She's the only one I have. I wanted to live with her."

"Why should you want to live with an aunt? Have you no parents?"

"I have no mother," I said reverently.

That touched the Commandant. The interpreter was not impressed. He was tough where other people were concerned. His chest was bare of medal ribbons. His had been an easy war.

"And your father?" he asked.

"He is the cause of all this," I said, with just the right amount of hate mingling with my fear.

"How is that?"

"He is so brutal," I said. "His cruelty was responsible for the death of my mother. He owns a café and is drunk every night and beats me without mercy. I hate him and shall never see him again. You would understand if he was your father." I had tears in my eyes. A few tears might save me from the firing squad. Pride was not so important. The Commandant might have children himself. He felt sorry for me. The interrogator looked at me distastefully. I could forgo his admiration.

The Germans talked together.

"You were running away from your father when you were caught then?"

"Yes."

They talked again.

"I would rather go to prison than return to him," I said.

"Where is your identity card?"

"I burnt it."

"You burnt it?"

"I knew I would probably be caught here. I was taking no chances that you would send me back to my father. He would kill me for running away."

The Germans talked again.

"You will undress."

I emptied my pockets. A cigarette case with my money in it, a dirty handkerchief, pencil, matches. They examined my jacket and trousers, my shoes. If they noticed the English trademark on my vest the game would be up. The guard held it at arm's length, shook it and threw it on to the growing heap. The secretions of fear and sweat had made it stink. They motioned me to dress. They kept the money but returned the matches, pencil and handkerchief.

"Can I buy some food?" I asked; "I have not eaten for two days." I was not hungry but wanted to keep up my strength.

The Commandant spoke to one of the guards who clicked his heels, left us for a few minutes and returned with some thick slices of hard, dry brown bread. I forced them down my dry throat. A spy, I thought, would be well furnished with money and false papers. I had neither!

I was taken out of the office up three flights of stairs and locked into a pitch-black room with no light. I struck a match and lit a piece of old newspaper. The room had several windows all of which were locked. There were several iron beds with stained dusty mattresses and blankets. I wrapped the blankets around me and fell asleep.

I awoke, cold but alert and refreshed, at the first light on the following morning. I broke an iron strut from the bed and levered a window open. A slated roof sloped ten feet down to a gutter. From the gutter a ramshackle drainpipe zigzagged sixty feet to the ground. The blankets in the room would not stretch that far and the drainpipe did not look safe. I closed the window. A few fields away a broad river meandered under a railway bridge. Judging from the position of the rising sun the railway ran from the south-east to the north-west and the river was at right angles to it. The road along which I had been marched the night before must be on the other side of the house. I memorized the land-scape from my vantage point.

Later in the morning a guard took me to the interrogator.

"You are going to work this morning. The guard will take you to the kitchen. We have a French cook, she will tell you what to do."

A French cook working for the Germans! This, although the Germans did not realize it, might be the worst interview of all. I prayed she was not a collaborator.

We descended into the bowels of the château through stone arches into a stone-floored kitchen large enough to cook for a feudal baron and all his retainers. A strongly built middle-aged woman stopped scouring a pan. She looked first at me, then at the guard. She said nothing. Behind her a young girl was sitting on a stool plucking a hen.

The guard spoke in German to the woman and pointed to me. The woman replied in German. She walked over to a bench and cut some slices of bread, daubed them with grease and beckoned me. She thrust the plate into my hands. The guard stood beside the buxom girl. She was giggling, nervous, afraid of his thick-fingered touching. I took an angry step towards them. The older woman grabbed my arm, her fingers were strong.

"Listen," she said, "eat your breakfast. Afterwards you will work for the Germans. Clean out lavatories, baths, scrub floors."

"No!" I said, drawing my arm away. The young girl jumped off the stool and ran through a door. The guard turned towards us, smiling, half-ashamed.

"Yes!" said the older woman. She looked unsmilingly straight at me. I had nothing to fear from her. She started scouring her pans. The guard lit a cigarette. I ate part of the bread and put the remainder in my pocket.

The guard led me to my work. The mere fact that they were making me work was a good sign. This might be part of my punishment. They could not regard me as a dangerous prisoner. In the bathroom I filched an old safety razor to replace the one I had thrown away. With the blade I could cut the blankets into strips. By midday I had finished and was back in the small room in the tower. How long was I going to be kept here? What was going to happen next? I paced the room, giving way to the depression that had threatened since my capture. I cursed. Scattered on the floor were several stained brittle butt-ends. I gathered them, unrolled the once spittle-soaked tobacco and wrapped it afresh in a piece of newspaper. I lay back on the bed, struck a match and inhaled. The smoke was acrid and strong but it satisfied a craving.

Later, I cut the blankets into strips and hid them in a cupboard. That was the last resort. If all else failed I would climb down the outside of the château as soon as it was dark.

The sun had swung across most of the sky before I was interrupted again. The corporal who had examined my clothes escorted me to the Commandant's office. The same interrogator was there. He was still suspicious. Instead of the Commandant were two other officers. The senior of them sat at the Commandant's desk. The other stood by the stove. Judging from the ribbons on their chests, both were fighting men, young, blue-eyed, strong-chinned. The master-race, I thought. I felt it, too. No word was spoken. The German at the desk just stared at me, noting my big build, my blue eyes, my brown hair. I didn't look like a Frenchman. If I pull this off, I thought, it will be a miracle. He spoke to the interrogator. The question was translated. "Where is your identity card?" Out of the corner of my eye I was aware of the other German, watching me from the side.

"I burnt it," I said.

"Who helped you cross the line?"

"No one. I know nobody here."

I repeated my story again.

"What is your address?"

"I can't tell you."

The headquarters officer jumped to his feet and started shouting at me in German.

"You must tell your address or it will be the worse for you," snarled the interrogator, copying the tone of his senior.

I remained silent, staring at the floor, shuffling my feet.

"I will give you the address of a friend."

They wrote down a mythical address in Lyons. They seemed satisfied. The Captain threw me a cigarette. My hand was unsteady. The interrogator handed me a light. As I·bent over, the senior officer barked at me in English.

"Are you English?"

I looked at the interpreter as if I thought this was one

more question in German. No one spoke. I dragged on the cigarette. Anything I said now would seem phoney. At last the Germans started talking among themselves. The interrogator turned to me.

"You are fined two hundred francs. If you try to cross the line again you will be sent to prison. Tomorrow, when the Commandant returns with the key to his safe, you will be sent back over the line."

I could scarcely believe it. They were actually sending me to Free France. I did not stop acting my part.

"Can I not remain in Occupied France?" I pleaded.

The Germans talked again. "No," said the interpreter. The interview was over.

On the way back to my room the corporal, who spoke a little French, told me he would try to arrange for me to stay on this side of the line if he had charge of me the following morning. I told him I had better return and acquire some fresh papers before I tried it again. He gave me a few cigarettes and patted me on the shoulder. I almost felt ill at ease deceiving such a kind-hearted fellow.

As the door locked behind me I went to the window. In the distance a line of fires burned along what I guessed would be the demarcation line. Tomorrow I would be in Free France. I lay on the bed wishing I had not cut up all the blankets. I lit a cigarette and thanked the god that protects escapers. Taking a small piece of paper I wrote, 'Sgt. Pilot D. D. NABARRO, R.A.F. Escaped from here, DECEMBER 1941.' On the wall was a small crucifix. I put the paper behind it.

Towards noon the following day the friendly corporal led me before the Commandant who handed over my money less the two hundred francs fine and fifty francs for board and lodging. Then the Commandant himself escorted me to the frontier post. The guard at the barrier came rigidly to attention under the German flag.

I shook hands with the elderly German officer. He smiled and said in French, "*Allez! Lyons!*" and pointed down the lane.

"You do not know what you have done," I replied in the same language.

He smiled again. I looked at the swastika and turned on my heels.

IV

ESCAPE FROM ST. HIPPOLYTE DU FORT

from

The Way Back

By VINCENT BROME

The Way Back *is the story of Dr. Albert Marie Guérisse, a Belgian who became a British Secret Agent during the Second World War, using the name of Pat O'Leary. Under this alias he ran an escape route with Captain Ian Garrow, a Scot who had survived the last stand of the 51st Highland Division at St. Valéry in the days of Dunkirk. Their organization was the means of helping numerous British and Allied soldiers and airmen to escape from France. In March 1943 O'Leary was betrayed to the Gestapo by Roger, one of his most recently acquired agents, who turned out to be Gestapo Agent No. 47. After being imprisoned and tortured for months in Fresnes prison in Paris, he was taken to various concentration camps in Germany, ending up in Dachau, where he suffered unbelievable brutalities and privations until he and other inmates were released by the Allies on 29 April, 1945.*

For his services to the Allied cause, Lieutenant-Commander Pat O'Leary was awarded the George Cross and the D.S.O.

The following pages describe his escape from St. Hippolyte du Fort after he had been captured in April 1941, when, as commander of H.M.S. Fidelity he was trying to rescue twelve Polish officers hidden by the Resistance in Vichy France.

IT was in St. Hippolyte du Fort that the plan to escape first became a serious reality. Transferred from Lamalgue to St. Hippolyte, the three officers found their new home more a barracks than a fort, with the entrance on a busy main street. On the first floor were large rooms with heavily barred windows destined to accommodate British officers, and from the inner windows could be seen the courtyard where 250

43

shoulders, gave his feet into O'Leary's hands, received a shove, and was half astride the wall. O'Leary grappled with the guard who came rushing up. Rogers took one long leap and was racing up the opposite street, snatching a bicycle and pedalling like a madman. On the ground a second guard was kicking O'Leary as a shot rang out and a flood of French blasphemy burst through the courtyard. Dragged off to the commandant, the interview which followed was ferocious. A plump, rosy-cheeked man, normally very polite, the commandant's threats were more ominous because delivered quietly, but above all, some sense of outraged morality drove him to say: "It just isn't fair."

"What's unfair about it?" O'Leary asked.

"The way you rushed off two seconds after seeing me."

"It's our duty to try to escape," O'Leary said.

"Not by a trick," snapped the commandant.

"It wasn't a trick, it was intelligence," O'Leary answered.

"We'll see about that," said the commandant.

Without another word O'Leary was taken off to solitary confinement. The guards had not dealt lightly with him, and he was bruised and shaken, but in St. Hippolyte solitary confinement did not, at this stage, mean continual darkness and no food in a rat-infested cell. For ten days O'Leary saw only the guard who brought very sparse meals, did not leave his cell and was cut off from the life of the fort. In that time he worked out the plan for his own escape. Already the primitive techniques of rush, surprise and bluster were out of date. The commandant had effectively sealed off escapes of that kind. A completely new approach had to be made and step by step Pat evolved his plan. Once out of solitary confinement, work began.

First a British soldier with an artistic bent set to work on a spare piece of linoleum with a stolen knife, and diligently chipped and trimmed until he produced a rough and ready linocut of a French identity card. Some debate followed as to how O'Leary should be named, but it was the artist who decided: "I'll call you Adolphe—Adolphe Lecomte, a fine, rich name," and Adolphe Lecomte, by profession an engineer, he became. Several times the lino was inked with stolen prison ink and a copy run off. At first it blurred and smeared, but half a dozen attempts at last produced a reasonable copy.

O'Leary was now equipped with an identity card and a profession.

As senior officer in the fort he was permitted to call occasional meetings to pass on orders and information from the commandant, and under cover of some small change in regulations, he held a quick and hurried conference with the men in a ground-floor room, explaining his plan to set up a complete escape organization once he himself was free. But he had first to escape and his plan depended on one thing. Somewhere at the back of the O.R.s' assembly room was a locked and disused chamber with a barred window giving on to the path of the sentries. Could they break into this and saw through one of the bars, carefully replacing it, making it look as if the bar were still intact?

Within forty-eight hours a key to the room was forged from old wire and successfully turned in the lock. From two French girls outside the camp came a small hacksaw which Maurice Dufour smuggled in one night. After the evening meal an N.C.O. and two men turned the forged key in the lock, slipped in, re-locked the door from the inside and with relays of men keeping watch outside, went to work. The room was pitch dark, low-ceilinged, smelling of damp and decay, and full of rusting old iron bedsteads. The dim light from the window made it possible to select the weakest bar and they sawed steadily in relays for two hours the first night. Progress seemed disappointingly slow. The cut in the bar was not more than an eighth of an inch deep, the screeching of metal on metal seemed to get worse as they penetrated deeper, and twice warnings from outside sent them scurrying into the darkest corner of the room. Worse still, barely three feet below them ran the sentry's path and it seemed impossible that he would not detect the noise as he paced up and down.

The second night they smeared margarine into the cut and began sawing more slowly to reduce the noise. Another eighth of an inch gave before their assault. When one cut had been carried right through the bar at one end, they reported that it was such a tough, thick bar of solid iron that it did not seem likely to yield to pressure and another cut at the opposite end would be necessary. Pat estimated that to cut the bar at both ends would occupy a week. He selected the day following its probable completion for his escape bid, and made elaborate arrangements with Hewitt and Parkinson. Zero hour would be 11.55, when the men queued up to get the midday meal in the main courtyard. Pat would use the faked key to lock himself in the room and at 11.55 Hewitt would give the signal to create a diversion of the most elaborate and noisy kind possible. A whole mass attempt to escape would be staged on the opposite side of the fort.

Night after night the sawing went on. As the cuts in the bar grew deeper it became necessary for the workers to conceal their handiwork from the guards on the pathway outside. They kneaded pieces of discoloured bread into dough and worked them into the cuts, spreading the dough like rust. On the seventh day Pat received a report that only a thin sliver of metal now held the bar in place. He went over every detail of the arrangements with Hewitt and Parkinson once more. Only one thing could give them away; the sense of expectancy in the atmosphere which always preceded any escape known to a mass of prisoners.

At 11.50 on the Friday morning Pat sat locked in the dank, dirty room, sitting on a fast decomposing iron bedstead, watching the guard through the window. A gentle test pull on the bar showed that it would give easily. He could hear the distant sound of feet, the usual clanging of heavy doors and the murmur of voices as the *gendarmes* talked amongst themselves. Outside, a thick-set soldier, his pistol very much in evidence, stood with his feet apart, hands clasped behind his back, staring towards the town. It was a beautiful day, the air crisp, the sun beginning to burn, and the sky brilliant blue. Everything depended on the reaction of that thick-set gentleman standing down there wrapped in contemplation. Taken sufficiently by surprise he might be thrown into confusion; given a chance to recover he might shoot at sight.

11.54. In the courtyard two hundred men were milling around, trying to form some kind of queue for lunch, when Hewitt looked at his watch, saw the minute hand creep to 11.55 and gave the signal.

Suddenly the mass of prisoners made a dash towards the outer wall, a dozen men climbed on the shoulders of others, a rope mysteriously appeared, was run up the wall, and a whole hysterical uproar of shouting and gesticulation began. It did not need much insight to detect the theatricality of the outbreak, but every guard within sight rushed to the wall, fighting broke out and guns were levelled.

O'Leary had stared tensely at his watch. 11.53 . . . 11.54 . . . 11.55 . . . 11.56. . . . At 11.57 he reached up and dragged the bar inwards. As he saw the guard outside running towards the courtyard he took a flying leap out and down. The guard swung round and saw him: "Stop or I shoot!" Pat staggered to his feet and raced away. A swerving zig-zag, the main street reached, the sound of shooting and he dived wildly into a side street. People pointed and tried to stop him. He crashed into and through a talking group; a man tried to cling to his arm and he brushed him off, sending him sprawling. Suddenly an old house barred his path, the door wide open in the hot sunshine. Straight into the cool black shadows he leapt and before he could stop himself saw a long trestle table with old people eating their lunch, barring his way. Carried forward by his rush he had no alternative but to leap on to the table. He dashed down the centre, trying to avoid the soup and the plates, aware only of faces aghast, of cries, of chairs falling backwards. Off the opposite end and into a small dark kitchen, where an old woman and a young girl were washing dishes. This was a hospice for old people and the girl one of the nuns, very correct in her white apron and bonnet. Pat seized her by both hands and babbled—"British officer escaped from the prison—help me—where can I hide?" The nun blanched and muttered, "I'll fetch Mother Superior." O'Leary pushed himself into the darkest corner of the kitchen, the older woman standing paralysed, as he listened, tense, for the cries of his pursuers. A second later an imposing figure entered the room. Stout, very calm, and clad from head to foot in black, she said: "You are a British officer?" O'Leary began to explain, but she took him by the hand: "Come with me." Up one flight of stairs and then another; more stairs, with twisted landings and dark old timbers, the house growing quieter the higher they climbed. At last they came to a huge attic full of every kind of junk, and in the centre at least twenty-five chests and coffers of all shapes and sizes, as though a bankrupt undertaker had left his stock to rot. She opened one of the chests: "Get inside," she said. "I'll come back later."

In the oldest tradition of concealment O'Leary lay

D

panting in the trunk. The footsteps retreated down the stairs and the house settled into silence again, with only the creaking of the ancient timbers remaining to try his nerves. Ten minutes and the trunk had become stifling; its gold vestments, musty with age, distilled a powerful odour. He raised the lid, looked round, took several deep breaths and sank back again. Presently the trunk became intolerable and every five minutes he raised the lid for a breather, but the atmosphere in the trunk grew thicker and thicker. One hour went by and there was no movement, no sign of life from the house below. Pat thought of creeping downstairs again. But supposing the guards had occupied the hospice and were waiting, supposing the Mother Superior was under arrest and the whole house surrounded. Lying there without news, not knowing what had happened, was a torment.

Another half hour went by before he heard footsteps on the stairs. He listened intently, trying to distinguish whether they were male or female. The steps came nearer. He pulled the vestments over his head and lay very still. Suddenly he felt the lid rising and a woman's voice said: "All right, but we must be very careful. Come with me." It was the Mother Superior. Climbing out, thanking her in whispers, O'Leary was at last told what had happened. The guards had raced in after him and she had admitted seeing him. "Yes, he was English and an officer—but he went clean through the house and out the other side." The guards had looked suspicious and the Mother Superior added: "In the sight of God, there is no Englishman here." Still suspicious, the guards had gone away but had thrown a cordon of soldiers round the entire hospice, in the belief that if they waited long enough, they would catch him. "But," said the big, composed figure in her nodding white bonnet, "there is still one way out." She showed no sign of alarm or even anxiety, and as she talked she walked steadily from the third to the second, and the second to the first floor. Quickly surveying the kitchen she hurried to the ground floor and down into a gloomy, musty cellar. There she went swiftly to a dark aperture at one side. "Follow me," she said. They entered a narrow tunnel and O'Leary suddenly realized where they were going. This was a tunnel running to the heart of a vineyard along which the harvest could quickly be gathered and brought to the house in former times. Everywhere the rich, heavy smell of grapes and the scent of wine permeated the earth, producing, in the confined space, an atmosphere heady to the senses. A great stillness and silence settled, the air grew thick, little trickles of earth ran down the walls as the tunnel narrowed, and presently they were walking bent double, and everything was black. Just the rustlings of the Mother Superior's habit, her deep breaths and the sound of her feet, sullen and heavy in the tunnel. Presently a dim light appeared ahead which strengthened and grew until Pat could see the sky, and a minute later the Mother Superior gestured to him to remain behind while she reconnoitred. A hundred yards back she could see the guards. O'Leary came out of the tunnel behind the Mother Superior's skirts, went down on all fours as she walked towards the boundary of the vineyard, and crawled along in the shelter of her gown. Three minutes later a whispered farewell—and he was free.

V

ESCAPE ACROSS THE U.S. BORDER

from

The One That Got Away

By KENDAL BURT *and* JAMES LEASOR

During the Second World War Lieutenant Franz von Werra, the Luftwaffe fighter ace, achieved notoriety as the only German airman who successfully escaped from British captivity, and several books have been written about his exploits. A film—produced in Britain—has also featured this intrepid escaper.

In September 1940 Franz von Werra was shot down near Maidstone and, after interrogation, was sent to a P.O.W. camp in the Lake District. Twelve days later he escaped while on a route march with other prisoners. He was recaptured, however, and transferred to another camp at Swanwick. From this camp he took part in a mass escape via a tunnel and, posing as Captain van Lott, a shot-down Dutch pilot, he successfully reached Hucknall aerodrome, where he bluffed his way into the cockpit of a Hurricane. But while fiddling with the controls, he was intercepted and forced to reveal his true identity.

In January 1941 von Werra was taken with other German P.O.W.s to Canada, landing at Halifax on the 23rd. On the train taking them to a camp on the north shore of Lake Superior, von Werra decided to make yet another bid for freedom.

The One That Got Away tells the full story of his extraordinary adventures, terminating in his illegal exit from the U.S.A. and his return to Germany via Mexico and Peru.

THE train clanked and lurched over the points outside the station. It was gathering speed rapidly. Manhard's thumb was up.

Wagner, holding two corners of his blanket in his lap, looked at von Werra in anxious inquiry. Von Werra nodded.

Wagner stood up, and opened out the blanket. Wilhelm slid along into Wagner's corner seat.

Masked by the blanket, von Werra stood up, caught hold of the outer window, and jerked upwards. It did not move. Another fierce jerk and then a steady, sustained lift. The window opened smoothly.

A rush of cold air pressed the blanket against Wagner's body. He continued to shake the corners up and down, looking up the coach towards the two guards.

Von Werra felt the icy blast on his face, heard the unexpectedly loud and hollow beat of the wheels over the rail joints. Snowdrifts flashed by at a terrifying speed. The train was still accelerating.

It was sheer madness. Suicide. He couldn't possibly do it.

The next moment Wilhelm saw von Werra's jack-boots disappear through the middle of the open window. For a split second, which he will never forget, he saw von Werra's body, rigid, arms straight out above his head, suspended almost horizontally a foot or so outside the coach.

It dropped back and was gone. There was nothing but the icy draught and the whine and the beat of the wheels on the rails.

Wilhelm shut the outer and inner windows and slid back along the seat. Wagner folded the blanket deliberately, slowly, and sat down.

No word was spoken.

All three were aghast, incredulous.

A few brief seconds ago von Werra had been sitting there with his head in his hands. Now he was gone.

The three of them watched ferns of frost sprout rapidly over the window. Inside a minute the glass was completely covered. It was as though the window had never been opened.

They never saw von Werra again. They had not even had time to wish him luck.

At daybreak, Major Cramer, who was officer-in-charge of the prisoners in that coach, walked down the gangway to see how the men who had been ill during the night were getting on. When he reached the bay occupied by Wagner, Manhard and Wilhelm, he paused. All three were lying on their bunks.

Von Werra's was empty. He raised his eyebrows interrogatively. Wagner nodded his head slowly.

Cramer passed on, smiling.

It was not until late the following afternoon that von Werra's absence was discovered. The train was then several hundred miles from the point where he had dived out of the window.

Von Werra landed on piled snow at the side of the track. The force of the impact drove all the breath from his body. He lay for a minute, feeling sick from the shock. He had ricked his neck in the fall, and he ached all over.

He stood up dizzily and looked around him. The cold struck him like a blow—he had jumped from stifling heat into thirty degrees of frost. The perspiration congealed on his skin.

There was snow everywhere, the smell of pine trees. In the distance, a red pin-point of light. The train's rear-lamp. Then it was gone.

He felt a sudden surge of exhilaration.

His temples throbbed, his neck ached, he was stiff, chilled to the marrow, and his nose stung like hell. But he was free.

He became aware of the silence—the silence of snow. It was as though his ears were plugged with cotton wool.

The sky was clear and the stars hung low and large. The snow reflected their diamond light.

Heavens, it was cold!

What a fool he had been not to think of getting a cap. He would have to do something or his ears would drop off with frost-bite. He pulled from his pocket the tartan scarf he had bought at Swanwick, and wrapped it over his head.

Having taken a bearing on the pole star, he crossed the railway track and set out southwards across a stretch of open country. The going was difficult. Each step he took he sank up to his calves in snow. The harsh, rasping sound of his boots in the snow seemed to fill the universe.

He began to imagine noises, and when he glanced back quickly over his shoulder, it was not only to check his bearing by the pole-star.

After about an hour he saw the serrated outline of a pine forest, black against the pale horizon. There was no road or track along the edge of it. There was nothing for it but to find his way through.

The forest was full of noises—creakings, scufflings, whisperings, sighings, rustlings—breaking the awesome silence.

Sometimes he was in the open, knee-deep in snow, sometimes groping, stumbling in the blackness under the trees. After a while he came to a broad avenue. It was a hundred yards wide—probably a fire break. The snow in the middle had been flattened by a tractor. It was like walking on a road. Ahead of him the tree tops formed an elongated V against the stars. Behind him the sky was paling. Dawn was near.

He hurried. The hard track was a godsend, but he was afraid that as soon as it became daylight he might encounter lumberjacks, or perhaps the man with the tractor. How could he explain his presence in the middle of a Canadian forest in such clothes at that time of day? He must get on to a highway. The sun rose. The tips of the trees on his right were edged with gold and silver. The pines cast gigantic shadows. He hastened onwards, sometimes running. He was reluctant to leave the hard track.

He must have walked several miles, but still the end of the avenue was not in sight. Suddenly he heard the sound of an engine. It sounded like a car, and it seemed to come from the trees on his right. He listened intently. The noise grew louder, and after a few moments a car flashed across the avenue half a mile away ahead of him, snow chains rattling.

A road! In a few minutes he had reached it.

For an hour he followed it without seeing any more vehicles. Then it joined a wider road. There was a signpost.

According to the announcement put out by the Canadian authorities, von Werra escaped from the train near Smiths Falls, Ontario, about forty miles south-west of Ottawa. If that is so, he had only about thirty miles to cover to reach the St. Lawrence which at that point forms the border between Canada and the United States.

When eventually he reached New York and was besieged by reporters, sensing the sort of story they were after, he gave it to them. He said he had leapt off the train 100 miles north of Ottawa; this gave him far more elbow room for an extravagant account, in the true von Werra manner, of his achievement and of the daring and aplomb with which he had brought it off. No one enjoyed more than von Werra telling a good story for the entertainment of his audience, and if their legs were pulled in the process, so much the better!

His story having been accepted by the American Press (which after all would have no means of knowing the real route taken by the prisoners' train and presumably did not bother to discover for themselves that no east-west rail track passes within a hundred miles of "a hundred miles north of Ottawa") there seemed to von Werra no reason to vary his account when he came to write it in book form for the German people. Indeed he improved on it.

First of all a truck had come along and he had thumbed a lift in the manner Wagner had taught him. He had a story ready for the driver. He was a Dutch seaman. He had been twice dive-bombed crossing the Atlantic and had seen too many ships sunk by U-boats. He had had enough. He had relatives in Ottawa who would help him get a land job.

After some miles the lorry driver set von Werra down where he was due to turn off the main highway. "Plenty of stuff heading for Ottawa on this route," had been the driver's parting remark. "You'll soon hitch a ride, bud."

Sure enough, after a quarter of a mile, von Werra had heard a rattle of snow-chains coming behind him. He removed his hand from his pocket ready to carry out the Wagner drill again. When he looked back his heart missed a beat. He quickly put his hand back into his pocket and turned his back on the approaching vehicle.

It was a big saloon car. On its bumper there was a large red shield bearing the word "POLICE".

Von Werra pretended to ignore the car as it drew level, but the driver braked and pulled in beside him.

So his third attempt had not been lucky after all. Had he been a fool to walk along the main highway instead of keeping to the forest where he would have been safe?

The policeman was beckoning him to get in. He had no option. Inside he noticed the radio receiver. That explained it. Police cars were probably out scouring every highway looking for a short, fair man wearing a blue overcoat and no hat.

But from the policeman's opening remarks it appeared that he was more concerned with von Werra's half complete hitch-hiking gesture. What Wagner had been unable to tell him was that since the beginning of the war begging a lift had been made illegal in Canada. "You changed your mind just in time," the policeman had said. "If you'd hailed me, I'd have run you in. As it is I'll run you in to Ottawa." For von Werra had told him about his "relatives" in Ottawa.

Whether any policeman ever did help von Werra on his way we are unlikely to know. If the policeman did not exist, at least he could not come forward to contradict von Werra's story! If, as von Werra said, the policeman dropped him off outside police headquarters, it was certainly not in Ottawa where he also placed some other daring adventures. He had gone into one of the big banks and asked to change English currency into Canadian dollars; he had not revealed that all he had to exchange was a ten shilling note. When the clerk behind the grille had demanded to see his papers, von Werra had once more escaped from a desperate situation. He had another story for American newspaper men, that he had narrowly escaped arrest by police guarding the Parliament Building while he was sightseeing in the capital; but this one he must have forgotten by the time he came to dictate the notes for his book.

If, as the Canadian authorities stated, and as his companion, Wagner, confirms, von Werra left the train near Smiths Falls, he certainly never went near Ottawa, which lay in the opposite direction—i.e. northward—to that in which he wanted to go.

What his object can have been in making up such a tale, is left to the imagination of the reader who has already had experience of von Werra's gift for extemporising.

One incident must have had some truth in it, for von Werra describes a ruse by which he acquired a road map from a garage, and an "Imperial" road map of Ontario State was among the items later found in his possession.

The indisputable fact remains that in due course, from whichever direction and by whatever means, von Werra did arrive at Johnstown on the north bank of the St. Lawrence and saw the twinkling lights of the United States beckoning him from the other shore.

He had no idea how he was going to cross the river. According to his map, there were international bridges at Cornwall, forty-five miles downstream, and at Thousand Islands, forty miles upstream. Between the two bridges there were ferries at Morrisburg, Prescott and Brockville. Prescott was the nearest, only a few miles away, and he decided to investigate that first. But would the ferry be working at that time of year? It seemed unlikely in view of the ice he had seen on the river from the train, farther downstream between Quebec and Montreal.

He walked south and came to what appeared in the gathering dusk to be a wide, flat, snow-covered valley. It was a few seconds before he realized that this was the River St. Lawrence. It was frozen over. He was tremendously excited. All he had to do was to wait until it was quite dark and walk across to the United States.

It was far better than a ferry or toll bridge where he would have had to run the gauntlet of customs, passport officials and police of two countries.

But the size of the river was terrifying. How wide was it? Five hundred metres? A thousand? The dusk and the snow made it impossible to judge. But it was a long, long way to the winking lights of the American city on the other side, which he reckoned from his map to be Ogdensburg.

He set out along the bank, wading knee-deep through the snow. He was dead tired and ravenously hungry. He had eaten nothing for nearly twenty-four hours. It had been cold enough all day, but with the approach of night the temperature dropped rapidly. There was a bitter wind at his back. It pierced his clothing like a knife. The cold and fatigue had made him drowsy. He fretted with impatience.

He had travelled so far; now there was only three-quarters of a mile at most between him and final freedom.

He struggled for about two miles along the bank. It was desolate and silent. There was only the hum of the wind round his ears, the occasional flurries of powder blown along the surface of the snow.

He waited until long after dark. A haze of light hung over Ogdensburg. Some distance to the east of it there were three isolated points of light forming a triangle. Perhaps they were street lamps. He made them his objective.

At seven o'clock he left the comparative shelter of the bank and set off across the open ice of the river.

The snow had been blown into deep drifts near the bank. He floundered, fought his way forward foot by foot. Fifty yards out the going became comparatively easy, but the wind swept over the ice straight up the course of the river. It seemed to be laden with splinters of glass. Ice formed on his eye-brows, on the scarf over his head and on the upper part of his coat. Snow from the drifts he had struggled through turned into ice as he walked; the flaps of his coat were like boards.

The glittering stars and the lights of Ogdensburg merged and traced scintillating lines across the snow. The merging of land and sky gave him the illusion that he was about to look over the edge of the world. The illusion vanished as the lights of the city ahead became more distinct.

Now and again he heard the sound of the ice cracking—a sharp snap followed by a rapidly receding rumble. He knew that cracking ice was not dangerous so long as it was freezing. But when he reached what he thought was about half-way, the sounds of cracking became very loud and menacing. Sometimes they were close and he could feel the slight sudden shock wave. An odd sensation.

He tripped over something and went sprawling. The ice was no longer smooth under its thin covering of snow, but jagged and rough as a road surface broken up by a pneumatic drill. He was so numb from cold that it was a minute or so before he felt the full hurt of his tumble.

He was winded and shaken. He lay for a moment, almost overcome by the urge to sleep, his senses pulling one way, his will the other. There came to his mind the memory of a summer evening on a lake near Berlin: green reeds rustling, sun-spangled water, white sails billowing, ripples lapping against glistening, varnished woodwork. Lapping . . . lapping. . . .

The wind dropped momentarily and he clearly heard the sound of a car horn. He got up, aching all over, slipping and stumbling on slabs of ice larger than paving stones.

He was only a quarter of a mile from the American shore.
Cars rolled along the waterfront, headlights blazing.

He hurried forward eagerly, then paused. Ten, fifteen
yards ahead the snow seemed to stop. Beyond was blackness.
The shore already? But why was there no snow?

Then he saw the lights reflected on the blackness: water!
He could not grasp it. How could there be water when the
whole river was frozen over? He frantically hacked with the
heel of his boot at a slab of ice. A corner broke off and he
tossed it forward into the blackness. It fell with a hollow
splash, like a pebble into a well.

There was an ice-free channel between him and the
American shore.

To swim in that temperature meant certain death. He
had to go back.

Von Werra returned to the Canadian bank and walked
along it towards Prescott. He came to a collection of chalets—
a deserted summer holiday camp. He floundered about in the
deep snow on the foreshore and eventually found what he was
looking for—a long, cigar-shaped mound of snow. He scraped
away the side with his boot and came upon something hard.
It was an upturned rowing boat.

He went back to the chalets and found a wooden fence.
After much kicking and wrenching he managed to free two
palings. They were too wide and too thick and ice made them
heavier still, but they would have to do. He used one of
them as a shovel to dig away the snow from the boat.

It was a large, cumbersome affair, and was frozen to the
ground. He had to lever it free, a little at a time, with one
board, using the other as a wedge. When he had freed it he
still had to turn it the right way up. It took all his strength
and the aid of the two boards but finally he righted it.

There were no oars or rowlocks. The boat was a six-seater.
How ever was he going to row it—even assuming he could
manage to drag it as far as the water?

He groped round, looking for another boat. He found
nothing, so returned to the six-seater.

He had got to do it!

In a sudden, desperate rage, he threw himself at the stern
of the boat and pushed wildly. It scarcely moved.

He felt a snowflake on his cheek. He looked up at the sky. The stars were obscured. He looked across the river. The lights of Ogdensburg were barely discernible through a curtain of flurrying snow.

It would be fatal to give way to rage and panic. He must conserve his strength, use his wits to spare his muscles, and make every scrap of effort count.

If he tried to *drag* the boat, he would waste a lot of effort, for he would tend to pull the bow down into the snow. He must *push* it. When he got out beyond the drifts, where the snow was only ankle deep on the ice, he could tie his scarf to the mooring ring in the bow and pull the boat behind him.

He tossed the boards into the boat and began pushing it towards the river. He advanced a foot to eighteen inches at a time. At first he thought he would never reach the river. But gradually he stopped thinking. He became an automaton, oblivious to everything except the rhythm of his movements, the rasping of his breath and the taste of his saliva. Fatigue, hunger, thirst and cold were forgotten.

At last he reached the open ice. He crouched down on the lee of the boat out of the wind and the driving snow, resting. When he got up again and tried to push, the keel was frozen to the ice. He had to wrench with all his might to free it. It was wasted effort—he must not rest any more until he reached the pack-ice.

He tried to tie his scarf to the mooring ring, but his fingers were without feeling and for the life of him he could not tie a knot. He would have to continue pushing.

Half-way across.

Sometimes for minutes at a time the lights of Ogdensburg were completely obscured by snow. Von Werra kept pushing. He dared not stop. Now and again he slipped and fell on to his knees. But he got up and went on.

He was brought to a halt by the pack-ice near the water's edge. How could he get the boat over the ice and into the river?

He pulled the boat back a few feet, then pushed it up on to the pack-ice using the two boards as runners under the keel. Again, using the boards alternately as runners, he managed to push the boat forward, a length at a time.

At last he reached the open river. He tipped the boat three-parts of the way into the water, jumped in and pushed off against the ice with one of the boards. The whole boat slid into the water, rocked violently and in the struggle to regain his balance the board slipped out of his numbed hand.

He sat down and picked up the remaining board, trying to use it as a paddle. But it was too long, too heavy and too clumsy. He could neither feel it nor grip it. It slid out of his hands into the water.

Rudderless, oarless, the boat floated away into the darkness, rocking and turning lazily round and round in the ten miles an hour current. Now and again small icefloes thudded against the sides.

An escaper must have luck. Farther downstream the ice-free channel followed the contour of a toe of land jutting out in the river. The boat, steadied now and facing upstream, gradually slid across the channel and eventually bumped and scraped along the jagged ice bordering one side of the headland.

Von Werra was no stranger to excitement. But even he found the thrill of that trip on the St. Lawrence a little too hectic and sustained. Time seemed to stop. He had the impression that the boat was spinning round and round in the darkness, and hurtling down to the sea.

When it bumped and grated against the margin of ice by the headland, he needed no time to make up his mind. The boat grated: he leapt. He managed to fall on the ice. The boat recoiled, then slowly returned. The last he heard of it, it was bumping and scraping slowly downstream.

He got to his feet, staggered across the ice and scrambled up the bank. He was very anxious. It seemed to him that he had been in the boat for hours, and that he had drifted miles. And he knew from the map that farther downstream the U.S.A. border was some way south of the St. Lawrence— that *both* banks were in Canada.

He saw a huge building some distance away on his left. The windows were ablaze with light. Then he had a shock. He noticed that every window was barred. Had he landed in the grounds of a penitentiary?

He moved away to the right as quickly as he could. He

was reassured when he saw a car pass by ahead of him. There must be a road. Then he saw two cars parked farther down on the right. He got on to the road and walked towards them. The leading car was unoccupied. The bonnet of the other was raised and a man was tinkering with the engine. A young lady in a snow-sprinkled fur coat stood by him and there was another girl sitting in the car.

On the licence plate of the rear car were the words: "New York". It was the same with the other car.

He dared not believe it. He had seen cars in Canada with New York licence plates.

The man went to the car ahead, presumably to get some tools. He looked hard at von Werra but did not speak.

Von Werra moved across in front of the car. The head-lamps shone on his overcoat, which was stiff with ice. His legs cast long shadows on the snow. The woman stared at him and then glanced in the direction of the river from which he had come. She laughed and asked lightly:

"What's the matter with you?"

"Excuse me. Is this America?"

"Are you sick, or something?"

"No, truly. What is that house over there? What place is this?"

The woman was struck by his accent and by the tiredness of his voice. She replied straightforwardly:

"That is New York State Hospital. I am a nurse there. You are in Ogdensburg."

"*Ogdensburg?* But——" Von Werra could not believe it. Instead of having drifted miles downstream, he had travelled barely half a mile.

But what did it matter? He was in America.

He smiled wearily.

"I am an officer of the German Air Force," he said. "I escape across the river from Canada. I am"—he corrected himself, "I *was* a prisoner-of-war."

The nurse gave him a cigarette. He had difficulty in holding it in his frost-bitten fingers. The nurse explained that she had been setting out "uptown" when her car had stalled. She had telephoned a garage and the proprietor himself, Mr. Al Crites, had driven out to see what was wrong.

There were, she said, many Canadians in Ogdensburg, including frontier officials.

It was not until some time later that von Werra realized that the nurse had been trying to tell him that Al Crites was a Canadian.

Crites gave von Werra a lift into the city. The German insisted on getting out at the traffic lights on the corner of Ford and Patterson Streets. Although he did not then know that Crites was a Canadian, he wanted to make sure that he surrendered to an American policeman.

A few minutes later Patrolman James Delduchetto, of the Ogdensburg City Police, having been tipped off by Crites, arrested Oberleutenant Fritz von Werra as a tramp, loitering in the precincts of the Presbyterian Church.

"Come on, you!" said Patrolman Delduchetto. "Headquarters!"

"Excuse me. You are American, or Canadian?"

The policeman tapped the badge on his cap. It bore an eagle and the letters "U.S.A.".

Von Werra smiled.

"Okay!" he said. "Sure!"

At police headquarters, von Werra was charged with vagrancy. But with the aid of his uniform jacket, complete with Iron Cross, and various censored letters addressed to him in British internment camps, he was able to convince the police he was an escaped German prisoner-of-war. The vagrancy charge was dropped, and he was turned over to Immigration Inspector David K. J. Benjamin.

An Immigration Board held a preliminary inquiry at Ferry House the same night, and von Werra was arraigned on a charge of illegal entry into the United States. The hearing was adjourned to the next day to enable him to get in touch with the German Consul in New York, and to obtain legal representation. Later, he was handed back to the police for safe keeping.

Since diving out of the train early that morning he had passed an eventful and utterly exhausting day. Physically, he was dead beat. Somehow he managed to keep going on nervous energy. His eyes pricked for want of sleep and he was in a waking dream.

Things had moved fast after his arrest. When he arrived back at Police Headquarters, photographers and reporters milled around him. He was given food and drink and then he told his story.

And now the other side of von Werra's character took over. He committed one indiscretion after another. He boasted, bragged, exaggerated outrageously and spoke of the British war effort with contempt. If this performance had been limited to the night of his arrival, it would be easy to overlook it, but it was continued throughout the next day, after food and a night's sleep, when some of the famous feature writers arrived from New York to interview him.

The following morning, Saturday 25 January, the story of his escape, and many pictures of him, were front page news throughout America. The local paper, the *Ogdensburg Journal,* devoted several pages of news and pictures to his "saga".

Following are a few extracts:

. . . Von Werra boasted of German supremacy in the present war and said his "big ambition" was to "get back to my squadron in time to take part in the all-out invasion of England." Asked by Police Chief Herbert S. Myers to "put it in writing", von Werra wrote out the date "May 12 1941" and said: "Remember what I am telling you, on May 12—that will be the big day and I will be back flying over England with my squadron."

. . . He boasted that he would get away from the States as easily as he had gotten away from the English in England on two occasions and from the Canadians . . .

. . . Von Werra was idolised as a hero and trailed by crowds of sympathetic admirers after he was apprehended by local police . . .

. . . At his mass press conference he spun stories that would have amazed Horatio Alger, Joseph Conrad or the author of the Arabian Nights.

On 27 January the London *Times* published an account from its New York correspondent, under an appropriate heading:

E

BARON MÜNCHAUSEN ESCAPES
GERMAN AIRMAN TELLS THE TALE

. . . He said that he shot down three British aeroplanes that day, but had come into collision with another German aeroplane when coming out of a dive. He said he had flown over England so many times that he was unable to count the flights. He had escaped this time, he said, so as to take part in a "knock-out blow" against England in March. The Germans had been experimenting with the transport of troops in gliders towed by bombers, each glider carrying 45 to 50 men. He asserted that United States help was "too late" to "save" England, and predicted a British capitulation in September. Praising British morale, he declared that German bombers had done "terrific" damage to London.

VI

ESCAPE FROM TOST BEI GLEIWITZ

from

My Purpose Holds

By Jerome Caminada

Jerome Caminada, a South African employed as a civilian war correspondent by The Times, *was arrested by the Germans in Boulogne in 1940 and interned in the castle of the Wülzburg. One of his fellow prisoners was Giles Romilly, with whom he talked over the prospects of escape. He was unable to do anything about it, however, until he was transferred in September 1941 to Tost bei Gleiwitz, a stalwart, dirty brown building, a former asylum for lunatics on the border of Poland.*

After an abortive attempt, when he got away two miles from the prison before recapture, he joined Andrew Strang and Robert Johnson (Johnny) in September 1942 in the plan related here.

He and Johnny reached Hungary. Adventures as English teachers in Budapest were followed by internment in Rumanian prisons and camps before they finally reached Italy and freedom in September 1944—four years after each had been taken into captivity and after they had travelled nearly 3,000 miles.

WHEN Strang had asked me to help him, he had said that he would need at least three men as well, and after hearing the details, I more than agreed. His idea was to use an immensely long and thick plank which he would get the others to push out of the office window. He would then crawl out and along it to the end. Here a rope would have been tied, and he would slide down the rope to the top of the wall, jump down on to the pavement and be out.

Thousands of prisoners spent months digging under their German guards; here was a way of going, in a few minutes, over their heads.

In theory the plan sounded simple, if ponderous, but in practice there were enormous difficulties. How, in a camp where any length of plank, any odd article, would attract the immediate attention of both German and internee, and where no spare wood could ever be found—how did he propose to acquire this monstrous, battering-ram apparatus? And having got it, how did he propose to keep it, and get it into place without attracting attention? And then, if it were used, what of the lights on the path and the sentries underneath?

Strang's answer to the first problem was a use of the obvious. He went to the camp carpentry shop, where two prisoners worked nominally under German supervision, and placed the order. I think he said that the plank was required for the camp stage, but in any case the carpenters did not ask questions. A plank some twenty-five feet long would be needed, and as they did not have such a piece, and if they had had could not handle it, they made two separate pieces, and a wooden sleeve to join them. The two pieces would be fitted into the sleeve at opposite ends to make the whole one piece. Normally it would have been out of the question for the carpenters to make anything so large, but it happened that timber had been sent in from Sweden for repairs in the camp, and they used some of this.

This done, they sent the apparatus over to the main building with the labour gang of internees used for rough work in the camp, getting them to store it against the wall in one of the passages. There could be no way of hiding a 'prop' so large, so the only thing to do was to put it openly against the wall where the Germans passed by several times a day, and hope that because of its very obviousness no questions would be asked. And that is what happened; not one German thought to inquire into the purpose of this object.

We realized that when almost the full length of the plank was outside the window, its weight, plus that of a man crawling along it, would make it impossible for a group of men holding on to the piece still inside the room to get enough leverage to keep the whole plank horizontal. More support would be needed to hold up the outward end. The best way to obtain this would be to tie our rope to one of the bars across the corresponding window on the floor above the window we were to use, hitch the middle of the rope round the outward end of the plank, and allow the rest to hang free. The room above the one we were to use was also an office, but had bars on the windows. We would still slide down the last piece of rope from the plank on to the wall.

This now meant that we required a rope much longer than the one we had made for the discarded plan, and as we had used all the string we could get, the only solution was to lengthen our rope by reducing it from a thickness of four strands to three. Back into the library we went next day, unplaited the rope, and plaited it again. I was doubtful that this would hold our weight, but we tested it on a hook in the wall and it seemed to pass.

We then selected four men to help us. Jack Ford and Charlie Averill were obvious choices, and were ready at once; so was Strube, a commercial artist who, with Ford, had already served a sentence for assisting in Romilly's escape. He bore the Germans no love, having previously been in a gaol for a year or more. He asked no questions and was invaluable at the crucial time. A fourth reliable man was hard to find, but we finally asked a young man who had come from France. His father was also in the camp, and the son was a little fearful of retaliations by the Germans on both of them, but the sense of adventure won him over.

Everything was now prepared. We each had a small bag filled with food, razor, soap, a spare shirt, and a pair of socks, and would carry this on the plank, tied, with our boots, round our necks. We would not be able to carry overcoats or anything else, but I decided to stuff a cap in my pocket, and to put on a rough pair of gloves.

Strang produced an old pair of wire cutters which he had long before found, or stolen, and we were ready. We left the cutting of the wire to the last minute because we feared that once cut it would be visible in the daytime. Things had moved quickly; our preparations had taken only two or three days, but we were ready. It was 7 September, 1942.

We waited one day more for a clouded sky. It was not as windy as we would have liked, but the best we could hope for.

"We'll meet at ten o'clock tonight outside the room, when the last stragglers are in bed," Johnny told Strang.

"Right. Have we got the keys?"

"I'll get the key to the room," I said. "Johnny has the key

to the room above. Lucky it's an office too, we don't want a crowd watching us from their bunks. But we had to ask Arnold for it. He wasn't too curious, and he's all right. The fact that he uses the office won't put him in the soup. There'll be no evidence there."

"Do the others know it's tonight?"

"Yes, they'll be there."

I went up the stairs at eight-thirty that night to give the news of the day to about two hundred men in the Festsaal. Perhaps the last time, I found myself thinking, as I looked at them grouped around me. I dare say I'll be moved after this effort. They looked so eager, as they stood there, so pathetically anxious for good news of the war. I tried to throw in a joke or two.

"We'll see what the situation is tomorrow," I ended glibly, talking about the Russian front.

I went downstairs to my room, and the tier upon tier of bunks. My boxes were on the shelf on the wall, and my bunk, a top one, in usual disarray. Hope I don't lose all this stuff, if they grab me and move me, I thought, looking at my new pair of black shoes, just arrived from England, and some superior undergarments sent by the South African Red Cross. Property, property, for ever tying one down, I tried to tell myself. Johnny at the far end of the room was fussing about his bunk too.

The man below me had gone to bed with his beret on, as he always did. Neat, methodical, punctual. "About time you turned in, son," he said looking at me over the blankets. He kept imprisonment at bay, at the age of sixty, by discipline.

At nine o'clock I fetched the key to the office, and at nine-thirty repeated the trick which had worked before, keeping the office key in my pocket. I then went into the cold corridor outside my room. The usual group of gossiping stragglers were there, their cigarettes glowing in the murky quarter-light of a little bulb high up. They congregated at the end of the passage as always. Johnny and I hung about, making small talk when necessary, but wishing heartily they would go to bed. There they sat on benches, talking, talking—what the missus said in her last letter, how long the war would now last—the same as ever.

At ten-ten the last man stamped out his cigarette and

went to bed. We slipped back into our room, wriggled around in the narrow space between the tiers, and changed into old flannels, pullovers, and jackets. At the last minute I pulled on a roll-top pullover also. My brown boots were still with me, and my cap in my pocket, also a couple of handkerchiefs and my camp identity disk No. 17932.

I went one floor up to the second floor. Everyone was already there, and the battering-ram was on the corridor floor, in two pieces. We entered the room, and everybody else sat down while Johnny began to cut the wire at the north window. Andrew sat at the east window to keep watch. The others were on the floor, their backs to office cupboards, the two pieces of the plank, the joining sleeve and the rope beside them. The lights outside shone fixedly on the street wall and on the building, and the two sentries paced their beats below, or stood talking at the corner of the building. I waited to relieve Johnny.

We had to cut several vertical and horizontal wires to be able to draw back a square of wire large enough for our bodies to pass through. We thought it would be done in an hour. Johnson grunted and squeezed; then gave up with aching wrists, and I tried.

"Wonderful cutters, these," I grumbled. "Blunt as hell."

Snip! A strand was cut, and the noise seemed like the report of a pistol. Surely the sentries must hear that? We tried to work only when they were pacing away, but could not be sure where they were. Nothing happened, and we carried on.

We had miscalculated. Instead of having a hole made within an hour, it took us three hours. By now we were all taking turns. Eagerly, and yet fearfully, we waited for each 'snip'. Six, seven, eight, nine of them. A hole large enough was at last made.

"What's the time?" I said.

"About one-thirty," answered someone.

"What do you think, Johnny? Can we do it tonight?"

"Don't think so. We've got to wait for a chance with these sentries—a chance for three of us in turn; and we've got to get clear of this area before light. I don't like it."

We discussed it, and tried to look out carefully through the hole to see what the sentries were doing. They were just approaching each other and began to talk. We gave up. It was too late to do more that night. We would have to wait one more day.

Someone produced bits of string from his pocket, and we tied the broken wire together as best we could. Our loyal helpers picked up the equipment, and went out into the passage with it to stand it where it had been before. Johnny took the rope, I locked the door, stole off once more to the custodian's bunk to hang the key over his head, took the dummy key away, and went to my room to bed.

"Bloody night walkers," mumbled the beret below me, and turned over. I climbed above him, and slept.

The following day, 9 September, passed hard. We were short of sleep, but could not compose ourselves to rest. Night came; it was very still, but pitch dark, and we were hopeful.

That night the usual group outside our bedroom seemed to have no intention of going to bed. Ten o'clock came and went, ten-thirty, still they sat there. I could not sit, and paced up and down. By five minutes to eleven three men were left— and an air-raid alarm was raised again. The guard was doubled—activity everywhere; once more the attempt had to be postponed.

Our nerves were wearing thin. An internment camp is not the easiest place to develop the art of waiting, and we were in danger of slipping over the crest—that timing point of fusion between complete preparation and confident anticipation—when all attempts should be made. We were approaching an anticlimax.

For one thing, the key problem was getting out of hand. The man who had charge of the key was by now suspicious of my comings and goings, and showed his disapproval by saying I should have to choose another time to read the newspapers. I made some half-promise, and obtained the key once more. Not daring to repeat the trick of the false key that night, I returned the genuine one just after nine-thirty, but left the door to the office unlocked. It was that night or never.

We assembled outside the office once more; it was becoming a drill. I went into the room and quickly untied the string binding the wire, while Johnny took the rope to the room above. He unlocked the door, went to the window

above the one where I was waiting, and tied one end of the
rope firmly to the iron bars. Very gently he then let the other
rope end down outside; I grabbed it and pulled it into the
room.

Johnny came back, and we put the two pieces of the beam
together, joined by the sleeve. The whole was then so long
that to do this we had to open the door, which was in direct
line with the window, and keep it open, allowing the rear
end of the beam to stick out into the passage.

"Interesting for any German who comes along," said
Charles.

Jack Ford then took the hanging rope and hitched it
round the end of the beam nearest the window, leaving the
greater part of it free. He was to hold the free section and
pay out as soon as the apparatus was pushed forward, the
rope being long enough to enable him to hold on to the
free end, even when one of us was sliding down the rope
from the plank to the wall. This would give better control
and enable the plank to be pulled back more quickly. Thus,
at the farthermost point of the acrobatic operation the rope
would lead from the window above to the end of the plank
over the wall, round the end, under it, with one of us (we
hoped) sliding down, and back in a bend to Jack standing at
the lower window. The other three helpers were to push the
beam out, and put their weight on the inner end as it became
shorter and shorter inside the room.

Strang settled down at the window overlooking the
censors' offices to watch the sentry patrolling at right angles
to the road, and Johnson and I sat at our street window,
straining to see or hear where the man was below. The
window-ledge was wide, so that when we leaned out through
the gap in the wire he would come into sight fully only at the
far end of his beat. We could do nothing until Andrew's
sentry was at the end of his beat farthest from the road, and
perhaps in his box there, so that the corner of the building
would obstruct his view of us; and the sentry below must also
be at the far end of his beat to allow a slight chance of his
not seeing or hearing us. Johnny was to go first; myself second;
Andrew third.

Everyone was silent. We soon found that it is not a
sentry's conception of his task to be as far away from his mate

as possible. Much more likely is he to stay close to the other; witness these two that night. If one was not at our end of his beat, the other was; and frequently they were both there. Then they would stay to chat, leaning their rifles against the wire and, as we could distinctly hear, telling each other of their family troubles.

Poor fellows! We hoped they would not have more troubles on our account. We did not recognize them by their voices, and were glad, because if they had been men we knew and liked we would have been embarrassed. It was a fairly strict point with every prisoner not to leave a guard he liked to "carry the baby". And this time there would be some baby.

Just before eleven o'clock, the time of the changing of the guard, Johnson saw his opportunity. "Let her go," he called. Like some great derrick the beam shot out of the side of the building.

Hunching himself up on the window-sill, Johnson crawled through the broken wire, and set off along the plank. He reached the end and started to slide down the rope. But he was not, as we had calculated he would be, over the top of the wall, nor was he low enough down. With the lights in the ground full on him, he hung in mid-air, turning slowly round, like a figure on the gallows. The horrible parallel flashed through my mind. We watched him dumbly.

He did not lose his head. He realized better than we— though we were in the room, and he was not—what was wrong.

"Let the rope go," he called softly. "Let it go more. Pay it out." He was right. In the excitement, or because he could not see properly, the man next to me at the window was holding on to the rope too tightly, and the beam had not gone out as far as it safely could. He gave the rope play, the beam went out another four feet, Johnson dropped lightly on to the top of the wall, and the next second was in the street. Everything, wood and rope, came back with a rush as we frantically pulled. No alarm was heard. Johnson was out.

We could not believe it. One man was out. We waited gasping. Still no shouts or shots. We had succeeded that far. Now it was my turn.

At eleven o'clock the guard changed. The new sentries

arrived and stood talking, rarely pacing their beat. When they did, they did not do so at the same time. I waited. For one and a half hours I waited. I could dimly see Johnson on the other side of the street, a crouching figure in the gutter. We had agreed that he should wait for me, but if the alarm was given at any time he should leave as fast as he could. As Strang was going independently, we were not to wait for him.

About half-past twelve footsteps were heard in the building; footsteps we knew well. The Germans were on their rounds—they often, but not always, went round in the night—and the door of our room was half-open. Nor could we shut it, with the piece of wood sticking through, unless we pulled the two pieces of the beam out of the joining sleeve. That I was not prepared to do. Would they pass our door? Would they discover us?

I was not there to learn for myself the answer to these questions. As we sat listening, Strang suddenly called out: "He's gone into his box." His sentry was in his box.

I pushed my head out through the hole in the wire to see what my sentry was doing. He was near the far end of his beat, walking away from us. This was my moment.

"Shove her off!" I called. And the great beam once more slid and slithered out over the window-sill.

My bag and boots strapped round my neck, I set off to crawl the plank. How far below the ground seemed to be, showing clearly in the electric light. I grabbed hold of the rope leading upwards to the window above to steady myself. But clumsy as I always was, I was soon half on the plank and half off. I slithered along as best I could, until well past half-way. It took two or three seconds.

Behind me came the noise as of a tree crashing down. A splitting of timber, a splintering that seemed to me must be heard all over Germany. I found myself, still on the plank, coming down—not on top of the wall, but inside. Soon I would be dropping, it seemed to me, at the sentry's feet.

The sleeve behind me, the joint into which the two pieces of the beam fitted, had broken, and the beam was slowly bending under my weight. I could almost hear, I could almost *feel* the sound of a rifle going off. But nothing happened.

My old gloves came in useful now. Reaching up with my left hand, as I slowly descended, I was able to grasp a strand of barbed wire running along the top of the wall. With this new purchase, and still holding on to the rope with my other hand, I struggled upwards until I had a leg on the wall. I then drew myself on to the top, gathered myself, and jumped down into the street on the other side.

Johnson loomed up, and began to run. In my stockinged feet I joined him.

We were out. We were free.

VII

ESCAPE FROM SHAMSUIPO

from

Hongkong Escape

By R. B. Goodwin

When Hongkong surrendered to overwhelming Japanese odds on Christmas Day, 1941, Lt.-Com. R. B. Goodwin, O.B.E., at that time a sub-lieutenant of the New Zealand Division of the Royal Naval Volunteer Reserve, had the misfortune to be in hospital with a leg wound. It was not until the end of February that he was fit enough to be taken to the overcrowded North Point Camp. In April he was sent with other officers to the Argyle Street Camp in Kowloon, where he remained for two years before being transferred to the Shamsuipo Camp. During all that time he had been contemplating escape, and at last on the night of 16–17 July, 1944, he was able to put his plans into action.

Following his escape, he made a hazardous journey across South China, was helped by guerrillas, and through them contacted British troops, eventually arriving at Kunming. From there he was sent to Auckland on leave, reaching home on 17 November.

On 30 August, 1945, he again anchored in Hongkong Harbour, and next day visited Shamsuipo Camp, where he met many old P.O.W. friends who had just been released— also Colonel Tokunaga, commanding officer of all prisoner of war camps in Hongkong, who was now a prisoner.

★

FOR weeks there had been electrical storms with constant rains, and Sunday, 16 July, 1944, was just another day of pouring rain, without, however, the usual display of lightning. In fact, when night fell, the rains came down with never a flash to break the darkness, a most unusual condition. Never before had there been such an opportunity.

Nothing could be done outside until after midnight, when the lights went out. Inside the huts all lights were switched

77

off at 10 p.m., and after that my work began. With neighbours so close, there was only two feet between the bunks, I had to move with great care to avoid arousing suspicion. Mosquito-nets over the bunks hid me fairly well, and under my sheet I slipped on a shirt and shorts, and a pair of rubber-soled shoes.

Rain beat solidly on the roof and squalls whistled about the camp, making the interior of the hut seem wonderfully comfortable by comparison with conditions outside. It would be so easy to slip off my clothes, relax the nervous tension, and settle down to peaceful sleep. Outside there was nothing but streaming wet discomfort, unknown and unseen dangers, death lurking in every shadow.

Lying there, listening to the sounds of tempest, straining my ears for any sounds to indicate the proximity of guards, it was grimly amusing to think of what might happen in the next hour or two. Having seen the reactions of the Japanese to previous alarms, it was easy to imagine the scene should a false move cause me to short-circuit the electrified wires on the fence. Before my frizzled body hit the ground there would be guards yelling and rushing about the camp. Dozens of extra troops would be pouring in from Headquarters, and the whole camp would be paraded over and over again. There would be no more sleep for anyone that night because there had been caused so much inconvenience, so much loss of "face", and such a display of panic and stupidity as to feed anew the smouldering sense of inferiority in our captors. Anything in the nature of an alarm caused such a pande-monium, and such a display of ineffective effort, that it was a dismal commentary on the ease with which they conquered all our positions in the East.

Suddenly the lights went out and the camp was plunged into intense gloom. There was no suspicious sound, only the noise of the wind and the rain. No one stirred inside the hut. Lifting the mosquito-net I slid silently off my bed, lifted my pack from underneath, and crept along to the door. There was no one in sight, and I passed safely through. To be seen fully dressed and with a large bundle in my arms at that hour of the night would have called for an awkward explana-tion, and I had a keen interest in avoiding everyone. There would be interrogations on the morrow, and it was better that nothing should be known.

Outside, a soft rain was falling and darkness spread an impenetrable cloak. A wayward squall whistled along the fence, rattled the lamp-shades, and was gone. No one was about. There might be sentries standing against the huts, they did that sometimes, but conditions were perfect and it was no time to hesitate. A few swift paces brought me to the bridge, and on the far side of that I dropped flat on my stomach to wriggle under the concertina wire. That was easy, for the wire had recently been raised a little by grass-cutters. By the time my pack had been pulled through, the rain had stopped, and just as I began to crawl towards the chosen lamp-post someone came to visit an open latrine that stood by the edge of the drain. From my position on the ground I could see him very clearly against the sky, but the darkness of the ground sheltered me. Then several more men came out to join the first, taking advantage of the lull between showers, and in spite of the dark it did not inspire me with any great confidence to be lying there, not more than twelve feet distant, with nothing but a few thin strands of wire to hide me. The intruders were much too clearly in view for my peace of mind, and valuable minutes were wasting.

When three or four of the nocturnal wanderers had returned to their huts I decided to wait no longer, and began to crawl cautiously along the narrow path between the wire and the fence. Then, having reached my post I was in the act of standing up, when approaching voices made me hug the ground again. This time it was the one o'clock change of guard going outwards, and it gave me a shock to know that already an hour of darkness had gone. Three soldiers filed past, ten feet distant on the other side of the drain, and I am afraid I took rather a morbid interest in their silhouettes, especially in their rifles and bayonets so clearly etched against the gloomy background. Rain was falling again, and lying there in the mud and water, scarcely breathing, it was not at all pleasant to think of the consequences should that party see me. I could do nothing until the relieved guards came in, and as it was a matter of only two or three minutes before they came trudging past, they were probably only too glad to return to the shelter of the guardhouse. It was then time for me to make the next move.

From long and close scrutiny I knew exactly what that

fence was like, but in spite of all my study I had been unable
to think of any way to pass the roll of concertina wire along
the top. But the four electrified wires were my immediate
danger, and I felt that if they could be successfully passed,
the concertina wire would be beaten too.

Having carefully adjusted the pack on my back to give
my arms greatest freedom, I lifted my right foot to the insulator, grasped the post above the top wire, and tried to climb.
Imagine my dismay at finding that the step was too high and
that my strength was unequal to the task. Here was a pretty
dilemma. Rain was runing down the post and wires, my shoes
were wet and muddy, the insulator had only a very small cap
above the wire, and it was imperative that my foot should
remain firmly on that little piece of smooth porcelain. Several
unsuccessful attempts to climb convinced me that it could not
be done, and then I remembered that it was my right leg
that had been injured. Though no weakness had been
apparent when working about the camp it was possible that
some infirmity remained, so, readjusting my balance I placed
my left foot on the insulator. Then, using my arms to their
utmost, I heaved myself upright.

That was an exhilarating moment, with the first really
dangerous step successfully completed. I was off the ground,
the insulator had not broken, I was not electrocuted. Now
for the next step. It had to be my right foot this time, but
the step was not so high. In poising for this step my bare leg
pressed hard against the third electric wire. There was no
insulator on that one, and it was standing out nine inches
from the post. Those were moments of supreme danger. All
my weight was concentrated on the small insulator top, little
more than an inch in diameter, and my left foot was rapidly
tiring. My bare leg was pressed hard against a live wire; my
right foot was precariously poised on the top insulator, and
my hands were grasping the post between strands of concertina wire. With my leg against the live wire one touch of
those invisible strands above would have been fatal, and even
without touching I was afraid that the running water would
complete a circuit. The situation was one of great delicacy,
and it seemed that Death looked on with more than passing
interest the while I tried to adjust my balance. Then, summoning every ounce of strength I straightened up, and stood

clear above the electric wires. As quickly as possible I stepped off the insulator on to the barbed wire fence behind the posts.

One major danger was passed, and then there began a most desperate struggle. Before I could stand up the roll of wire had to be forced outwards with all my strength, and it was pressing hard against me as I clung to the post. My only foothold was on top of the fence directly below the middle of the roll, and since half of it overhung either side of the fence my feet were resting under the middle of it, while my chin was resting on the top. I began a fierce struggle to transfer my body from the camp side to the outside of the roll. It was a war of attrition, won by pushing one leg down through the wire, then drawing the other one out and pushing it down again a few strands farther on. The hard steel wire was relentless, and it was an operation fraught with the utmost difficulty and pain.

The whole fence was swaying precariously, the lamp shade was rattling loudly, and the wires of the fence were slipping and squealing through their holding staples. I was doubled up over the roll of wire, with my shirt, shorts and flesh caught in a dozen places by barbs that sprang at me afresh with every movement. No matter how hard I pushed and trampled, the steel wire flew back to gain fresh grips the moment the pressure was released.

After several minutes of that exhausting fight I had to rest, and my heart sank for the first and only time on my journey. Would I never escape from that subtle enemy, which struck from every direction with a hundred invisible fangs? Where was the sentry who should have been at his post, twenty-five yards away at the end of the fence? At every moment I expected a torch to flash upon me, and to feel the thudding blow of bullets. It seemed impossible that he could not hear the noise, yet nothing happened.

Inside the camp another group had gathered at the latrine, and I felt certain from their animated voices that they could hear, and were discussing, the racket on the fence. That further added to my disquiet, for their talkative meeting at that hour of the night would be likely to attract the guards.

After a brief rest my struggles were resumed, the wires

F

squealed again, and nothing less than a miracle could save me. Casting all caution to the winds I plunged and tore and strained with all my might, preferring to be shot struggling rather than just hanging limp in the wire. At last both legs were over the outside of the wire, and there I crouched with both feet on the top of the fence, my hands gripping the post, knees and chin almost touching, and with a dozen barbs gripping clothes and flesh with equal fervour.

My intention had been to climb down the outside of the fence, but I was quite unable to push the wire away to make that possible. The situation demanded a desperate remedy, so, straightening my knees, I let go with my hands, and hoped for the best. There was a tearing of cloth, the fence jerked violently, and I dropped seven feet to land with a tremendous thud on my back. Tins in my pack rattled loudly at that harsh treatment, and certain that an alarm *must* then be raised, I raced for the second fence. Finding the gap at once I dropped my pack and slid under the bottom electric wire, with my face scraping the mud and I know not what fraction of an inch between my back and eternity. I pulled my pack through and stood up, and then suddenly realised that my noisy though unceremonious departure had evidently passed unheeded.

How had it happened? The sentry could not have been asleep as the guards had just been changed, and my only thought is that he had left his post to yarn with one of the other sentries farther along the sea-wall. Whatever the reason, there I stood safely outside the two most dangerous fences, with comparatively easy going ahead.

To reach the sea-wall at a point beyond the electric fence I had to cross diagonally over that ground where petrol had been stored, and great care was needed to avoid its deep trenches. The intense darkness was my best friend, but it was also a great hindrance, for I had to feel for every step. The obstacles at the sea-wall were up to that time unknown, so it was with great satisfaction that I found nothing there but a broken barbed-wire fence with only three loose wires remaining between the posts.

Before leaving the hut I had stuffed a waterproof hat and a pair of stockings inside my shirt, and as it was raining heavily again I decided to put on the hat to keep my head

warm. It gave me a rude shock to find that in falling from the
fence my shirt had been ripped out, and the hat and stockings
had gone. The discomfort which the loss would cause was
nothing compared to the danger that the lost articles might
indicate my route, for above all else the Japanese must be
prevented from knowing the direction of my flight. Without
that knowledge they must of necessity disperse their search
over a wide area, and my chances of success would be so much
better. My first impulse was to go back for the lost articles,
but second thoughts convinced me that any such attempt
would be foolish, since valuable time would be lost and the
chance of finding them in the dark was remote.

Now for the last fence. Lying down I pressed the lowest
wire into the grass and, as I started to roll through, my whole
body contracted under the impact of a powerful electric shock.
The current cut out immediately, and I was out on the top of
the concrete wall, my mind racing with confused thoughts.
Was it a trap wire? Had the shock recorded at the guard-
house? I remembered that at Argyle Street it had been said
that tell-tale lights showed any interruption on the fence
circuit. Haste to depart was my most urgent need, and I
crawled along the top of the wall to a post which would serve
as an anchor for a light rope. Below me was a black void in
which was an unknown landing-ground. It might be rocks, it
might be sampans with sleeping owners on board, or it might
be just plain sand. The tide was out, so of one thing I was sure
—there would be no water there. That much information
had been gathered on one of the drain-cleaning expeditions.

Having made sure that the rope ran freely I dropped both
ends over the wall and prepared to slide down. Accustomed
as I had been all my life to rowing dinghies and climbing
about the rigging of yachts, it had never entered my head that
that would present any difficulty, but on trying to take my
weight on the thin rope I was quickly disillusioned. My hand
could not grip hard enough, so to hold on, while swinging my
body over, I put a turn round my right hand, thinking that it
would be a simple matter to take it off before starting to go
down. Again, much to my surprise and discomfort, my
strength failed and I had to slide down with the turn still
round my hand. The result was inevitable, and I reached a
beach of firm sand with the skin torn from both palm and

back of the hand, an injury that gave me a great deal of pain in the days to come.

Matters of greater urgency left no time for regrets so, coiling my rope, I began walking towards the sea, keeping in deep shadow under the wall. Small waves were rolling on shore in bright lines of phosphorous, and when close to them I sat down to make ready for swimming. It took me two or three minutes to fasten one life-jacket on myself and one on the pack, and while I was engrossed in that job a sudden flashing of lights a few yards along the fence gave me a great fright. In a moment my fears were at rest, for the flashes were caused by a loose wire swinging in the wind against the electric fence. Every time the wires met sparks were flying, and there lay the explanation of the shock I had received. Each time the wires made contact a shock was sent along the barbed-wire fence, so my fears of a trap were unfounded. It was blowing hard and raining heavily again, so there was no danger of being heard. That was comforting knowledge, for in watching the flashing wires I had seen the sentry, who should have heard my departure, standing directly above me.

When the life-jackets had been inflated I tied my rope to the pack and set off towards the sea, passing close to grounded junks on the way. There were a great many craft in the bay, both ashore and afloat, and I had no wish to be seen by the people on board. In spite of the darkness there was a sheen on the water, and when looking seaward dark objects could be seen for some distance. It was not at all reassuring to know that while wading out through the shallow water I was plainly visible from junks on shore, for a person deliberately walking out to sea on a wet and stormy night could hardly fail to arouse comment, even in China.

The pack floated buoyantly, and when it had floated back clear of my feet I fastened the rope round my neck and started to swim. Brilliant phosphorous marked every movement with a trail of fire that made me proceed with care when passing close to anchored vessels. When viewed from the camp in daylight it did not seem to be far across the bay, but it seemed to be a long way then, with nothing but stormy night all about. Intense blackness hid the shore, and there was nothing to indicate my progress save junks that, as they swung towards me in eddying squalls, seemed bent on my destruction. The

wind had its advantages, for besides covering my noise, by
swimming almost at right angles to its direction I was able
to keep to my course.

My sense of time had gone completely, and I had no idea
how long it took me to cover the half mile to shore. At last my
foot touched bottom, and I stood up to wade out on what
looked like the beach. Fifty yards away a small sampan was
high and dry, a small lamp burning beneath its matting
cover. Nothing else could be distinguished, so turning my
back to the sea I began to stumble up the sloping shore,
making an inordinate amount of noise by tripping over
empty tins and other rubbish lying there. I expected to find
a bank sloping up directly to the road, but a few paces took
me into a cultivated garden, with banked rows of sweet
potatoes. That was not in my reckoning at all, and it made
me think that the beach must be farther west.

Having returned to the sea I was wading past the stern of
a junk on a slipway when I fell with a resounding splash into
a hole of unknown depth. Bobbing to the surface it took me
only a moment to reach the other side and scramble out, but
after taking a dozen steps more the same thing happened
again. That would not do, for there was no wind under the
shore and there would be watchmen on the junks. A continuous noise like a porpoise floundering in the shallow water
would be bound to attract attention, so I lay down to paddle
and swim again. Soon the trend and nature of the shore convinced me that my first landing had been correct, so making
out to deeper water I swam back to the beach, guided by the
light still burning in the sampan. This time I continued
across the potato patch, and soon reached the road.

Now what to do? The road was flanked on both sides by
buildings, and directly behind those on the northern side
steep hillsides rose to the Kowloon range. The salient featues
of those hills had been memorised, but how did one pass the
buildings? I could see nothing and had no idea which way to
go. My feet had been hardened by continuous barefoot
walking while in camp, so, as my shoes were squelching
loudly at every step, they were taken off and slung round my
neck. I was still undecided which way to go when someone
came clumping along the road in wooden clogs. As the walker
approached I stood quite still, until he reached a point on

the road directly opposite. Suddenly a brilliant torch-beam streamed from right alongside me, and it held a Chinese coolie for some distance, at the same time lighting up the buildings opposite. Among mingled feelings of surprise and fright came the realization that I was standing within two feet of a Japanese sentry, and also that some thirty yards to the right a narrow lane ran in towards the hills. There was my route.

VIII

ESCAPE FROM DEVIL'S ISLAND

from

Dry Guillotine

By René Belbenoit

Devil's Island, the infamous penal settlement on the shores of French Guiana, is a name that used to strike terror in the hearts not only of criminals but of all reasonably-minded people.

René Belbenoit, who was sentenced to life imprisonment in this hell hole, was transported there in 1920 at the age of twenty-one. From the moment of his arrival there was only one thought in his mind—escape. Four times he made the attempt, and four times he was recaptured. But at last, in the company of five other convicts, he made a fifth effort and succeeded.

Dry Guillotine is a horrifying account of this "death in life", which will always be associated in many minds with the case of Captain Dreyfus—one of the world's most appalling miscarriages of justice.

I LIMPED down the hot roadway along the outskirts of Saint Laurent, the village of the condemned, thinking that I would have to do something quickly to get funds to finance an escape before I went crazy. To escape through the jungle, I had learned, by three terrible experiences, was impossible. To escape by sea required the assistance of seamen partners. I would have to obtain a boat. I would have to seek companions who, like myself, preferred death at sea to life in Cayenne—men whom I could trust not to whisper my plan to any Corsican guard. To escape by sea required, in addition to a good boat and good companions, a substantial amount of food and supplies. It would require at least ten days of favourable weather and wind before we could reach a safe landing place. These three requirements seemed impossible to satisfy.

A man in freshly washed and ironed linens and a white sun helmet, which marked him immediately as being some sort of a tourist, stopping for a moment or passing through the penal colony, crossed the sunbaked roadway and beckoned to me.

"Where can I find a prisoner who speaks English?" he asked in schoolboy French.

"I speak a little English," I said. Perhaps this stranger would give me a tip for some chore.

"I want to find a prisoner named Belbenoit," he said in English. "The man about whom Blair Niles wrote her book, *Condemned*. I want to talk to him. Guide me to him or bring him to me, and I will give you five dollars!"

I looked around hastily. No guard was in sight. "Give me the money," I said. He peeled a note from a fat bundle of notes and handed it to me. "Which way?" he asked.

"Right here!" I said, laughing for the first time in years. "I am Belbenoit!"

"You?" he asked, looking down at me disparagingly. "Are you the prisoner who has escaped four times?"

"Who are you?" I asked.

He seemed a little taken back, but finally announced that he was an executive of an American motion picture company. His company, he explained, was going to make a motion picture based on Blair Niles' book—a film story about Devil's Island—one that would feature a dramatic escape. He had flown down to French Guiana to study the convict colony at first hand. He wanted the picture to be accurate, he said, a true-to-life portrayal of a man's sufferings in the worst prison in the world. Would I be interested in giving him information, supplying him with additional factual material which could be used in his forthcoming picture? If a prisoner tried to escape, how would he do it?

"He'd escape by the sea—in a sailing boat," I said, voicing the thought which had been racing through my head for many long days. "He'd . . ."

"No!" he interrupted me. "This must be an escape through the jungles . . . combat with fierce animals, snakes, swamps . . ."

"Nobody has ever escaped through the jungles!" I insisted. "I tried it three times. I ought to know!"

"Maybe so!" he said. "But it makes a better picture. In our picture the hero has to escape through the jungle. I've heard that you've had more dramatic escapes than any other convict," he added. "If you answer all my questions, I'll make it worth your while!"

Well, Fate for the first time in my life was offering me a helping hand. It was not for me to quibble over a motion picture hero's ability to escape through the jungle! I spent the whole night sitting at a table answering his questions, making rough drawings of prison cells, punishment racks, describing in detail my three attempts to escape through the jungle, giving him details of horrible backgrounds, answering every question while he took a bookful of notes. By dawn he said that he had enough. He peeled some bills from his money roll and handed them to me. The aeroplane in which he had arrived soon was but a speck in the Caribbean sky. I would have given my soul to have been as free as he, privileged to soar through the heavens to pleasant lands. A lump was in my throat as I realized how casually this man had landed, asked questions and flown away, as though he hadn't a moment's thought to waste on me as a brother man. To him I was but an information bureau, something he could pump dry, transmit profitably into continuity and impersonal celluloid.

But in my hands he had left two hundred dollars! With so much money—I knew a Chinaman who would get me a boat and package together food—and with such an outfit I knew I could find other penniless _libérés_ who would join me. I made up my mind that this time I must not fail. There was to be no recapture. I must make my way first to temporary freedom, some West Indian island that would give us temporary sanctuary, and then to the United States. Thousands of miles lay between French Guiana and New York, but with each mile gained I felt that I should escape that much farther from inhuman, atrocious existence and should gain that much towards civilization—and liberty. The people of the United States, I'd heard, would not deport a _libéré_ who had gained its shores—from Devil's Island.

"This time I'll make it!" I whispered over and over again to myself as I set about organizing my expedition.

I searched through the penal colony like a hawk for men

whose plight was most terrible, for companions I thought
would be of great physical aid for my escape. At last I selected
four convicts: Dadar, a young *libéré* whom I had known for a
year, who had served a five-year sentence for a first offence
robbery; Casquette, who had served fifteen years for killing his
mistress; Bébert, who had struck a cruel Corsican guard in
the face and nearly had his head blown off by a blast from the
guard's gun—after release from the hospital he had served an
additional four years of solitary confinement; and "Panama,"
a convict whose name none of us knew, but who had once
escaped and lived happily for twelve years in Colombia only
to be apprehended at last by a new French consul and
returned for Devil's Island punishment. Four men who
promised me that they preferred freedom or death.

But none of us had any knowledge of navigation. None of
us was a seaman. So I looked farther and finally selected
Chifflot, who had been sentenced to five years at hard labour
for killing, in self-defence, the son of a powerful negro chief
of a Congo protectorate tribe, who, subject to the influences of
modern civilization, had become a procurer of white women
in Montmarte. Chifflot had been a sailor. If I furnished the
boat and food, all he'd need, he promised, was the sun and the
stars to guide us to safety over the horizon of the Caribbean
Sea.

"We are going to Trinidad first," I said. The people of
that British island I knew loathed the existence of the French
Hell and would allow escaped men a safe resting place.

At six o'clock on the night of 2 May, 1935, we six men met
stealthily at a Chinaman's shop in the penal colony village of
Saint Laurent. The night grew black. Noiselessly we glided
into the forest and made our way to Serpent Creek. The boat
which the Chinaman had promised to hide for us proved to
be only half the size of the craft bargained for—a dugout
canoe barely three feet wide. In disgust I examined the packages of provisions, found them to be less than half of the
things agreed upon before I had passed my cash to him. I had
a terrible sinking feeling as though my escape had failed
before it had begun. My companions talked about postponing
the attempt. Even a little shark, they said, could overturn such
a craft—we would all die at sea.

But something told me not to let myself turn back. I got

into the canoe, urged them to take their places; and soon we were out of the creek and paddling noiselessly down the centre of the night-shrouded Maroni River. The tide was with us and we moved swiftly. Now and then we passed a canoe manned by wild blacks or Indians. They called to us but we did not answer. The Chinaman had supplied us with a water keg, but to make sure the water hadn't been poisoned we stopped at a fresh water creek and filled it with water that I knew would be safe.

At the mouth of the Maroni we hoisted our patchwork sail. Chifflot took the home-made tiller. The long slender canoe began to dance upon the water like an eighteen-foot cigar. Chifflot pointed out a star which he said would guide us due north. Waves began coming over the side of the canoe. Two men sat close to Chifflot to keep him company at the tiller and to make sure he didn't fall asleep. Others began bailing.

Men in their right senses would never have gone out on the merciless Caribbean Sea in such a craft, but we were driven by a quite insane desire to put Devil's Island and the Penal Colony behind us—to seek freedom at any price. The night passed all too quickly, as we looked over our shoulders constantly to make sure that a power boat was not coming out into the night after us. When the dawn came we were far out at sea, and there was nothing save a querulous gull to spy on us.

We complimented Chifflot, and Casquette took his place at the tiller. I volunteered to be the expedition's cook. Charcoal was lighted in a kerosene tin and strong tea soon revived us. The Chinaman had cheated me thoroughly on the food supply; I would have to stretch it out very thin during the coming days. But no one, during the first day, grumbled. We all talked with nervous gaiety; we were, at last, free of French Guiana! The fiery red of the setting sun made us work carefully to tie down all our supplies. Chifflot warned us that following such a sunset we could expect rough weather.

At eight o'clock the wind began to blow, helping us forward as it came from the continent behind us. The stars disappeared. I crept to the stern and sat beside Chifflot with a little compass in my hand. The canoe went faster and faster over the waves. I judged that we must be racing over the sea at about fifteen miles an hour. The other men became frightened as waves wet us, but to me every mile we gained ahead of the growing storm took us that much nearer freedom. Casquette was supposed to relieve Chifflot at the tiller, but to do this would have been too dangerous. We were precariously riding foaming waves; the least false move with the tiller would have caused us to capsize. Chifflot sang songs all night, his voice rising louder and louder in competition with wind. Then, shortly before dawn, the wind miraculously died down, the brassy sun rose over the horizon, and we set about removing our clothes and hanging them up on paddles to dry.

We had to repair the sail. A mattress cover and several old shirts had been used to make it. The cloth was so old that many of the patches had been torn apart. Not a sign of a ship was seen all day. The sun and glare of the sea burnt our flesh. The wounds on our legs, inflicted first by the iron bands that were welded about our bare ankles during our early prison days and aggravated by constant rubbing of our shackles, began to open and run and burn under the intermittent soaking of salt spray.

The third night found us not such good friends. Each of the six men, cramped for fifty long hours against his neighbour, had first talked himself out of joviality; and then everyone began to find fault with something or someone. Chifflot's hands were so blistered with holding on to the tiller that Casquette had to relieve him. Clinging desperately to the tiller in the darkness and on a sea more turbulent than it had been the previous night, Casquette had all he could do to keep us from being swamped in the deep sea troughs. We did not attempt to keep a course. The sea washed the compass from my hands in one mighty wave, and not a single star was to be seen.

When dawn came at last we were drenched, stiff, hungry, thirsty and sick at heart. I dipped some water out of the water keg and discovered that the sea water had got in and turned it salty. I mixed it with condensed milk and passed it around to my companions. They said it tasted terrible.

"We'd better turn and try to reach the mainland!" said Bébert. "We'll get fresh drinking water and put out again."

"We are probably off Demerara," Dadar guessed. "That's

less than half way to Trinidad. I'd rather take a chance on the jungle; there's at least plenty of water to drink!"

"We've only been gone three days!" I said, "and you speak already of turning in towards the coast. I told you when we started that I would not turn back. If we reach Trinidad we are safe. If we land anywhere on the mainland coast, we will be turned over to a French consul. I know. I've tried it!" Thus, we quarrelled all day long.

The fourth night was increasingly cruel. The fifth, sixth, seventh, eighth nights were nightmares; we became like six beasts. Eight more days we lived, how I do not know. Many times I thought the canoe would be buried in a black wave but as though some kind power lent it at the last moment a charm, the frail craft magically came up over the foaming crests, quivered for a moment and then plunged into another wave.

"Trinidad! Bah!" Dadar growled. "We'll never make it! And if we do, what surety have you, Belbenoit, that we won't be arrested? There's a French consul in Trinidad, isn't there?"

"Yes, but the British people, I believe, won't turn us over to him," I insisted. "They'll allow us to rest a few days, replenish our food; those Britishers, they're sportsmen. They'll grant us a few days' refuge! Stop worrying and I'll show you!" I was at the tiller and kept the bow pointed steadily north-west.

"Bah!" Bébert in the bow of the canoe snarled. "Change the course!" I've had enough of this. I'm going to land on the coast and take my chance—with my feet on the ground!"

"Stop!" I yelled at Dadar, who began crawling towards the sheet of the sail. I reached into my shirt and drew out a small pistol which I carried next to my skin, wrapped in oil cloth. I aimed the pistol at Bébert and then at Dadar. I am a very little man. I should have been no match for any of my companions in physical strength. But I had made up my mind to turn neither to the right nor to the left but keep heading towards the British island of real security. The five big men glowered at me but even a mouse can become brave when his freedom is at stake.

"Rush me if you like," I said, looking over the muzzle at my companions. "Here are six bullets, and I will kill each one of you if you insist!"

I did not want to kill my five companions. As I looked at them over the barrel of my stubby pistol, I realized that, like myself, they had swallowed much salt water from the angry sea, that they were hungry and scared of the shark-infested water. Their insistence on my shifting the tiller, altering our course and heading in for land was born of desperation and not of personal animosity.

"You are mad!" I said to them. "The coast is Venezuelan territory. You will surely be arrested and returned to Devil's Island. We cannot be far from Trinidad. There we'll be safe. I promise you, in Trinidad we will be safe to rest, eat good food, revive our strength before taking to the sea again."

"Put the sail over!" Bébert shouted to Chifflot. I aimed my pistol at Chifflot, but at the same instant Dadar jumped up, tried to spring past him and snatch my gun. Before I could fire Dadar had slipped and fallen against Chifflot, and both of them tumbled against the half-submerged gunwhale.

"Beasts!" yelled Casquette. "You're going to capsize us all!" He seized Dadar by the ankle, hit him behind the ear with his bony fist.

"Better tie him up!" Panama cautioned, throwing Casquette some wet cord. The unconscious man was securely tied, hands and feet together so he couldn't move. Then Casquette put his hand to his forehead and looked over the horizon.

"Look over there!" he yelled. "It's land!"

The others stood up and looked, but I, thinking it was a trick to get me away from the tiller and off my guard, didn't budge.

"It's Trinidad!" shouted Chifflot. "Come, Belbenoit, and see for yourself!" The sail obscured my vision of the horizon to which they pointed. Cautiously I tried to get a clear view without risking a sudden onslaught. I turned the tiller sharply to swing the bow over a big wave, and as we crested the foaming whitecap I saw that they were not trying to outwit me. There, against the horizon, were high, green mountains outlined against the blue sky.

The sight of those mountains wiped out all animosity, all evil talk, all quarrelling, from our minds and voices. We all shouted joyously, smiles replaced anger-drawn scowls. I pulled the tiller back and set the course again. The wind grew stronger behind us. We had been at sea fourteen days in a canoe that needed constant bailing, but now each of my companions except Dadar bailed happily as the sail bulged under the pressure of the breeze.

A few hours later we were riding the swells off shore. A thatched house set in a grove of coconut palms seemed deserted. I turned the tiller and steered the bow through the waves until the canoe, like a surf board, was shot up on the glistening white beach. My companions tried to leap ashore eagerly, but they were so weak that they stumbled and fell sprawled out on the dry sand like men suddenly robbed of all strength.

"Now do as you please!" I said. And I cast my pistol far out into the sea.

Some negroes, fishing along the beach with nets, passed us, circling us warily; but I called to them, begged them to climb the trees and get us some water coconuts to drink and eat. They put down their nets, climbed the trees and secured the nuts. But they would not approach nearer than fifty feet. They rolled the nuts down the beach to us and then went off hurriedly.

I hacked off the tops of five nuts, passed one to each of my companions. I cut the cords that bound Dadar and lifted him out of the slimy canoe, held the cool sweet liquid to his mouth as he drank. We drank the water of two nuts apiece, ate the white meat, then started to wobble across the sand like drunken scarecrows. The earth seemed to dance under my feet—to ebb and flow as the sea for such long terrible nights and days had done. In the hut there was a big black kettle full of rice and salt fish. We dug our hands into it and ate like wolves until, stuffed and drugged with relief, we rolled over on the floor of the hut and fell into a drunken sleep.

When we awoke I suggested that we go immediately to the nearest town and announce our arrival. At first my companions didn't like the idea at all. They insisted that we'd probably be arrested. It would be better, they said, to spend a few days here, eating coconuts and foraging for other food and supplies without the authorities knowing about us. But I insisted that this would not be as good for us as going to the authorities immediately—before they had heard indirectly of our arrival.

"I'm going to report myself!" I said, starting into the coconut grove. "You can stay here if you like."

But they fell in behind me and soon we were walking over a narrow road. We saw no one but negroes, very black and big negroes, speaking English in broad accents, who looked suspiciously at us with big eyes and gave us most of the road when they passed. After two hours we reached the little hamlet of Moruga, which, I learned, was the administrative centre for the south-east coast of Trinidad.

I went directly to the police station. The constable of Moruga sat behind an old table. He was a tremendous negro with the face and neck of an ape. He was dressed in a military uniform spotlessly clean. We stood before him while he summoned two policemen, who towered over us like ebony giants.

"Where do you come from?"

"From French Guiana," I said.

"Where are you going?"

"To the United States."

"For what reason have you landed in Trinidad?" he asked as soon as he had laboriously pencilled the previous information on his blotter.

"Because we have been at sea in a canoe for fourteen days. We were half-drowned. We had no fresh water. No food."

The constable stood up, went to the telephone nailed on the wall above our heads, turned the handle. "Six French fugitives landed here last night," he said. He listened to instructions from some superior, then hung up the earpiece.

"Get eighteen loaves of bread," he said to his policeman. "Get six pounds of rice, six pounds of sugar, six pounds of coffee, six pounds of codfish, twelve packages of cigarettes." He made out an order of some kind and signed it with a rubber stamp. "Give this to the storekeeper," he ordered, and when the two policemen had left he turned to us and began reading from a notebook.

"Hear ye the law of Trinidad and be guided accordingly!" he said. "No French convict escaping from Devil's Island and reaching the shore of Trinidad will be arrested by any authority unless after landing on Trinidad he breaks a law, regulation, or disturbs the peace. If the fugitive arrives by a boat which is still seaworthy, he will be given food and allowed to embark again. If the boat is not seaworthy, he will be given transportation to Port of Spain, accompanied by a police officer who will escort him directly to the Controller of the Port. Is your boat seaworthy?" he said.

"No!" I almost shouted.

"I will have to inspect it and make sure," the constable said. When the food had arrived he took us down the road in an old car, then we walked down the path to the sea. He looked at the canoe.

"Would you like to go to sea in a thing like that?" I asked. "Look, the hull is already splitting open!"

The giant negro scratched his head, looked for a few moments out over the wave-chopped sea and then shook his head. "I'll take you to Port of Spain!" he said.

Back at the police station he gave us each a bottle of beer. A negro woman prepared a meal for us—rice and baked plantains, fresh fish, steaming coffee, preserved mangoes, salt beef. She would accept no payment.

We drove during the afternoon through the island, passing a constant stream of negroes and donkeys, until we reached Port of Spain. Here we were taken to the military prison. Our things were searched, our names taken, and we were locked up in one of the guard rooms.

"This is to notify you," said the sergeant in charge, "that you are not under arrest. But you must stay here—where the French Consul can't get you—until the Controller looks into your case." A large meal was served to us in the guard room, and after eating it we fell asleep and we slept soundly until nine o'clock next morning.

Shortly after ten o'clock, a man in civilian clothes was admitted to the guard room.

I nicknamed this man, after a short while, 'My Friend.'

"Where are you going, my friend? . . . What can we do for you, my friend? . . . I will see what I can do for you, my friend," he said, asking endless questions, all of which I answered frankly.

"Follow me, my friend," he said at last, knocking on the door. It was opened immediately. He led us out of the military prison, walked with us down the street until we came to a place where a sign with "Salvation Army" painted on it hung over the pavement. We apparently had been expected,

G

because a dining-room table had been set with six plates. A Captain Heap and his wife introduced themselves to us. Mrs. Heap, in spite of our insistence that she should not do so, began waiting on us, serving us with better food than we had tasted in many cruel years. Neither Casquette nor Bébert had eaten at a table for fifteen years, and all of us, accustomed to being treated like beasts, had tears in our eyes.

"This is where you will stay, my friend," said the plain clothes officer. "I will return to talk with you tomorrow, my friend," he added as he took his departure.

Captain Heap told us that he was an intelligence officer assigned to the special supervision of administering to the needs and fate of fugitives from Devil's Island. Before 1931, he said, fugitives were not allowed freedom on Trinidad. Up to that time Venezuela welcomed escaped prisoners and let them live in freedom. But now Venezuela had passed a law ordering the arrest and imprisonment, at hard labour, of all French Guiana fugitives; and Trinidad and its people, who had continually criticized the existence of the French penal colony and the methods used there, had passed a law under which French Guiana fugitives would be given a twenty-four-day permission to reside and a means of continuing their flight to some other country.

We lived in the Salvation Army's depot now, without a care in the world for our present safety, free to come and go as we pleased, to visit the cinemas or any other place which we desired. Several people visited the depot and left food, cigarettes and clothing for us. But after the first day of excitedly sampling our freedom, we went to work writing letters to friends and acquaintances, seeking funds for buying passages on a friendly steamer to another port. Panama wrote to a friend in Colombia; Dadar, Bébert and Casquette hadn't any friends and expected nothing.

Chifflot, I discovered, had 4,000 francs in a suppository! He said he would buy passage on a German ship and go to Europe to see his mother before she died. But to do that he needed a passport. We went to the Spanish quarter to see whether we could get one. As usual in such matters, it proved to be simply a matter of price. A Venezuelan barber gave us the address of a former Venezuelan general, now in exile from his own country but apparently still having some friends across the Gulf. The general had his headquarters over a drug store. He told us to come back in three days.

In three days Chifflot had a Venezuelan passport with all the necessary visas; he was now a Venezuelan citizen named Chifflara!

"My mother will be glad to see me no matter what name I arrive under!" he said. "Better to live a Venezuelan than a dead Frenchman!"

A week after our arrival he boarded a ship for Hamburg. I saw him off at the pier, hoping that I too would receive some money from my cables and airmailed letters and be able to embark like a human being and not a slinking beast.

I went to the bank every day. "Nothing, sorry!" said the teller each time. My companions begged me to stay with them and with them seek a better boat in which to continue our flight. I waited until 6 June and then went to the office of the Inspector General of Police. 'My Friend,' to whom I had talked, made the appointment and accompanied me.

The Inspector General, an elderly British Army officer, who spoke beautiful French, talked with me for half an hour.

"Two things about the French I cannot understand—or stomach!" he said with a twist of his moustache. "One is their French Foreign Legion—and the other is Devil's Island!"

Then he asked me to wait in an antechamber while he talked with 'My Friend.' When he came out I stood stiffly to attention.

"We are going to give you a boat. Go through the harbour and see if you can find a boat such as you will need for sale." Then turning to 'My Friend' he said, "There ought to be some fisherman's boat that would serve admirably."

At eleven o'clock the next day, we had a boat. Casquette had spied it a few feet off the dock where several police launches were tied. It was a lifeboat, rigged with a mast and sail. "With such a boat," Casquette laughed happily, "we can go to China!"

A naval officer inspected the boat with us. He authorized its purchase by the government from its owner, then ordered a government carpenter to be put at our disposal.

"Tell the carpenter what you want done with the boat, and he will do it," he said. Then he asked me to make a list of materials and supplies which would be needed for the trip.

A policeman would buy them for us from the wharf-front stores.

On a dining-room table at the Salvation Army depot I spread out a marine chart which a man had given us.

"We must not let ourselves be swept on a beach in either Venezuela or Colombia," I said. "We can reach the United States by skirting the West Indies, putting in now and then on a British island for rest and supplies and continuing through the Caribbean until we reach Miami."

I picked out the islands on the chart—Tobago, one hundred miles north of Trinidad, then Grenada, seventy-five miles farther, then Saint Vincent, then Saint Lucia, Saint Kitts. The Salvation Army captain said he would write the depots in these islands to be on the lookout for us—to help us.

"We'll have to keep clear of Martinique and Guadeloupe!" Casquette warned. "If we land in the French Islands we'll get a quick ticket back to Devil's Island."

"Puerto Rico is American!" I said. "Nothing to fear there. Haiti will be safe. Cuba we'd better skirt until, off Havana, we head north for Key West. All the journey," I said, "will be in frequent sight of land. When we lose sight of one island another will appear ahead of us! It's not too bad a road to freedom!"

IX

ESCAPE FROM INDIA

from

Seven Years in Tibet

By HEINRICH HARRER

In September 1939 Heinrich Harrer, an experienced Austrian mountaineer who had taken part in the Nanga Parbat expedition, was in Karachi, preparing to return to Europe, when he was taken into custody and put in a large internment camp at Dehra-Dun on the slopes of the Himalayas. Escape was never far from his mind—escape through the tantalizing mountains always in front of him— and to prepare for it he set himself to learn a little Hindustani, Tibetan and Japanese. After two abortive attempts, he finally made the successful bid related in the following pages.

Harrer's escape from Dehra-Dun was only a prelude, however, to the strange experiences which awaited him over the Tibetan border. Eventually he became tutor and confidant of the young Dalai Lama, of whom he gives a fascinating and sympathetic account, and from whom he parted with regret when the Chinese Communists invaded Tibet in 1950.

"YOU made a daring escape. I am sorry, I have to give you twenty-eight days," said the English colonel on our return to the camp. I had enjoyed thirty-eight days of freedom and now had to pass twenty-eight in solitary confinement. It was the regular penalty for breaking out. However, as the English took a sporting view of our bold attempt, I was treated with less than the usual rigour.

When I had finished my spell of punishment I heard that Marchese had endured the same fate in another part of the camp. Later on, we found opportunities to talk over our experiences. Marchese promised to help me in my next attempt to get loose, but would not think of joining me. Without losing any time I at once began to make new maps and to draw con-

clusions from the experience of my previous flight. I felt
convinced that my next attempt would succeed and was
determined this time to go alone.

Busy with my preparations I found the winter passing
swiftly and by the time the next "escape season" came round
I was well equipped. This time I wanted to start earlier, so as
to get through the village of Nelang while it was still uninhabited. I had not counted on getting back the kit I had left
with the Indian, so I supplied myself afresh with the things I
most needed. A touching proof of comradeship was the gener-
osity of my companions who, hard up as many of them were,
spent their money freely in contributing to my outfit.

I was not the only P.O.W. who wanted to get away. My
two best friends, Rolf Magener and Heins von Have, were
also engaged in preparing to escape. Both spoke fluent
English, and they aimed to work their way through India to
the Burma front. Von Have had already escaped two years
before with a companion and had almost reached Burma, but
was caught just before the frontier. During a second attempt
his friend had a fatal accident. Three or four other internees,
it was said, planned to escape. Finally the whole seven of us
got together and decided to make a simultaneous break-out
on the grounds that successive individual attempts increased
the vigilance of the guards, and made it more and more difficult to get away as time went on. If the mass escape succeeded
each of us, once out of the camp, could follow his own route.
Peter Aufschnaiter, who this time had as his partner Bruno
Treipel from Salzburg, and two fellows from Berlin, Hans
Kopp and Sattler, wished, like me, to escape to Tibet.

Our zero hour was fixed as 2 p.m. on 29 April, 1944. Our
plan was to disguise ourselves as a barbed-wire repairing
squad. Such working parties were a normal sight. The reason
for them was that white ants were always busy eating away the
numerous posts which supported the wire and these had to be
continually renewed. Working parties consisted of Indians
with an English overseer.

At the appointed time we met in a little hut in the
neighbourhood of one of the least closely watched wire corridors. Here make-up experts from the camp transformed us
in a trice into Indians. Have and Magener got English officers'
uniforms. We "Indians" had our heads shaved and put on

turbans. Serious as the situation was, we could not help laughing when we looked at one another. We looked like masqueraders bound for a carnival. Two of us carried a ladder, which had been conveyed the night before to an unguarded spot in the wire fencing. We had also wangled a long roll of barbed wire and hung it on a post. Our belongings were stowed away under our white robes and in bundles, which did not look odd as Indians always carry things around with them. Our two "British officers" behaved very realistically. They carried rolls of blue-prints under their arms and swung their swagger-canes. We had already made a breach in the fence through which we now slipped one after another into the unguarded passage which separated the different sections of the camp. From here it was about three hundred yards to the main gate. We attracted no attention and only stopped once, when the sergeant-major rode by the main gate on his bicycle. Our 'officers' chose that moment to inspect the wire closely. After that we passed out through the gate without causing the guards to bat an eyelid. It was comforting to see them saluting smartly and obviously suspicious of nobody. Our seventh man, Sattler, who had left his hut rather late, arrived after us. His face was black and he was swinging a tarpot energetically. The sentries let him through and he only caught up with us outside the gate.

As soon as we were out of sight of the guards we vanished into the bush and got rid of our disguises. Under our Indian robes we wore khaki, our normal dress when on outings. In a few words we bade each other good-bye. Have, Magener and I ran for a few miles together and then our ways parted. I chose the same route as last time, and travelled as fast as I could in order to put as long a distance as possible between me and the camp by the next morning. This time I was determined not to depart from my resolve to travel only by night and lie up by day. No! this time I was not going to take any risks. My four comrades, for whom Tibet was also the objective, moved in a party and had the nerve to use the main road which led via Mussoorie into the valley of the Ganges. I found this too risky and followed my former route through the Jumna and Aglar valleys. During the first night I must have waded through the Aglar forty times. All the same, when morning came I lay up in exactly the same place which it had taken me four days to reach in the previous year. Happy to be free, I felt satisfied with my performance, though I was covered with scratches and bruises and owing to my heavy load had walked through the soles of a pair of new tennis shoes in a single night.

I chose my first day-camp between two boulders in the river-bed, but I had hardly unpacked my things when a company of apes appeared. They caught sight of me and began to pelt me with clods. Distracted by their noise I failed to observe a body of thirty Indians who came running up the river-bed. I only noticed them when they had approached dangerously near to my hiding-place. I still do not know if they were fishermen or persons in search of us fugitives. In any case I could hardly believe that they had not spotted me for they were within a few yards of me as they ran by. I breathed again, but took this for a warning and remained in my shelter till evening, not moving till darkness had fallen. I followed the Aglar the whole night long and made good progress. My next camp provided no excitements, and I was able to refresh myself with a good sleep. Towards evening I grew impatient and broke camp rather too early. I had only been walking for a few hundred yards, when I ran into an Indian woman at a water-hole. She screamed with fright, let her water-jar fall and ran towards the nearby houses. I was no less frightened than she was and dashed from the track into a gulley. Here I had to climb steeply and though I knew I was going in the right direction my diversion represented a painful detour that put me back by several hours. I had to climb Nag Tibba, a mountain over 10,000 feet high, which in its upper regions is completely deserted and thickly covered with forest.

As I was loping along in the grey of dawn I found myself facing my first leopard. My heart nearly stopped beating as I was completely defenceless. My only weapon was a long knife which the camp blacksmith had made expressly for me. I carried it sheathed in a stick. The leopard sat on a thick branch fifteen feet or more above the ground, ready to spring. I thought like lightning what was the best thing to do, then, masking my fear, I walked steadily on my way. Nothing happened, but for a long time I had a peculiar feeling in my back.

Up to now I had been following the ridge of Nag Tibba and now at last I tumbled on to the road again. I had not gone

far when I got another surprise. In the middle of the track lay
some men—snoring! They were Peter Aufschnaiter and his
three companions. I shook them awake and we all betook
ourselves to a sheltered spot where we recounted what had
befallen us on the trek. We were all in excellent shape and
were convinced that we should get through to Tibet. After
passing the day in the company of my friends I found it hard
to go on alone in the evening, but I remained true to my
resolve. The same night I reached the Ganges. I had been five
days on the run.

At Uttar Kashi, the temple town which I have mentioned
in connection with my first escape, I had to run for my life.
I had just passed a house when two men came out and started
running after me. I fled headlong through fields and scrub
down to the Ganges and there hid myself between two giant
blocks of boulders. All was quiet and it was clear that I had
escaped from my pursuers; but only after a longish time did I
dare to come out into the bright moonlight. It was a pleasure
for me at this stage to travel along a familiar route, and my
happiness at such speedy progress made me forget the heavy
load I was carrying. It is true that my feet were very sore, but
they seemed to recover during my daytime rest. I often slept
for ten hours at a stretch.

At length I came to the farmhouse of my Indian friend to
whom I had in the previous year entrusted my money and
effects. It was now May and we had agreed that he was to
expect me at midnight any day during the month. I purposely
did not walk straight into the house, and before doing anything else I hid my rucksack, as betrayal was not beyond the
bounds of possibility.

The moon shone full upon the farmhouse, so I hid myself
in the darkness of the stable and twice softly called my friend's
name. The door was flung open and out rushed my friend,
threw himself on the ground, and kissed my feet. Tears of joy
flowed down his cheeks. He led me to a room lying apart from
the house, on the door of which an enormous lock was hanging. Here he lit a pine-wood torch and opened a wooden chest.
Inside were all my things carefully sewn up in cotton bags
Deeply touched by his loyalty, I unpacked everything and
gave him a reward. You can imagine that I enjoyed the food
which he then set before me. I asked him to get me provisions

and a woollen blanket before the following night. He promised to do this and in addition made me a present of a pair of hand-woven woollen drawers and a shawl.

The next day I slept in a neighbouring wood and came in the evening to fetch my things. My friend gave me a hearty meal and accompanied me for a part of my way. He insisted on carrying some of my baggage, undernourished as he was and hardly able to keep pace with me. I soon sent him back and after the friendliest parting found myself alone again.

It may have been a little after midnight when I ran into a bear standing on his hind legs in the middle of my path, growling at me. At this point the sound of the swiftly running waters of the Ganges was so loud that we had neither of us heard the other's approach. Pointing my primitive spear at his heart, I backed step by step so as to keep my eyes fixed on him. Round the first bend of the track I hurriedly lit a fire, and pulling out a burning stick, I brandished it in front of me and moved forward to meet my enemy. But coming round the corner I found the road clear and the bear gone. Tibetan peasants told me later that bears are only aggressive by day. At night they are afraid to attack.

I had already been on the march for ten days when I reached the village of Nelang, where last year destiny had wrecked my hopes. This time I was a month earlier and the village was still uninhabited. But what was my delight to find there my four comrades from the camp! They had overtaken me when I was staying with my Indian friend. We took up our quarters in an open house and slept the whole night through. Sattler unfortunately had an attack of mountain sickness; he felt wretched and declared himself unequal to further efforts. He decided to return, but promised not to surrender till two days were up, so as not to endanger our escape. Kopp, who in the previous year had penetrated into Tibet by this route in company with the wrestler Krämer, joined me as a partner.

It took us seven long days' marching, however, before we finally reached the pass which forms the frontier between India and Tibet. Our delay was due to a bad miscalculation. After leaving Tirpani, a well-known caravan camp, we followed the most easterly of three valleys, but eventually had to admit that we had lost our way. In order to find our bearings Aufschnaiter and I climbed to the top of a mountain from which we expected a good view of the country on the other side. From here we saw Tibet for the first time, but were far too tired to enjoy the prospect and at an altitude of nearly 18,000 feet we suffered from lack of oxygen. To our great disappointment we decided that we must return to Tirpani. There we found that the pass we were bound for lay almost within a stone's throw of us. Our error had cost us three days and caused us the greatest discouragement. We had to cut our rations and felt the utmost anxiety about our capacity to hold out until we had reached the next inhabited place.

From Tirpani our way sloped gently upward by green pastures, through which one of the baby Ganges streams flowed. This brook, which we had known a week back as a raging, deafening torrent racing down the valley, now wound gently through the grasslands. In a few weeks the whole country would be green and the numerous camping-places, recognizable from their fire-blackened stones, made us picture to ourselves the caravans which cross the passes from India into Tibet in the summer season. A troop of mountain sheep passed in front of us. Lightfooted as chamois, they soon vanished from our sight without having noticed us. Alas! our stomachs regretted them. It would have been grand to see one of them stewing in our cooking-pot, therby giving us a chance, for once, to eat our fill.

At the foot of the pass we camped in India for the last time. Instead of the hearty meat dinner we had been dreaming of, we baked skimpy cakes with the last of our flour mixed with water and laid on hot stones. It was bitterly cold and our only protection against the icy mountain wind that stormed through the valley was a stone wall.

At last on 17 May, 1944, we stood at the top of the Tsangchokla pass. We knew from our maps that our altitude was 17,200 feet.

So here we were on the frontier between India and Tibet, so long the object of our wishful dreams.

Here we enjoyed for the first time a sense of security, for we knew that no Englishman could arrest us here. We did not know how the Tibetans would treat us but as our country was not at war with Tibet we hoped confidently for a hospitable welcome.

X

ESCAPE TO SPAIN

from

Nancy Wake

By RUSSELL BRADDON

Nancy Wake, one of the heroines of the French Resistance, is an Australian who married Henri Fiocca, a rich Frenchman of Marseilles, in 1939. She joined the Resistance movement, and then aided Ian Garrow and Pat O'Leary with their escape-route. As Mme Fiocca, her French nationality was a great help in their organization; but her activities became suspect by the Germans, and it was decided that she had better leave Marseilles. She was arrested at Toulouse, however, and imprisoned and beaten up. Rescued by O'Leary just before his own arrest—she then made her way into Spain, accompanied by some escaping airmen, as described below.

After being imprisoned by the Spanish authorities and treated abominably, Nancy Wake reached England. She joined the F.A.N.Y.s and Colonel Buckmaster's Special Operations Executive. After intensive "commando" training, she was parachuted into France, where she worked with the Maquis d'Auvergne. In the autumn of 1944 Nancy and her Maquis triumphantly entered Vichy, which had been vacated by the Germans; but on the following day she received news that her husband, Henri Fiocca, had been tortured and executed by the Gestapo on 16 October, 1943, almost a year before.

★

IT was to the home of Mme Sainson that Nancy and her friends, once they had reached Nice, now walked. 'Sainson' being French for 'Samson', Madame's Resistance *nom-de-guerre* was inevitably 'Delilah'.

There can have been no more reckless enemy of Hitler's Reich in the whole of France than Mme Sainson. Both she and her husband were active members of the Resistance, her flat was always full of escaping airmen and the whole population of Nice knew that if ever they saw anyone who looked foreign or lost, the place to send them was to her apartment in Rue Baralis.

She had a daughter aged twelve and a son aged fourteen, both of whom had frequently carried messages and helped her outwit the Germans. Once, when the flat was surrounded and being searched, and in it was a radio transmitter that would have meant death to them all had it been discovered, it was her young daughter who carried it out of the house. Deceptively childlike and innocent, she walked straight past the sentries at the front door with the transmitter concealed in a pail of rubbish.

On another occasion Mme Sainson had sheltered thirty evaders at once in her flat. It was an uncomfortable and dangerous time; but all thirty were eventually sent safely on their way towards freedom.

In 1942 alone, sixty-three men passed through her hands. From the end of 1942 onwards it was Nancy who always took delivery of her 'guests' and each woman had conceived an undying admiration for the other.

Mme Sainson's brother, Raoul, had escaped to London in 1942 and her husband was to be arrested in 1943 and later executed. Yet right through till the end of the war she carried on—with a maximum of gossip and ostentation—her escape-route work.

She was a humorous, volatile woman with heavy black eyebrows, calculating brown eyes and strong white teeth. Running her husband's garage in her spare time, her greatest pleasure in life was to give the fuel the Germans left with her (for the exclusive use of their own vehicles parked there) to the fishermen of Nice: the missing quantity she would replace with water! She worked in close association with the district priest and her lack of any sense of security was the despair of her chief, Arnoul.

Her worst weakness was a passion for being photographed with groups of Allied escapers. She would take them down to the beach for a breath of fresh air and then she would ask the nearest Italian soldier to photograph them. Once she even suggested that three of the enemy soldiers should join her group. The result is a handsome portrait of a mischievously smiling Mme Sainson with three slightly disconcerted-looking

Americans, who spoke neither French nor Italian, for whom three flattered Axis soldiers are making a willing background.

When Arnoul heard of this episode he was extremely displeased: but the expression of his displeasure made no impression at all on his exuberant subordinate. Unrepentantly she showed him the photograph and remarked that she thought it a very good likeness, except for the Italians who were imbeciles and of no importance.

This, then, was the atmosphere towards which Nancy and her four friends walked from the station at Nice. They entered the apartment doorway, climbed up the stairs and Nancy looked at the doormat. It lay squarely against the door. This was one of Mme Sainson's only three gestures towards security. If there was any danger, she kicked the mat crooked: then she chained the door firmly (which was her second precaution) and laid a hand grenade ready inside the door (which was the third). Anyone mad enough to knock when the mat was crooked merely invited Mme Sainson to open her door the few inches allowed by the chain and to deposit an exploding bomb at their feet.

"We're safe," Nancy sighed with relief and knocked. Mme Sainson opened her front door and peered out suspiciously. "Nancy!" she exclaimed with delight. "How are you? Come in." Without asking for any explanations she ushered in the troupe of strangers behind her friend as well.

"A brandy?" she offered. They all accepted. "I'm sorry Nancy that we have no *pastis!*" The two women laughed uproariously at this and the men looked puzzled. Mme Sainson hastened to explain.

"Nancy is very fond of *pastis,*" she said, "but of course it is forbidden. Once she had a small flask of it and the police caught her with it. They ask her, this is *pastis,* no? And Nancy says, 'Certainly not, it is only perfume and anyway I never drink,' and puts it in her handbag and they believe her and let her go! Ah," she concluded, "*elle est formidable, cette Australienne! La plus formidable de la Résistance!*"

Between the two women there was a strong bond of affection and confidence. This was not surprising. They were very alike. Arnoul regarded them as his two best agents and respected their talent for imagination and initiative in the work they did.

Fortunately for him his respect was amply returned—although that was not surprising either. At the age of sixteen Arnoul had won a British Military Medal in the last year of World War I. In 1940, to quote his own picturesque English, he 'had been obliged to go very quickly from Paris where the Germans did not like him'. Friends in Nice gave him a job running a macaroni factory and, under cover of that, he continued his resistance work.

In 1941 Claud Bourdet, then leader of the Resistance in that area, became a national Resistance officer and appointed Arnoul (whose real name is Major Comboult) as his successor.

Thereafter this slim man, who looked ten years younger than his real age, ran the organization in Nice. Occasionally Mme Sainson would have him wringing his hands in despair at her recklessness but more often he blessed the fates that had given him so courageous a lieutenant. Whenever, in her profligate fashion, she took in excessive numbers of 'boarders', so that she was unable to buy sufficient food for them all on the black market, he himself would make up the deficiency with huge donations of macaroni. To over a hundred evaders, as a result, he was to become known disrespectfully as 'The Macaroni Man' or M. Macaroni. Americans and Britons particularly found the diet he provided hideously monotonous. But they were grateful to him that they ate at all—and to Mme Sainson that they had a roof over their heads and a hostess who apparently loved entertaining them.

Let it not be thought, with all this gossip and lack of security, that the Gestapo never heard mention of Mme Sainson. They did, frequently. In fact all the time. And quite often they took her away for questioning. But Mme Sainson had a great facility for tears and as soon as they picked her up, and right through her interrogation, she would sob moistly and noisily. Invariably they decided that she was a cowardly blabbermouth, worthy only of contempt, who boasted of non-existent Resistance work to boost her own prestige—and so they would release her. Immediately she would stop her weeping and return grimly to work.

Nancy stayed with Mme Sainson for three weeks. During that time she bought new clothes, acquired a set of false identification papers and endeavoured to find out exactly what the position was about the circuit.

Soon she discovered that guides were again escorting escapers across the Pyrenees. Bernard, therefore, made some exploratory trips and eventually declared that the time was ripe for Nancy's seventh attempt at getting out of France.

He declared that he wanted to go to England with her and she suggested that the New Zealander and two American airmen should accompany them. She herself escorted the non-French-speaking Allied airmen to a big store to be photographed, so that false papers could be made for the three of them.

In her spare time she cooked or gossiped with Mme Sainson, or went to the cinema with the Sainson children whom she adored, so that the days passed quickly and happily and eventually she was almost sad to have to leave. She and her party took the train from Nice to Perpignan.

At Perpignan they picked up two French girls who also had pressing need to leave the country. The next difficulty that confronted them was to locate guides. Because of the breakdown of the circuit, they had no passwords and no contacts. Nancy, however, knew the address of one of the guides so she volunteered to try and persuade him to take her party into Spain—a dangerous business because, without a password, it was quite possible that the gentleman concerned would regard her as a spy for the Gestapo and shoot her out of hand.

Eventually she contacted the guide and, without any preamble, said, "Look—I haven't got a password. You don't know me, but I know you. You've worked for O'Leary and I've worked for O'Leary too. Now don't give me any nonsense— I want to go to Spain."

Such blunt candour was too much for the guide. He asked a few cautious questions: Nancy gave the correct answer to each. He went with her to collect the rest of the party and then they began the trek into Spain.

They walked in the darkness for about three hours, then they met the main group of guides. These were all men who, before the war, had made their living entirely by smuggling across the frontier. Then it had been contraband: now it was bodies. Some of them were a cut-throat-looking crew but they knew their job—and their mountains—perfectly.

Nancy and her party were hidden for the rest of the night in a hollow on the hill-top and at dawn were pushed into the back of a coal lorry. Coal, loose in bags, was then packed all around and over them. The lorry drove off. Soon they entered the twenty kilometre strip of French territory which the Germans had made a forbidden zone to anyone who did not actually live in it. At the end of this zone lay the frontier: on the other side of the frontier was another forbidden zone to a depth of fifty kilometres. These seventy kilometres in all, and the Pyrenees (which were heavily patrolled with sentries and dogs), were the danger areas.

The coal truck was frequently checked on its run through the French zone but no attempt was ever made to search the coal in the back. At last the truck halted and they were told to get out and take cover in the bush. Wearily they flopped to the ground and allowed a sickly sun to warm their grimy bodies.

At sunset two guides and a dog called for them. The senior guide was a Spaniard whose Resistance name was Jean. He was wanted in France by the Gestapo for espionage and in Spain by the police for murder. He was tall and thin and dark, about thirty years old, and seemed unperturbed by the price that lay on his head on both sides of the frontier.

The second guide was a girl, Pilar. She was a good-looking peasant girl, as strong as a man and just as taciturn as Jean. The dog belonged to her and it knew its way backwards and forwards across the mountains even better than did the Spaniards. Somehow Nancy felt that the presence of this dog, a mongrel fox terrier, was a good omen. Sadly, though, she wondered how things were going with Picon . . . and Henri . . . and her friends.

All of them were instructed to remove their shoes and put on rope *espadrilles* instead. These were better for rock climbing and quieter. They had to go by the rockiest paths because these alone could foil the soft-padded police dogs of the Gestapo. They had to march silently because sentries on the dark mountain-sides relied even more on hearing movement than they did on seeing it.

They set off. For forty-seven hours on end they marched

H

and climbed with only ten minutes rest every two hours. Jean and Pilar were implacable about this—and the little terrier pranced with impatience at every stop.

Each time they rested they had to take off their wet socks and put on dry ones—otherwise the wet socks would have iced up and frostbitten their feet. They would keep the wet socks in their pockets and then put them on again, after removing the dry ones, just before the march resumed.

Jean allowed no talking or coughing or smoking. If anyone wanted to cough he had to smother it completely under his coat or with his fist, anything, so long as there was no noise.

All of them began to be afflicted by colic. The had eaten some black-market lamb and it had apparently been tainted. The trip became hellish. One guide always went ahead, preceded by a silent, prancing mongrel dog, and the other always flogged them on from the rear.

They clawed their way up into the highest, craggiest reaches of the Pyrenees, using their hands and their feet equally, panting and despairing. They were hungry, which was bad, but they were also thirsty, which Nancy considered worse. She ate handful after handful of snow. The others argued at her about it but she ignored them. Nothing would stop her walking but she must have something to drink. It was a bitter, alpine climb.

Time after time they would ask Jean or Pilar how much farther.

"One more mountain," they were invariably told. But each time they crossed a mountain, a valley and another mountain lay ahead. Ruthlessly they were driven on.

On the second part of their forty-seven hour trek they were lashed with a biting snowstorm. A blizzard raged and the ice and snow cut into them like needles. But they pressed on through it. One of the Americans cried out that they must halt, he could go no farther. Nancy slapped him savagely and he went on. One of the girls said she could go no farther. Nancy whispered to Jean, and Jean calmly tripped the girl into an icy stream. Then she had to go on or freeze to death.

But finally it ended. They reached a hut, lit a fire, dried their clothes and waited till nightfall. Ahead lay a river. When they crossed that river they were out of German-controlled Europe and into Spain. Nancy slept badly as she waited on this last leg of her dash for freedom. There were several alarms, but nothing came of them.

Then, under cover of darkness, they eluded the sentries, crossed the river and left the sentries behind them.

"Henri, my dear," Nancy muttered as she reached the other side, "I hope you'll be as lucky in your journey as I've been."

XI

THE COFFIN PLAN

from

Dare to be Free

By W. B. Thomas

*Wounded in the leg during the fighting in Crete in 1941,
Second-Lieutenant W. B. Thomas, a young New Zealander,
was captured by the Germans and flown to a hospital in
Athens. His leg took months to heal, but eventually, when he
was able to get about, he made plans to escape with one of
his men, Private Stan Schroeder, who had also been
wounded. Their attempt miscarried, however, and they were
put in the cells.*

*After the failure of 'the coffin plan', told here, W.B.
Thomas was sent to a P.O.W. camp at Salonika, from which
he finally escaped. Helped by friendly peasants and sheltered
for a time by monks in a monastery on Mount Athos, the
Holy Mountain of Greece, he fell in with two other Allied
soldiers, John and Niki; and after various adventures in out-
witting the Germans they succeeded in reaching Turkey.*

WHEN we were released from the cells and sent back to our
wards in the hospital, I found that life there had assumed an
entirely different aspect. Existence as a prisoner was no longer
humdrum, small annoyances and quarrels no longer a worry.

Everything had become a stupendous adventure, a sort of
real-life game with definite rules and penalties. The goal at
the end was freedom. But one had to dare to be free.

The piquancy of having duty on one's side in law-breaking
was exhilarating. The mind seemed never free from some
thrilling or amusing idea which would help towards the goal.
To steal the German pay-roll and use the funds to hire a boat
for Eygpt, to lock the guard in their guardrooms with the
great iron doors which led into their quarters, to purloin a
German uniform from the hospital store and walk out at

night unmolested, to go out concealed in a large bundle of hospital laundry with the connivance of the Greek contractor, or buried under the rubbish of the rubbish cart—all these were almost feasible. To explore their possibilities kept the mind healthy.

Schroeder's departure from Athens, which happened soon after our attempt, threw me in with a group of officers who were all bent on escape. Their enthusiasm made life very pleasant indeed. The leader, or rather the older member of the group, was a Captain Shannon.

We had a great number of ideas, some of which were put to the test with varying degrees of failure. The first really sound idea, however, was one which would fire the imagination of any lover of adventure.

It arose from an inspiration of 'Skipper' Shannon's after he and I had been to a funeral. A young Maori officer, Lieutenant ——, who had been grievously wounded in a bayonet charge on Crete, died peacefully, having struggled valiantly to live for five long months. We had all thought a lot of ——, and admired his cheerful pluck during the period at the end when he knew there was no hope. Consequently twelve officers applied for permission to attend his funeral. It was granted on sworn parole.

The funeral took place only a few hours after the certification of death, a necessary custom in the heat of Athens. We draped the secretly held Union Jack over the rude coffin, knowing that the Germans would not object. Then we carried him down from his ward and out to the main entrance.

An army truck was waiting there with a guard of a corporal and three men, all armed. We stowed the coffin aboard carefully and clambered on. The truck drew out of the gates and down a series of secondary roads until we approached a small suburb of Athens.

When the truck drew up we found ourselves at the gates to a walled cemetery. The walls were ten feet high and of stone and mud.

I could never subscribe to the popular opinion that all Germans were bad. On the contrary, I often found men in their army whom I could respect. On this occasion the guard did not come into the cemetery at all, but contented themselves with leaving the truck at the gate and placing a sentry at the four outer corners. Thus the whole of the ceremony inside was British.

We carried —— up a lane of cypress trees until we were met by two Greek priests who, without speaking, guided us to where a shallow grave had been prepared. The priests joined us in sympathy as one of our own padres committed —— to rest. We saluted at attention for two minutes and then left him. It was a simple and touching ceremony.

Before we left the cemetery the two priests invited us into a small annex to the chapel and offered us *ouzo*. In the absence of the Germans they were very friendly and full of confident stories of the arrival of the Allies in the near future. Just before we left we realized that we had not brought the Union Jack, and were somewhat surprised when the priests offered to return it with the coffin. They explained that, for the sake of economy, bodies were removed from the army coffins before the grave was filled in. All the many dead from the hospital had used the same coffin.

We returned to the gate, in no great hurry, and the Corporal of the Guard recalled his sentries. In half an hour we were back at the hospital.

That night Shannon came up to my ward, acting in an excited and mysterious manner. I was convinced that he had hit on something. We went up on to the roof, by then deserted, and Shannon revealed his plan.

"Sandy," he said, "I've discovered the perfect escape route! It's absolutely foolproof; it's a certainty if there ever was one!"

This from 'Skipper' was startling. He was usually so conservative—even pessimistic. I pressed him to go on. But he could be a tantilizing person, and he took his time.

"There's no possible way it could go wrong," he declared emphatically, nodding his head at each word.

"What is it, 'Skipper'?—are you going to let me in on it?" I demanded.

"Of course. Do you know, Sandy, if this comes off it will make headlines; it will make a best seller of any 'Escape' book."

I noticed the 'if', but my impatience got the better of me. I pummelled him on his ample waist line until he surrendered. Even so, he went about his explanation at his leisure.

"That's just the trouble with you youngsters," he grimaced, "you get brainstorms about impossible schemes and when they all fail you bully us old-stagers into giving you the perfect solution—do you mean to say you didn't get any ideas today?"

"Well, if one was prepared to break a sworn parole. . . ."

"No need for that," 'Skipper' broke in, "*think* man. Use your grey matter."

Finally he gave up teasing. He had enjoyed his fun. He said very quietly.

"There was one of us in the party today who did not give a parole."

"Who?—the Padre?—yes, he did," I said, a little at a loss.

"No, not the Padre." He paused. "What about W—— in his coffin? Did he give a parole? Eh?"

He stood back and let the full significance of this take effect. I saw it all in a flash.

"Of course not!" I cried. "And had he been alive he would be free in Athens now. And the Germans would never know that he was around—never look for him!"

I stopped to give 'Skipper' an excited hug. "Old man, dear old Methuselah, you have hit on an idea in a million. We can die off one by one, or somehow take the place of patients who die, and the rest will be easy. If things go anything like today we will only have to get out of that shallow hole and drink *ouzo* with the priests until the guard takes all the mourners back."

"Yes. It's not bad, is it?" 'Skipper' beamed his pleasure. "The coffin could be loosely lidded with a few airholes for comfort. A chap could stow all his escape kit in easily. It is really a *de luxe* way of going."

"I expect every case of death is the same. What I mean is, do they let our doctors make out the certificate?"

"Well, I've known of three officers dying here, and in each case the Germans left it entirely to our own doctors."

"That seems OK. But what about putting the corpse into the coffin? Is that a British fatigue or a German?"

"You can be sure that any dirty work such as that is left to our own orderlies. No, if the doctors will play, the scheme is foolproof."

"Now what about details at the cemetery? Suppose some

dumb-cluck of a gravedigger buried one of us just to be a bit different?"

"That's not so difficult. We would have to take Padre ——— along with us: he speaks good Greek. He could get hold of the two priests and they would fix it. The only dirt that need go on the coffin would be the stuff they throw during the 'ashes to ashes, and dust to dust' part of the ceremony.

In the morning we approached the doctors. They were vastly tickled with the originality of the plot, but were rather hard to pin down for co-operation. We had to appreciate, they pointed out, that failure would bring a large measure of blame on to the doctors concerned. The Germans were particularly harsh in punishment of any abuse of the privileges accorded to protected people.

However, a young New Zealand doctor, Ron Granger, was willing.

We drew lots to decide who should have first turn, and I won.

In half an hour I was in bed and it was generally known around the ward, and later round the hospital, that I had a temperature of a hundred and four.

For a whole week the chart over my bed showed alarming temperatures, and people started talking in low whispers about my condition. Some of the medical orderies who were not in the know became really worried, and helped to create the atmosphere we wanted. The Padre became a constant visitor.

At three o'clock in the morning of Friday, 14 September, 1944, I died peacefully in my bed from pneumonia. Friday was a good day to die, because on that day Lieutenant Bruning left early for Athens and did not get back until night —so it gave a man a decent twelve hours to be buried in.

As dawn crept into the ward a group of mournful figures could be seen standing around my bed. Their voices were respectfully lowered and probably only I from under my shroud could tell that their sympathetic whispering consisted mostly of derogatory remarks about me. As it grew lighter I could see that I would have trouble to prevent the sheet over my head from rippling up and down as I breathed.

Ron had come up at three. I heard him now saying that

the German sergeant had been very sympathetic and was arranging for a later afternoon funeral. That sounded very satisfactory. 'Skipper' Shannon was heard saying in sepulchral tones that he thought it would be difficult to get a Greek coffin long enough for me, and in the event of it being too short, did Captain Granger think he could take off the feet, or perhaps the head? Ron thought that would be easy enough. After a pause he sent off one of the orderlies to bring a padre. I cursed them all. It was difficult enough not to giggle as it was.

An hour dragged slowly past. Breakfast arrived and, hungry as I was, I had the infuriating experience of hearing the orderly say with an unmistakable sniff and almost a break in his voice:

"Here you are, Goodwin"—sniff—"you'd better have poor Mr. Thomas's breakfast this morning. He"—sniff—"won't be wanting it."

I was snoozing complacently about ten o'clock, when I heard the orderly whispering urgently as he scrubbed the top of a dresser near my bed. I could not make out all he said, but his message came through like this . . . ". . . worried . . . German doctor . . . grey hair . . . maybe coincidence, but . . ." and then he was interrupted by a shout from the far end of the ward.

I immediately thought of the portly, grey-haired doctor who had dressed my wound in Corinth and later showed a kindly interest in me. What if he should choose today of all days to visit the hospital!

There was a commotion at the end of the ward and, oh horrors, someone was coming towards me speaking German. I froze stiff—I was not acting; it was sheer panic. As they came nearer someone said to someone else in a very German accent, *"Parlez-vous Français?"* and I knew that my worst fears were realized. It was my doctor friend. The party clattered to a halt at the foot of my bed.

Someone said, *"Et si jeune, il n'a pas vingt-deux ans."*

Someone moved quietly down to the head of my bed and stood there a moment. I could hear him breathing. Then, very gently, the sheet was raised from above my head, drawn reverently back and down my face. I could stand that. Then though I had my eyes closed I felt a hand coming near my face. It was too much. I gave a snort and a giggle and looked up into the startled blue eyes of the German doctor.

There was a moment of utter consternation. What was going to happen now? But the German doctor just stepped back a pace in fright, and then broke into peal after peal of uncontrollable laughter. He sat down on the next bed, held his ample waist with both hands, and just shook and shook as though he was unable to stop. Of course, we all joined in. Soon the whole ward was rocking with merriment. I think the last to join in was the German sergeant, who gaped at his senior uncertainly before blending his guffaws with the rest.

The Germans took no action whatsoever. I doubt whether Lieutenant Bruning was ever told. But, of course, the coffin plan was hit on the head. We swallowed our disappointment and looked around again.

XII

ESCAPE FROM THE WÜLZBURG

By GILES ROMILLY

from

Privileged Nightmare

By GILES ROMILLY and MICHAEL ALEXANDER

In 1940 Giles Romilly, a war correspondent, was captured at Narvik. As a nephew of Sir Winston Churchill, he was regarded by the Nazis as a possible hostage, and interned in the castle of the Wülzburg in Bavaria with hundreds of civilian prisoners. Like his uncle, Romilly did not take kindly to imprisonment. After the attempted escape, described below, he was taken to Colditz, where he shared a small room with Michael Alexander, a relative of the Field-Marshal. They and other Prominente, who included Viscount Lascelles (now Earl of Harewood), the Master of Elphinstone, a nephew of the Queen Mother, and Earl Haig, son of the Field-Marshal, were kept apart from the other prisoners.

Two days before the Allies reached Colditz, the Prominente were taken to an old castle in Bavaria for safer custody. And from that castle Giles Romilly finally made a successful escape.

I NOW loathed the Wülzburg and began to dream of escape.

Escape I must! But not talk about it. 'P.G.s' apart—I did not really worry about them—the merest hint of escape talk was pounced on by appeasing voices (as in the ghetto business) that said, 'It's selfish. The Germans will cut down the privileges of the rest of us.'

The germ of a plan survived from the time, more than a year earlier, of my abortive conversation with the called-up Bavarian. Now, I knew, as then I had not, that Wülzburg prisoners whose homes were in Germany were allowed to be visited by their families; that visits took place every Thursday; that visitors came in through the main gate and went out through it; that consequently there was, almost every Thursday, a dribbling in-and-out traffic of pedestrian civilians.

The very great majority of them were women. That might not matter. The Wülzburg amateur theatricals were well-established, and I had played a saucy servant in 'Twelfth Night' and an American girl in an adaptation of a novel by P. G. Wodehouse. Moreover, Wülzburgians, owing to the links that some had with outside German life, had been able to send for stocks of actual clothes, and the *Kommandantur* had allowed these to be brought in. There were high-heeled shoes, silk stockings, handbags, dresses in styles commonly used, sets of ordinary make-up.

I thought. I had a friend, John Ford. He had volunteered to fight for Finland, had reached that country when the war with Russia was over, and while retracing his steps had entered Oslo in time to be picked up by the Germans as they entered it. He (with four others in identical plight) had then been posted to the Wülzburg. He was a person of versatile talent and also of character. If I had to trust anybody I would trust him; I had to trust somebody.

John was a star of the Wülzburg football field whose nets had been woven by seamen from the string of Red Cross parcels. I, an inglorious spectator, hung about, while enthusiasts stamped on the touchline. Whistle blew. 'Out to your wing, man!' 'Pay attention to that wing, Frankie!' The Prefect, alongside two TocHers, strained vociferous. I nursed my scheme.

The match over, I told John my plan which hinged on the fact that Frau Scharre's canteen-shop was bisected by a ground-level corridor of which one entrance was in the prisoners' enclosure, the other in the outer *Kommandantur* area. Departing visitors emerged into this outer area through a guarded gate in a continuous fence. All things being helpful, the same effect could be achieved by someone who came out through Frau Scharre's corridor.

With John I noted habits of the guards and office-soldiers of the outer area and of visitors as they walked away. Often a departing visitor turned her head to wave to a high window.

It was early September. In the hot weather theatrical varieties were given in the grounds; a goal canopied with blankets made a blackcloth, in its shade a tiny piano, drum and percussion-set. The producer, a slight, nervy, brow-mopping man, invariably compèred turns with apologetic references to 'very trying conditions' and 'exceedingly difficult circumstances'. The French contributed a trick-cyclist, the Egyptians a team of acrobats and a Strong Man with a prodigious stomach whom the compère always introduced by regretting that 'exceedingly trying conditions' made it impossible for him to perform his principal act, which consisted of allowing a car to run over him, any horse-power. There was a West Indian, Jeff Luis, who sang the Wülzburg signature-tune *The Castle Could Hardly be Called a Hotel*. Jeff also had charge of all costume and make-up and the time had come to broach my plan to him.

Jeff, who was enthusiastic, concluded after many things had been tried on that the disguise ought to suggest the character of a young, respectable married woman. That meant that I could not wear a richly-curled barmaid-blonde wig, pride of the wardrobe, and so would need to hide my hair, especially at the back of the neck, with a converted scarf. There were no coats. Jeff said he would make one. But out of what? I had a camel-hair blanket, teddy-bear colour, a present from home. With this Jeff made in less than a week a superb coat with a belt and large, disc-shaped woolly buttons.

The business of dressing-up had next to be co-ordinated with that of getting from the prisoners' quarters into Frau Scharre's door. I could not trip downstairs and cross the grounds in full costume, nor could the whole change be done in the exposed doorway. The main change—stockings, frock, basic make-up—could be made upstairs in the empty theatre provided that there was a screening escort from there to the shop. John chose three people besides himself and Jeff. In the doorway finishing touches—shoes, coat, lipstick, cowled scarf—would need less than half a minute and would be screened.

A date was fixed. Intervening days went like dreams. There was an outdoor concert party. Everyone was merry, everything seemed funny. The producer-compère, dripping with success, mounted a shaky stool to announce that the party would close with English community-singing "if our Dutch, French, and Egyptian friends will bear with us for just a very few minutes". *Roll out the Barrel, Nellie Dean, If*

You Were the Only . . . The singing was thin. The little man, perilously asway, made inhibited, frantic conducting movements crying "Come on, now, sing it as though you meant it!" with the result, truly English, that the singing died altogether.

What was extraordinary was that everything worked as hoped. The din of Dutch clogs roared round on the stone stairs as I descended semi-transformed, huddling, unseeing. At the shop door hands flashed. In the passage a little white dog, not reckoned with, yapped. Feeling suddenly the sun-white gravel of the *Kommandantur* area I turned my head right and up and did not cease agitating a tiny handkerchief until cool shade intimated that I was in the vaulted tunnel leading to the main gate. I faced a vast blank door in whose wall-like front there was a small wicket-door. I turned a handle. The wicket opened outward and revealed a sentry. I hesitated. The sentry sprang forward, opened the wicket wide and stood back, holding it open.

I was on the drawbridge. The morning was golden. The air was heavenly. The warm stone parapet wanted to be leaned on. The basking moat begged for a lingering look.

The track-like road whorled down. In the rough, pine-needles glinted like pins. Now I stepped confidently. Another bend. Whistles! My heart seemed to stop. Ahead, almost blocking the track, stood uniformed men. I drew level, they stood watching, waiting, unmistakably waiting to detain me. I was in the thick of them, as in among a herd of cattle when they, just like cattle, barged reluctantly outwards. Growls of voices, then aimed whistles hit my moving back. Suddenly, suddenly I understood. Those whistles—they were wolf-whistles! Those uniformed men—loutish *Luftwaffe* youths looking for a pick-up and very likely knowing that on Thursdays women had to walk down this hill. *Women!* In the joy of freedom I had utterly forgotten my revised exterior. Young respectable married woman—what a test!—what a triumph! Not the kind that she would care for, she would be feeling indignant now, at least looking it. I looked indignant.

Indignant I tripped through Weissenburg, rich hub of a rich plain. I was looking for a bicycle. I meant to bicycle north to a Baltic port and get aboard a Swedish ship. I had no German money, the speed of cycling might just cover my small stock of food; I had no papers and guessed that a cyclist was less likely to be stopped than a pedestrian. I approached a bicycle, untended against a wall, and was about to grasp the handle-bars when a woman no doubt its owner appeared out of a door, mounted, looked back at me severely, and pedalled away.

I was out of Weissenburg. The bicycle incident had made me timorous. They were few now and far between and those I saw seemed always too close to harvesting parties in fields. This was a big road to Nuremburg, glistening with tarry heat, thundered on by heavy lorries: never a pedestrian. I trudged stupid, increasingly planless, feeling the heat, trying not to limp on blisters made by the pinching shoes.

A man on the road, 190 yards further, was scanning the country with field-glasses. He turned them towards me. Then he seemed to go away. I knew somehow that he had not gone away. All the same I was startled when a voice at point-blank range shouted, "Heil Hitler!"

There he was, jacked out from behind a trunk, a uniformed Teuton with blue aggressive eyes.

"Heil—Hitler!" I answered. The 'Heil' was a young married woman, the 'Hitler' unfortunately was not; it was a basso croak.

I walked past.

"Wo gehen Sie hin?"

My unanswering silence and my demure though now torturing steps were meant to suggest unapproachable dignity.

I heard him pounding up, as I had known that he would, and there again he stood. "Papiere!" I said that they were in the bottom of my bag.

Blue eyes bored.

"Sie sind keine Frau!"

"Doch!" I protested.

With a spring he ripped back the cowl, reducing me to a hybrid state. I felt defeated. A moment later I was in a lorry covering the twenty-two kilometres back to Weissenburg with no feeling except that it was nice to sit down.

The police chief to whom my captor took me happened to be a man who liked a joke. He bellowed with laughter at my appearance, now not even 'respectable', and when he had wiped tears of laughter out of his fat eyes he telephoned the castle and said that the Weissenburg police department

desired that a certain prisoner, 'Herr Rommillee', should be
fetched to speak on the telephone. He had grasped the point
that the Wülzburg *Kommandantur* might not yet realize that
I had gone, and he intended to elaborate his fun. At the other
end there was a long, long pause followed suddenly by faint
quackings into which the policeman, beside himself with
mirth, roared "No, of course you can't find him. He's sitting
here with me. He left your castle at eleven o'clock this morning by the front gate."

I enjoyed this too, but back in the castle I experienced the
disadvantages of the policeman's humour. A frog-shaped
cavalry-moustached German, swollen with fury, set on and
pommelled me. Then came the castle cell, every bit as cold as
it was rumoured to be, warmer clothes refused, shivering days
and nights in the caked sweat of my hot excursion; after
which, a sentence of eighteen days' *Zellenarrest* was formally
pronounced, and a closed car carried me thirty-three kilometres to a place called Eichstätt, where it seemed that there
were some approved cells.

The first day there, which was my birthday, I saw silly hat-
clutching German women running crying "Sondermeldung!
Sondermeldung!" The barred window looked on a sweep of
forecourt to a drive-in and a road faced by a house whose radio
carried audibly. The *Sondermeldung*[1] was the capture of Kiev
with 600,000 prisoners. I learned that I was to live on bread
and water. Those eighteen days were certainly in no hurry,
and I welcomed occasional calls paid by Hauptmann Sichel,
the Wülzburg security officer, though his face suggested
security as a rat-trap suggests it, and he called mainly to
inquire, others attending, why I had been walking inland
instead of towards a frontier. The suspicious implication
being clear, even on bread and water, I explained my plan.
The captain was not a man who took a point readily. Who
had helped me to escape? Nobody. It was suggested, with
humiliating accuracy, that I would have been incapable of
making the camel-hair coat; which rebutted, the captain
kindly offered to bring scissors, wool, and sewing kit so that I
could spend the long hours making a new coat. No, thank you,
I did not need a new coat just now.

[1] Special communique of the OKW—to announce some big
success or victory.

I knew to a minute at what time of which day the sentence ought to end; and the eighteen days seemed less long than the eight hours of overtime during which no tread came. Forgotten, I was sure. But later that night I was in Nuremburg station with a corporal and a guard. Entrained, trundling overnight to goodness knew where, I looked at a small photograph which showed the cavalry-moustached lieutenant puffing angrily over against me in camel-hair coat. The corporal had taken it as ordered, then the officer ordered him to destroy the negative and all copies because he did not like the result. The corporal could not let me keep the picture in case of search but he said that he would send it to me after the war. We detrained next day into dreadful-looking flatlands cut by an un-Bavarian wind and plodded in cortège towards a dreary mass of purple brick like a school or mental hospital. I was taken over from the unobnoxious corporal whom wearily I had begun to like and shown into an empty cell where the stone floor was inches deep in water. As usual night seemed to be falling. It fell. Unlockings occurred; there stood a guarded English prisoner with a pot of tea which he had most thoughtfully brought. The almost black tea made me ecstatically drunk. The watery bed was a luxury, I could not imagine anything more delightful.

This place was called Tost, 'bei Breslau', in Silesia. The first thing I saw was a cage with John Ford in it, looking through bars sad, devoted, suffering on behalf of another, who perhaps had forgotten . . . ? I felt very guilty and still did after John had explained that on the Wülzburg the Germans had threatened to punish the whole castle if those who had helped me did not confess.

I

XIII

THE GREAT ESCAPE FROM NEWGATE

from

The Road to Tyburn

By CHRISTOPHER HIBBERT

*One of the most picturesque figures of the London under-
world of the early eighteenth century, Jack Sheppard, the
notorious thief, had become a legend by the time he was
twenty-two. Many of the real facts about his short life are
shrouded in this legend and in the books written about him
afterwards; but it is known definitely that he made four
daring escapes from prison. The first was when he broke out
of St. Giles's Roundhouse in April, 1724; the second was
when he and his doxy, Edgworth Bess, made a getaway from
the New Prison, Clerkenwell, while awaiting trial a month
later. A few weeks afterwards Sheppard committed the most
daring burglary of his career, but was betrayed to the
officers of the law by Jonathan Wild, another underworld
figure, of whom he had made an enemy, and lodged in Newgate, the largest, oldest and best-known of the London
prisons. On 13 August he was tried at the Old Bailey and
sentenced to death. While awaiting execution, he escaped by
the aid of Edgworth Bess and her friend, Poll Maggot, but
was recaptured and lodged again in the condemned cell.*

*Jack Sheppard's second and greatest escape from Newgate
is told in the following pages. It was a bold adventure which
ended, however, in disaster, and after being tried a second
time he journeyed along the dreaded road to Tyburn on
16 November, 1724. Even on the scaffold he was confident
that he would still escape—a confidence which was mis-
placed, for the plans of his would-be rescuers miscarried and
he paid the supreme penalty.*

W<small>HEN</small> the information that a new trial would be necessary
reached Newgate, Jack was taken from the Condemned Hold
to the Castle, a cell high up on the third floor above the
prison gate and believed to be the strongest and most impreg-
nable part of the whole prison.

Here Jack was, as before in the Hold, chained down to the

floor, and fettered. He offered the usual fee for 'easement of
irons', but his goalers had orders to refuse the fee and in no
circumstances to allow him to be released from his chains for
any reason at all.

As money was of no use to him he asked his visitors and
friends to bring him tools so that, as he could not buy his way
out of his irons, he might force his way out of them. Within a
few days he was brought a small watchmaker's file which he
was able to conceal in a Bible which the prison chaplain had
given him and which was the only thing he was allowed to
have near him when he was alone. He made some headway with
the padlocks by means of this file, but just as he was beginning to get the hang of them, his file was discovered by the
chaplain who, taking the Bible from him one day, found it
concealed between the pages and handed it over to a turnkey.

Some time after this Jack was supplied with several
stronger and more useful tools including some nails, a
hammer, two files and a chisel which he managed to hide
between the rushes of the seat of a chair which was provided
in the cell for the use of visitors and gaolers. With the help of
these tools Jack was able to escape completely from his irons
and made a practice to walk about his cell of an evening 'for
the ease of his legs'.

One evening as he strolled about his cell taking his customary exercise, he was surprised by a turnkey who came in
unexpectedly with a meal for him at an irregular time.

The turnkey looked in amazement at Jack, who greeted
him as if his wandering about the cell was the most
natural thing in the world. "'Twas troublesome," the prisoner
complained with a disarming lack of emphasis, "to be always
in one posture."

After Jack had been secured once more the turnkey sent
for Mr. Pitt, the Keeper, now recovered from his illness, and
his deputies so that it could be decided how the tiresome
fellow could be more effectively confined.

While the officials were discussing their problem Jack
asked them if they would like a demonstration of how he had
managed to release himself from his irons. They watched in
amazement as the extraordinary youth used his tools with
such remarkable strength and skill, amounting to a 'Magick
Art', that he was free again within a few minutes.

Pitt immediately gave orders for the felon to be loaded with even heavier irons and a larger and unbreakable padlock, and for his movements to be further restricted by encircling his wrists in an enormous pair of handcuffs.

No prisoner, so far as one of the chaplains could recall, had ever been so heavily ironed before. William Kneebone, who had arrived on one of his regular visits to Jack as the handcuffs were being padlocked, interceded for his former shopboy with tears in his eyes. He was in spite of the recent robbery, for which Jack appeared genuinely sorry, still very fond of the boy and felt a regretful responsibility for his present hopeless condition. His earnest pleadings and offered bribes did not, however, have any effect upon the gaolers, who not only feared the consequences of another escape but who were anxious not to lose so profitable an exhibit.

And so for the next week Jack languished in acute discomfort in his cell, sometimes lifting himself up to sit in a chair, more often lying down on his back on the stone floor. The visitors who still flocked in scores to see him noticed with pity the raw scars round his wrists where the iron of the handcuffs had cut his skin and gave him money for which he had no use and which he immediately sent away to other prisoners who were able to buy themselves some degree of comfort with it.

Without an implement of any kind to pick the locks which fastened the heavy chains around him he was unable even to attempt an escape. Visitors were now carefully watched by the turnkeys to see that they did not pass him any tools which would, as he later said, have been "more useful to him" at that time "than all the mines in Mexico". And then one day during the second week of October a friend was able without being seen to leave within Jack's reach on the floor of the cell before he left it an old and rusty but strong and useful nail. If the turnkey noticed the nail, which is unlikely, he disregarded it and when Jack was alone he was able to stretch out and pick it up and hide it in his stocking.

On 14 October the Old Bailey Sessions began and for the next few days Jack knew that the turnkeys would be busier than ever with a full prison and with the additional duty of escorting prisoners backwards and forwards from the Sessions House. If he was to escape at all, now was his chance.

At about two o'clock on 15 October Jack's dinner was as usual brought to him by William Austin, one of his gaolers. Jack set to with a good appetite and Austin sat down in the cell to talk to him while he was eating. Before he had finished Captain Geary of New Prison and Mr. Gough of Westminster Gate-House together with one or two other prison officials who were giving evidence at the Old Bailey Sessions called in to see the famous thief. The prisoner and his visitors laughed and joked together until nearly three o'clock, when Austin stood up to take away Jack's empty plate and to make his usual careful examination of the handcuffs, fetters and padlocks. Before leaving him Austin asked Jack to let him know now if there was anything he wanted because he would be too busy to come back again to see him until the following morning. Jack affected both annoyance and disappointment at this and begged Austin, if he really had no time to call in to see him again that evening, to be sure to come good and early in the morning because he was so lonely lying there by himself in the dark with nothing to occupy his mind.

Austin nodded and with a final glance at Jack's chains left the cell, locking and bolting the great door behind him. Jack listened for the rattle of the key in the lock and then set immediately to work.

There were, he guessed, no more than two hours of daylight left and he was determined to do as much as he could before it was dark. First of all he escaped from his handcuffs by means of the nail which he had kept concealed in his stocking. He clenched this nail firmly between his teeth and using it with practised dexterity he picked the lock. Then using the same nail he opened the immense horse padlock which secured the chain round his ankles to the staple in the floor. He was free now to hop about the cell, but there seemed at first sight no chance of breaking the chain which still linked his ankles together. On examining the chain, however, he found a link which appeared weaker than the rest and by twisting the chain backwards and forwards between his legs so that the weak link was further damaged by the strain which his frantic strength brought to bear on it, suddenly it broke and he was free. He was, of course, unable to squeeze his feet through the thick iron collars which encircled his ankles and to which the ends of the broken chain were still attached, so taking off his stockings he used them to bind up the links of the chain round his legs.

He had already decided that the only possible way of getting out of the prison was by climbing up the chimney into the room above and from there making his way on to the roof. The narrowness of the barred window ruled out any chance of escape by that means and although he could, he knew, break open the door of his cell, having done so he would still be on the same floor of the prison. Furthermore, opposite that door was the door leading to the quarters occupied by the Master Debtors, who would certainly hear him and might unintentionally betray him to the turnkeys.

Having already, during one of his nightly peregrinations the week before, poked his head up the chimney he knew that across the flue about six feet above the level of the floor was a thick square iron bar the ends of which were buried into the brickwork of the chimney on either side. This had obviously been built into the chimney to prevent prisoners escaping by squeezing up the flue as Jack intended to do. There was nothing to do then but to pull down the chimney brick by brick. So setting to work with the broken link he scratched away at the mortar joints until he had at last worked one brick loose. The job was not so difficult now and by means of his broken link and the horse padlock which he used as a sledge hammer he soon had a pile of bricks and mortar at his feet and the thick iron bar in his hands. Taking the bar with him he clambered up the chimney and using the end of it as a battering ram he smashed his way through into the room above.

This was a rectangular room measuring about twenty feet by ten feet known as the Red Room which had not been entered or used since 1716, when some rebels had been imprisoned there after the defeat of the Lancashire Jacobites at Prestonpans. Dust lay thick on the floor, but Jack, who was by this time covered in brick and mortar dust himself, noticed nothing as he climbed through the hole that he had made, for it was now pitch dark. From now on he was working in complete darkness. No light from the new moon came through the small prison windows and he had, of course, no means of making a light for himself. With his finger-tips on the walls he felt his way round the cell to the door and on the way his foot struck against a large nail which he picked up and put into the pocket of his apron, with his broken link and the other nail, in case he should later find a use for it. Soon he came to the door and with expert sensitive fingers he felt around its edges for the lock box. Using his three makeshift implements he had, within less than a quarter of an hour, bent aside the plate covering the lock box, picked the lock and forced back the bolt. The door creaked open on its rusty hinges and Jack walked out into the passage.

He turned left past a staircase and came to another locked door, the door to the chapel. Turning aside for a moment from this door he felt his way around the passage in an attempt to find an easier way of getting up on to the next floor. But there was no other way out of the passage and he came back eventually to the chapel door. Once more he felt its surface and ran his finger-tips round its edges, but this door appeared to have no lock and it was bolted on the far side by a bolt which he could not budge. It seemed very quiet in this part of the prison and he decided to take the risk of battering a hole in the brickwork beside the door. He knocked and rammed the wall, making a frightening noise in the darkness, but no one heard him and soon he had made a hole large enough to get his arm through. Pushing his hand through this hole in the wall he felt for the bolt on the far side and pulled it back. He passed through into the chapel.

The chapel, which he knew only too well, was a macabre and forbidding room divided by high partitions topped by iron spikes into separate pens for the different classes of prisoner. It was on the top floor of the prison and there was another door at its far side leading to the passage which gave access to the roof. To reach this door Jack smashed his way through into the pen reserved for prisoners condemned to death. He had been in this pen before and the curious distasteful smell of it, and of the whole chapel around it, was unpleasantly familiar to him. He was reminded of the horrifying sermons which the prison ordinary preached from his safe pulpit in a voice full of gloom and malice. He was determined to waste no time in the dreadful place. Although he could not see them he remembered the spikes that were ranged above him along the top of the partition and standing on top of a replica of a coffin, placed there to remind the convicts of their terrible fate, and grasping his iron bar firmly in both hands he hit furiously at one of the spikes until he had knocked it off. Then climbing up on to the top of the partition in the gap he had made in the row of spikes he jumped down on to the far side. Putting the broken-off spike into his apron pocket with his other tools, he felt his way forward to the next door. When he had reached it it took him only a few seconds to discover that it was going to be the most difficult door of them all so far. He tried without success for more than half an hour to pick the lock, but his old rusty nails were neither thin nor pliable enough and the lock was a strong one. Eventually changing his tactics he was able with his bar and spike to lever the lock box far enough aside and to pick the lock from the inside. The door rattled on its hinges and pushing it open he hurried along the passage to the door at the far end.

When he touched this door his heart fell. The immense iron plated lock box was clamped to the door by iron hoops and beneath the lock box an enormous bolt was fastened into its socket by a hasp secured by a strong padlock. The door itself was strengthened by four vast metal fillets.

He had broken through four stout doors, and beyond this one was the roof. He was nearly free. But he was tired out and to break through this fifth door, heavier and better secured than any of the others, in complete darkness and without proper tools, seemed even to him impossible. For a moment he hesitated wondering what to do and then he heard the clock bells of St. Sepulchre's Church chiming the hour. He counted the chimes. Only eight o'clock. The thought that he had come so far in five hours and that he still had the whole night before him put new hope into him. He picked up his bar and with skill and determination attacked the door. Deciding that the lock could not be picked and the bolt could not be forced he concentrated on the colossal metal fillet to which they were both attached. After long and anguished efforts he managed to force his bar into a position in which he could use it as a lever and then applying to the end of his lever his frenzied and scarcely human strength he wrenched it from the door. The lock and bolt were torn away with it.

He pulled the massive door open and walked along the corridor towards the roof. The door at the end of the corridor was bolted only on the inside, so having found the bolt he shot it back and came out gratefully on to the roof and into the fresh and sweet night air.

He was now on top of the gateway and many floors above the Lodge from which he had made his last escape. Surrounding him on every side were high walls shutting off his escape. Emptying his pockets he climbed up on to the top of the door which he had just opened and from there leapt to the top of the wall. He jumped down on the far side to the lead roof between and crawling across the tiled roof of the Common Felons' ward he came to the parapet wall of the gateway. Now for the first time he could see below him the houses and shops in Newgate Street. The shops were still open and the lights from the houses shone out into the street. The roofs of the houses were, he judged, about twenty-five feet below the place where he knelt and were too far away for him to jump down to them. Reluctantly he decided that he would have to go back for his blankets, so leaving the relative security of the roof he made his way back through the prison towards his cell. Feeling his way in the darkness he passed carefully but swiftly through the shattered door into the grotesque and silent chapel, along the stone corridors to the Red Room where the disturbed dust had settled mustily back on to the floor and down the chimney into his cell where the great pile of broken bricks lay heaped in front of the fireplace; expecting all the time for a door to open suddenly, for his escape to be noticed, his plan to fail.

Quickly he picked up his blankets and clambering up the chimney again he lost no time in getting back on to the roof. No one saw him. He sat against the parapet wall and tied his blankets together to make a rope. Then having driven the spike from the chapel into the wall, he tied the end of his blanket round it and climbed down on to the roof below.

He crawled quietly across the slates until he came to an attic window. There was no light inside and as he pressed his hand against the unlocked window it gave way and he climbed inside into the garret. He crept to the door and waited there listening for a few moments and then, hearing no sound, he opened it and went stealthily down two flights of stairs on to the first floor landing. As he moved to the head of the next flight of stairs the links of one of the chains round his legs clanked. He stood quite still where he was as he heard a woman's voice ask in alarm, "Lord! what was that?" Still not moving he heard the gruff less distinct voice of a man replying, "Only a dog or a cat."

Thinking it was unsafe to go any farther until the household had settled down for the night he went back to the attic room which he had just left and locking the door behind him he threw himself on the bed in complete exhaustion and slept for two hours.

He was awakened by the sound of opening doors and voices on a lower floor and getting up again he crept once more downstairs. He heard the voices more clearly now saying good-bye to a guest in the hall and the front door opening and closing. He decided to make a run for it. Making sure his fetters were securely tied he rushed silently downstairs across the hall and through the front door into Newgate Street. He left the door wide open behind him and later on at midnight Mr. Bird and his family were knocked up by a watchman who found it open. Mr. Bird blamed the carelessness of a servant and went back unsuspectingly to bed.

Meanwhile Jack was walking unhurriedly across London. He had strolled past St. Sepulchre's watch-house and had wished the watchman good night. By way of Snow Hill and the Fleet Bridge he had made his way up Holborn Hill and was now heading for the open country beyond Gray's Inn Lane. By two o'clock in the morning he had reached the village of Tottenham and here entering a cowshed he went to sleep on the earth floor for three hours. He woke at dawn in great pain, for his ankles, still encircled by the heavy iron collars in which he had escaped, were cut and bruised and swollen. Once more he tried to escape from these fetters, but he could not get them off by himself and now that it was light he knew that the search for him would be on and that it would be dangerous for him to leave the shelter of his cowshed for help. Fortunately at seven o'clock it began to rain and all day long the rain poured heavily down.

From time to time Jack looked out gratefully at the driving rain and the waterlogged fields. Anxious as he knew his gaolers would be to recapture him they would not find it easy to organize search parties in that weather. It was a comfort of a sort. He waited alone for nightfall, hungry and in pain.

XIV

THIRD ESCAPE

from

Where Bleed the Many

By GEORGE DUNNING

L/Cpl. George Dunning, D.C.M., *was made prisoner during the retreat to Dunkirk in 1940 and taken to Stalag VIIIB in Upper Silesia. He escaped into Poland, but was recaptured and tortured by the Gestapo before being sent back to the Stalag. He escaped again, was recaptured, and then sent to a camp at Rouen, where a number of prisoners were awaiting release on a Repatriation Scheme. When negotiations for repatriation failed, he made his third escape.*

Dunning got through unoccupied France and reached the Spanish border—only to be picked up by gendarmes and imprisoned in the notorious St. Hippolyte du Fort near Nice. A fourth escape again led to recapture and removal to Campo 73 in North Italy. He was there when Italy capitulated, and to avoid transfer to Germany he made a final bid for freedom. The story of these escapes and his adventures with various partisan groups makes Where Bleed the Many *one of the most exciting books about the Second World War.*

AUTUMN merged imperceptibly into winter and still we waited. We were restless, but despite the long delay our belief in ultimate repatriation obstinately persisted. Two factors helped sustain my morale. Firstly, the valuable advice and encouragement received from the British M.O. and from a major in the Loyals, both of whom took the keenest interest in our welfare and regularly passed on to us up-to-date information concerning the negotiations. Secondly, our proximity to the ordinary day to day life of Rouen

There was always something for me to see. West of the camp the Rouen-Elbeuf road was always busy. To the east I enjoyed vicarious shopping expeditions and café-crawling along la Rue Madeleine. To the north, where a row of houses backed on to the race-track, I could study, when curtains were not properly drawn, amusing and sometimes intimate vignettes of French family life.

To the south was the gap in the wire. . . .

Then there was the incident of the dung-cart. This weird vehicle called daily, driven by a nervous Frenchman whom we christened Alphonse, to empty the latrines. A vacuum contraption sucked the foul accumulations into a 'large barrel affair with a heavy iron lid. While his friends attended to Alphonse, offering him chocolate and cigarettes, one of the prisoners, evidently deciding not to wait for the repatriation deadlock to end, concealed himself inside the tank after what turned out to be an unfortunately bulky collection. At the gate one of the sentries stopped the cart and lifted the lid. Discreetly withdrawing to windward, he cried, "Komm', Engländer!"[1] The would-be escaper emerged like a bedraggled merman. His punishment was five days' solitary confinement under close guard.

Soon after 'Operation Merde' I was put in charge of the camp wood-cutting party. There were nine others, but the ones I best remember were Jimmy Matthews, Larry Mason and a fat little Aussie named 'Silver' Harrison. We were escorted by guards out through the main gate, round the outside of the wire between the camp and the street connecting the Elbeuf road with la Rue Madeleine and so to the trees behind the stables. Another guard, whom we knew as Willi, drove round with a horse and cart, but he passed along the street and part of la Rue Madeleine, branching off from the latter where it was joined by the cart-track.

We felled trees, sawed them into suitable lengths for loading on the cart, and Willi drove back by the same route to the camp, where another party would split the sawn trunks into logs. Then he returned for a second load and sometimes, if we felt particularly energetic, for a third. We marched back under the watchful eyes of the guards, while Willi stuck to the road.

When we got to know Willi better, he allowed some of the boys to perch on the timber and be driven back to camp. One guard sat up beside Willi and the other walked alongside the cart. I brought up the rear to keep a check on the load.

[1] Come, Englishman.

Then, one day in November, we were paraded outside the hospital and the Kommandant, whose name was Martin, made a brief announcement.

"I regret to have to inform you that the repatriation negotiations have broken down entirely and will not be resumed. You must believe that I am genuinely sorry about this. I myself have a son and a daughter interned in England and, like you, I entertained hopes that will not now be fulfilled." He shrugged resignedly, then went on, "Severely wounded prisoners will be sent at once to another camp where they will be more comfortable. The rest of you will move into the huts near the hospital and this part of the camp will be sealed off. Eventually, of course, you will be sent back to Germany. You will go now and pack your belongings. Dismiss!"

Some of us went to the hospital wards to give what assistance we could. It was painfully evident that the patients already knew that there would be no Christmas in England for them. They lay there—withdrawn, passive, unresponsive—indifferent to our ministration. One youngster, with stumps for arms, was fighting to hold back the tears he could no longer wipe away. Another, his glazed eyes fixed on the ceiling, muttered over and over again, "Jesus Christ! Jesus Christ!" At the far end of the ward the M.O., who had just broken the grievous news, was watching them compassionately.

We gathered together their few possessions and, when the transport arrived, acted as stretcher-bearers. Before the convoy moved out, a cutting wind sprang up and the squally gusts of rain beat fitfully against the tiny windows of the ambulances. We lined the route, bare-headed, but did not cheer our departing comrades. Their lament was the keening of the wind against the wire. . . .

Next morning we transferred our belongings to the quarters below the hospital block. We of the wood-cutting party were given permission by the Kommandant to sleep in the hut where the logs were stored. Fuel was short and there had been several cases of thieving, not by us, but by the German guards. There was an old boiler in the part of the hut reserved for the logs and we soon had it working. Later on we found a rusty iron bathtub in one of the stables. The Kommandant allowed us to have it, so we organized a regular system of hot baths.

Our behaviour on the tree-felling sorties had been so exemplary that the Germans now thought one guard and Willi sufficient escort for us. The guard took charge of the walking party, whilst Willi was left to keep an eye on those of us who rode on the cart with him. The guard—it was always the same one—was a hydrocephalic with a head like a pumpkin. He invariably smoked a pipe which curved over his pendulous lower lip. We called him Droopy.

As our cart rumbled along the streets French civilians frequently waved to us, but actual physical contact was strictly forbidden. On one of our trips, however, I was tagging along behind the cart as usual—Willi was driving and Jimmy Matthews sat beside him—when a girl of about eighteen gestured with a small parcel, indicating that it was for me. I looked behind me. Droopy and his party were hidden by the stables. I peered round the load, but Willi was arguing heatedly with Jimmy. I nodded to the girl. As we drew level she darted across, thrust the parcel into my hands and ran swiftly back to the pavement.

I promptly hid the package inside my battledress blouse. I turned to wave and saw that the girl was talking animatedly with a young man of perhaps twenty-six and another girl of roughly her own age. Now, I had noticed these three not only in la Rue Madeleine but also along the Elbeuf road, and had remarked the unusual interest they displayed in us and in the camp itself.

We off-loaded near our wood-shed, where I took the opportunity of nipping over to my bed and secreting my unexpected gift under the palliasse. When we went back for another load, the man and the two girls had vanished. At the end of the afternoon we all returned with the cart, half the party riding and the others ambling along ahead of Droopy, but again I saw no sign of the trio.

As soon as Willi and Droop had departed I called the boys together in the hut. "Listen, you chaps," I said. "I've just had a parcel shoved into my hand back on the road there."

"Who shoved it?" asked Matthews.

"The tall brunette I pointed out the other day."

My reply evoked a variety of ribald comments, but they quietened down when I produced the package and opened it. It contained three items: a small packet of cube sugar, a tiny

jar of butter and a meat-paste jar filled with jam. Jimmy
pointed to the sugar, his finger trembling with excitement.
"There's a paper in it, George!" he gasped. "A message!
Shufti quick!"

I unfolded the scrap of paper. On it was printed 'LOOK IN
THE BUTTER'.

I dug out the butter with a teaspoon and scraped out a
screwed-up ball of grease-proof paper. Feverishly I smoothed
it out. It contained another printed message—'LOOK IN THE
JAM'.

Feeling a precious fool by this time, I scooped out the jam
into the lid of my mess-tin. At the bottom of the jar lay a
folded note. Slowly I read it to the others.

> "We are very sorry to see the English soldiers in such a
> sorry plight. If we can help you in any way, you must let us
> know somehow. We shall be on the road where you received
> this parcel nearly every day. Burn this immediately.
>
> Christine-Gloria."

We looked at each other in amazement. "What are we
going to do?" piped up Larry Mason.

"Write back and thank them," I said. "Give me a pencil."
On a sheet of Red Cross writing-paper I wrote this reply:

> "Thank you very much for the food. We need nothing
> at present, but when we do we shall let you know and shall
> be grateful if you can pass it in the same way. Be careful.
> Don't let the Germans see you near the cart. Vive la
> France!"

We all signed our Christian names. Then I folded the note
very small, put it inside a flat Horlick's tablets tin, sealed it
round the edge with the original tape. Christine-Gloria's letter
I burned in our boiler.

The following day I had the tin ready in my pocket. A
search at the gate was always possible, of course, but I took the
risk and nothing happened. I looked for the girl on the road
all the way round to the tree-felling area, but she was not
there. Throughout the day's wood-cutting I kept one eye on

la Rue Madeleine, but she still didn't show up. When I went back with the first load I left the Horlick's tin under a fallen tree, picking it up when I got back. I carried out the same procedure each time we delivered a load.

Going round the circuit for the last trip, I saw the girl and her two companions looking into a shop window on la Rue Madeleine. Jimmy, who had providentially joined us for the ride, was sitting beside Willi, pulling his leg in execrable German. I was seated on the tailboard. As we passed our would-be helpers I motioned to them that I had written something and would deliver it on our return journey. The girl nodded understandingly.

We completed the final load for the day and Jimmy, on my instructions, clambered up beside Willi with the intention of keeping him distracted, especially along la Rue Madeleine. I walked behind the cart, the tin burning in my hand. Droopy and his charges were already disappearing round the bend of the track.

The three people were still dallying outside the same shop window. We drew level with them. The girl flew to my side, seized the tin and was away like the wind. I glanced round and the man waved to signify that all was well.

She was there again the next day but only the man was with her. Skilfully biding her time, she again managed to reach me undetected by Willi and Droopy. She handed me the Horlick's tin. I pushed it into the small message pocket under my belt.

Back in the hut at the end of our day's labours, I opened the tin and found a few more words of comfort and promise:

"We shall be very pleased to help you in any way we can. We shall be careful of the Germans. If there is any-thing you require, let us know in the usual way and we shall do our utmost to get it for you.
Vive les Anglais!
Christine-Gloria."

When I had relayed the contents to my room-mates I dropped the note in the boiler. Then I decided to go round to see the officers. My reasons for this were twofold. I was deter-mined to escape rather than be taken back to Germany and I wanted the Senior British Officer to know what was going on. Then again, I had a profound respect for the major from the Loyals and I hoped he would join the enterprise. He was certainly the right type—shrewd, forceful, fearless and thoroughly reliable. He had lost his right eye in the 1914-18 war and the black patch he wore gave him a piratical swagger.

I went to the hospital and knocked on the M.O.'s door. He asked me in and, when I had apologised for disturbing him, I told him briefly what had happened.

He listened with a judicial air. "Well," he said at the end of my narrative, "we'd better see what Bob has to say about it."

He called in the major from the next office and passed on all I had told him. The major's one good eye glittered exultantly as the story unfolded.

"Jolly fine show!" he enthused. "Obviously you must keep in touch as long as you can, but don't get rumbled, or we shall all suffer. If I were you, I'd carry on asking for unimportant stuff—fags, for instance, and unrationed food—just to see if the system works over a period. Once the line is firmly established, we can put it to more useful purposes as and when the need arises. In the meantime, if you have no objection, I should like your contacts to deliver messages from me to friends of mine in Paris. Could they do that, do you think?"

I said I could only try them. He scribbled a note there and then, which he entrusted to me. I in turn handed it on to Christine-Gloria on the next wood-cutting expedition. In fact, letters and parcels were passed with impunity for several days, including a number of notes addressed to 'Bob' which I took to the major.

Then, early in December, came the news that shifted the escape plan into top gear. We were informed by the Kommandant that at the end of January we should all be sent back to Germany. Within ten minutes of this momentous announcement I was closeted with the M.O. and the major 'Bob'.

The M.O. opened the proceedings. "You have heard about your imminent return to Germany. You must act now, while the chances of success are reasonable. Obviously I can't go with you. I have medical duties to perform both here and wherever I may be sent in the future. However, I'll do everything in my power to facilitate your departure. I take it you'd

J

both go, with or without my blessing. Now, Bob, it's your turn."

"I shall leave the details to George," the major began. "He knows exactly what we want—wire-cutters and overalls mainly. Ask your pals if they can get us away safely once we're through the wire. Fix the exit point, a suitable rendezvous, and go into the question of timings. I suggest just after Christmas. That will give them time to take their fingers out."

That night I wrote to some purpose.

"I am now going to ask you something that will really test your loyalty and co-operation. We have decided to escape. Later we shall arrange details. Meanwhile we must have wire-cutters and dark blue dyes. We shall trouble you as little as possible, but we hope you will be able to put us on a safe escape route once we are out. You are no doubt aware that helping prisoners to escape is punished by death. From what I know of the Germans, such a death would be most unpleasant and would probably embrace innocent members of your families. If therefore you wish to withdraw now and have no further contact with us, we shall understand. Whether you help or not, we shall go ahead with the escape. Destroy this.

George."

I did not ask for overalls because I had hit on a better idea. Our Red Cross pyjamas, properly dyed, would make admirable boiler suits if we stitched the jacket to the trousers. Our tin bath could be utilised as a dying vat. The log store, once our boiler was well stoked up, would serve as a drying room. All we needed were dyes. The question was—would our French friends oblige?

On the morrow the man was there alone, sitting nonchalantly outside a café in la Rue Madeleine, sipping an apéritif. As our cart trundled by, he was up like a rocket and by my side in a flash. I gave him the critical letter and, at the same time, he passed me a folded sheet of paper. I did not see him again that day.

His note was short but, in view of my urgent appeal, charged with significance. It ran:

"Do not be afraid to ask for *any* favours. We are prepared to do *anything* for you. We hear you will soon be
returning to Germany. We feel you would be much happier
in France. The girls are not with me today. We do not want
to arouse the Germans' suspicions at this stage. In future
you will see only one of us each day.
                              Don't forget.—*Anything!*
                                            Raymond."

I burned the letter, then I hurried across to the hospital to
tell the major that the people outside had been put in the
picture. "And I'm sure they'll help us, sir," I concluded
enthusiastically. "The man wrote today's letter. Signed himself ' Raymond '. If he gets us the cutters, we'll be out of this
apology for a concentration camp before——"

"Just a minute, George," he cut in. "I've decided to let
you into a secret. You keep saying ' we ' and ' us '. I think I
ought to tell you that, until yesterday, I had no intention of
going out with your party. I proposed to make a solo break.
Oh, I might conceivably have used the same exit, but I should
not have remained with you. My objective would have been
Paris where my friends would have taken care of me."

He stood up abruptly, walked across to the window and
stared into the gathering murk. "Yesterday you brought me a
letter. It was not from my friends in Paris. It came from your
pal Raymond. He said he had passed on all my letters faith-
fully, but his Paris contact had informed him that the Gestapo
had raided my friends' house and removed them to a concentration camp. They were suspected of being active agents
in the Resistance Movement."

"Did the Gestapo find any of your letters, sir?"

"Fortunately not. The fellow who delivered them can
vouch that they were destroyed as soon as read." He swung
round, his eye-patch giving him an oddly sinister look. "The
point is, George, that my solo flight has been knocked on the
head. If it's all right with you and the others, I'd like to come
in as a *bona fide* member of your escape party. In other words,
I go out with you and, if Raymond plays ball, I rely on his
organization once we're out. One thing I would stress. We
haven't much time left, so work fast."

When I left him I put into operation a plan I had been

working out for some time. My mind was still obsessed by the
gap near the stands. I had studied the area thoroughly both
by daylight and at night and I was confident that I could get
out if three conditions were fulfilled. Firstly, I had to have
wire-cutters. Secondly, I had to have darkness. Thirdly, I had
to lure the guards away from the wire. That night I tackled
the problem of the guards.

Briefly, the position in the area of attack was this. Between
the hospital block and the stands ran the double apron wire
fence with the intervening Dannerts. Joining this at right-
angles was a single apron wire fence, directly opposite the
entrance to the German bath-house under the stand. Immediately beyond this corner was my gap.

I reasoned that, if the inner fence were breached, a man
could crawl through, into the coil of Dannerts, along the wire
tunnel it formed, emerging at the gap leading to the bath-
house. He could then either risk taking the path used by the
officers and cutting across the front of the stand towards the
Elbeuf road or, if he decided that course was too dangerous,
he could keep *inside* the fence, and follow it round to where
it ran parallel to the Elbeuf road. No guards patrolled there
and the escaper could cut his way through the fences at
leisure, hiding if necessary behind the logs stacked just inside
the wire.

The first problem, then, was to distract the two guards
responsible for patrolling what we began to refer to as
'Dangerous Corner' and, if possible, draw them away from the
hospital area altogether.

I waited until Willi and Droopy, with whom we were on
reasonably friendly terms, were on wire duty near the gap.
Then, in the darkness I slipped along to their posts and asked
each in turn if he would like a hot drink. I explained that
they would have to move away from the lights of the hospital
so that I could get the drinks to them without being spotted.
They accepted the arrangements unquestioningly, so I went
back to the hut and made cocoa.

Filling up a couple of army water bottles with the steaming brew, I gave one to 'Silver' Harrison and told him how
and where to deliver it. The other I took across to where Willi
was pacing up and down trying to keep warm.

"Cocoa, Willi!" I whispered hoarsely.

"*Jawohl, Georgi.*"[1]

"Komm'," I bade him and, without waiting to see if he followed, I moved along inside the fence for about thirty yards. When I stopped, Willi was there all right, a dark shape waiting eagerly on the other side of the wire. I threw the bottle over to him. I lit a cigarette, cupping the flame in my hands, and puffed away contentedly until Willi had disposed of the hot cocoa. With a muttered "*Danke schön,*"[2] he flung the bottle back and I returned to the hut in time to meet 'Silver', whose delivery to Droopy had proceeded along the same lines.

We kept this up for nearly a month, sometimes with tea, sometimes with cocoa, until the guards had acquired the eight to eight-thirty hot drink habit. In fact the system worked better than I had ever imagined, for it was not long before the two guards who received the bottles moved even more than thirty yards from 'Dangerous Corner' so that they could share their drinks with their friends stationed farther round the wire. I learned, too, that the two guards farther on still also took advantage of the scheme. This meant that every night for at least a quarter of an hour six out of the eight patrolling guards were immobilized and the vital corner was left clear.

Raymond had passed over the dyes and wire-cutters only two days after I had asked for them, so the rest of the team occupied themselves with preparing our boiler-suits. On bath nights lookouts were posted some little distance from the hut and, grouped about our 'devil's cauldron', the boys went into the dyeing business with zest. The dyed pyjamas were hung on a line behind the wood pile, with sawdust scattered below to catch the drips. The dye was disposed of in the soft ground outside the hut and wood ashes scuffed over any tell-tale patches.

During the day a New Zealander on the inside working-party hid the pyjamas, bringing them back at night to continue the drying process. When they were completely dry, each man in the escape organization took over his own suit. Most of my personal possessions I kept in a small fibre suitcase purchased from Droopy for fifty cigarettes, but my dark blue

---

[1] Yes, George.
[2] Thank you.

boiler-suit I rolled up into a ball and hid inside my palliasse. I ripped the casing along the seam, stuffed the pyjamas in amongst the straw, then sewed up the palliasse again.

Whilst all this activity was taking place I picked up another message from Raymond to the effect that everything had been laid on for the break-out and that he and his friends were willing to help us. We had to be concealed in their houses before 9.30 p.m. because of the curfew for civilians, and he insisted on our getting out not later than 9 p.m. He could not guarantee any of his men waiting after that hour. Lastly, he wanted to know whether we proposed to make the attempt near the Elbeuf road or la Rue Madeleine.

On my next trip with the wood-cutting party I managed to pass my reply to Raymond.

"We shall attempt the break-out on or about the 9th of January. We shall let you know by signal at the end of afternoon work. The major and I will be standing together near the end hut. From outside your usual shop in la Rue Madeleine you will be able to see us. If you see the major take out his handkerchief and flick it about, you will know that the escape is for that same night. We shall leave at 8.45 p.m. at the latest, probably before. We shall let you know whether it will be towards the Elbeuf road or the Rue Madeleine. I think it will be the former.

A bientôt,

George."

Our boiler-suits were ready and our outside contacts prepared. Thanks to our hot drink service we had nothing to fear from the guards. The time and place for our break were more or less fixed, and we had a perfectly good pair of cutters.

All that remained to be done was the cutting of the wire. . . .

A week before the big night 'Silver' and I began taking our stand-ins with us on the evening cocoa patrol. These were two young fellows from another hut who had no wish to escape, but who had watched our preparations with interest and enthusiasm. They had volunteered to do the drink-slinging on the actual night of the attempt as 'Silver' and I, with the major and Larry Mason, would be amongst the first through the wire.

While these two were learning their rôles Jimmy Matthews, an Australian from our hut, and two look-outs were crawling across to the inner fence at 'Dangerous Corner'. They had the cutters and a dozen ferrules 1½ inches long which I had manufactured from the tops of tins. I had burnt these ferrules to the same dark colour as the wire. I had told them to cut the strands in the shape of a small door. Jimmy was to cut each wire and the Aussie, after guarding against possible twanging, was to slip a ferrule over the two broken ends so that there would be no sign of a break. I had worked out that a dozen cuts would do the job—three at the top, three at the bottom and six at the side. It would then be feasible to swing the whole section inwards, thus leaving an aperture large enough for us to wriggle through. Two quick snips on the Dannerts would allow us to get inside the coil and worm our way to the gap in front of the stands.

Such was the plan in all its simplicity. Jimmy and the Aussie knew that their time was strictly limited. I had told them that when the guards had finished their cocoa—which incidentally was scalding hot—I would light a cigarette and 'Silver' would do the same. The look-outs would warn them when they saw our signals and it was up to them to get away smartly from the fence. I laid down one unbreakable rule— they must not leave any cut wire without its covering ferrule.

On that first night they used five ferrules.

Next morning the major and I were admiring their work from a safe distance when a wounded fellow, who had recently lost a leg, hopped over to the fence and, before we could move to prevent him, suddenly pushed one of his crutches up against the section we had started to cut.

We gasped with relief when the wire did not budge. The tightly gripping ferrules had saved the situation.

White with rage and looking more like a devil-may-care buccaneer than ever before, the major beckoned to the man.

"Why did you do that, soldier?" he demanded icily.

The wounded man, leaning on his crutches, was shaking his head in a bewildered manner. "I heard the wire had been cut, sir," he said stupidly. "There's an escape coming off soon. It's all round the camp."

"And why should you try to sabotage the effort?"

"Because we'll all be punished, see? They never think of those who are left behind. I've had it before, sir. Red Cross parcels stopped, no letters from home, treated like——"

"Come with me, soldier," the major interrupted. "You too, George. I'd like the colonel to have a word with this chap. Come along."

A silent procession of three, we went straight to the M.O.'s office. When the major had finished, the Medical Officer eyed the offender tolerantly. "I think I understand," he said quietly. "I don't propose to go into the ethics of what you did. Perhaps the individual prisoner-of-war evolves some code of his own and fundamental decencies go to the wall. I would, however, suggest to you that any lapse on our part from ordinary civilized behaviour is a new defeat inflicted by the enemy. I tell you, too, that if you hadn't been a wounded man, you yourself might very well have been a member of the escape party whose plans you so very nearly frustrated. Finally, soldier, I can assure you that had you organized a method of escape for yourself, there is not a man in this compound who would have interfered. Think over what I've said, there's a good chap, and keep away from the wire in future. That's all."

In the evening the wounded man came round to our hut and apologised handsomely for his childish action. We all shook hands with him and told him to forget the whole incident. He begged us to let him help in some way, so I promised I'd make use of him on the night of the escape.

When he had gone we busied ourselves with the guards' cocoa. 'Silver' and I, again accompanied by our stooges, carried out successful deliveries, whilst Jimmy and the Aussie fixed up four more ferrules. We decided to leave the last three cuts until the evening previous to the break.

The time dragged along until 8 January. Notes had continued to pass and that afternoon I received Raymond's last message and an extra pair of wire-cutters.

"We shall be waiting as arranged on the Elbeuf road. There are no houses and it will be safer than the Rue Madeleine. When you approach the road, cough. Advance when you get an answering cough. Bring no food, but my organization would appreciate a few English cigarettes. You must be out not later than 8.45 p.m. My men now say they will not wait after that time. I shall look for the signal tomorrow. If it is not given, I shall communicate with you again. If it is—then *bonne* chance!

Raymond."

That meant we had to push our timings forward a quarter of an hour. No doubt the curfew was worrying his organization. We discussed the matter thoroughly and made the necessary modifications to our schedule. We could see no snags.

When 'Silver' and I and our stooges returned to the hut after the customary cocoa diversion the major was there, sitting on my bunk.

"Have we finished cutting, George?" he asked as soon as I had shut the door.

I looked across at Jimmy Matthews. "Everything's fixed up," he said with a grin. "God help us if any of those ferrules give way though. I've cut the Dannerts too. If you'd left us another five minutes we'd have laid a red carpet as far as the Elbeuf road, wouldn't we, Digger?"

I turned to our two stand-ins. "Now I'll just run over your instructions for tomorrow. Come here at 8 p.m., just after the guards are changed. The cocoa will be boiling hot, all ready for you. You must then take it to the guards exactly as you've seen us do. When they throw back the empties, light your fags and puff hard. And remember, the rest of you, if the fag signal is given you must leave the wire immediately and come back here. Otherwise you'll jeopardize the chances of those already out. Any questions?"

"Just one," said the Major. "Suppose we all get out safely. What about the hole in the fence? Wouldn't it be a good idea to have somebody shove the wire back and hook it somewhere to stop it flapping?"

"I'll find somebody to do that, sir. The longer it remains unnoticed the better. I think I know the very man for the job." I looked round the circle of intent faces and went on briskly, "This is the form, then. We get the water boiling for the cocoa at seven. Then we put on our dark suits and either gym shoes or civvy shoes. Ammo. boots will not, repeat NOT be worn. If any man is afraid of his face being seen, he can black

it, but if you keep your heads well down that won't be necessary. Balaclavas and gloves are essential. When you get
through the wire dive into the Dannerts and crawl along it as
far as the gap. Don't go towards the stands or you might bump
into officers using the bath-house. Keep *inside* the fence and
make for the far corner of the racecourse towards the Elbeuf
road where my friends will be waiting. Lie low behind the
logs there until I've cut the wires. There's no need to take any
food, but load up with as many fags as you can carry. Destroy
important documents you would otherwise have left behind.
Be sure you have your identity discs and, once the escape is
on, no talking. Lastly, all orders must be obeyed implicitly
when we contact the civvies."

Then the major stressed the more salient features of the
plan, again emphasising the value of obedience, co-operation
and strict attention to details, and so we broke up for that
night.

The morning and afternoon of the 9th wore on into evening. Seven o'clock found all eleven of us sitting around the
hut in boiler-suits, balaclavas and gloves. Conversation
spurted in nervous irrelevant bursts, embracing any topic
other than the business in hand. The water for the cocoa was
already bubbling in a smoke-blackened dixie. Bob had already
flagged Raymond.

At eight precisely the two stand-ins took away the water-
bottles of scalding cocoa and we slipped on our greatcoats and
crept over to the hospital block. We crouched down in the
shadows, waiting for our look-outs to give the signal that the
corner was clear.

A minute later, in the light from the hospital windows, we
saw the stooges returning with the bottles!

Wondering what could have gone wrong, we flitted across
and joined them in the hut.

"What's happened?" exploded the major. "Why have you
come back?"

"It's the guards, sir. They won't take the cocoa!"

The major swore vividly. "They've rumbled us. Some
bastard's given the game away. What the hell do we do now?"

I snatched the bottles from the trembling stand-ins, poured
the contents back into the dixie and put it on to boil again.
" 'Silver' and I will take the cocoa," I said briefly. "The

Jerries don't trust these two. Nobody's blown the gaff, sir. There isn't a man who——"

"What about the fellow with the crutches?"

"He's out there now, sir, waiting to crawl to the fence. He volunteered to hook up the wires after we're through. He's a good chap. Get over there again and carry on as planned. 'Silver' and I will make it somehow, but in any case don't hang about for us. Remember that Raymond can't stay after 8.45 p.m. Here—better take the spare cutters."

They padded softly out and 'Silver' and I took off our balaclavas. Our greatcoats concealed the boiler-suits. We separated to deal with our respective guards.

When I saw a dim shape outside the fence I called quietly, "Cocoa?"

"*Bist du's?*"[1] came the reply.

"*Ja. Georgi. Mit cocoa. Willst du?*"[2]

"*Jawohl. Komm'!*"[3]

He moved down towards the next guard post and I kept parallel with him. He halted.

"*Warum du nix haben cocoa von meinem kamerad?*"[4] I asked him.

He chuckled. "*Bin nicht krank,*" he said slyly. "*Dich kenne ich. Aber deinen kameraden nicht.*"[5]

"*Ich arbeiten. Senden kamerad.*"[6]

"*Ist gut. Dann trinke ich deinen cocoa.*"[7]

As I flung the bottle to him I heard the heavy tread of his fellow-guard approaching. "Chocolate?" I whispered insinuatingly. "*Zigaretten?*"

"*Ja. Wo dann?*"[8]

"*In kaserne. Ich hollen. Hir warten. Zurück kommen!*"[9]

Like an arrow I sped between the huts, shedding my greatcoat *en route*. By the hospital I paused to put on my balaclava and gloves. Then, crouching low, I made for the wire.

Lying flat on his face beside the hole in the fence was a

[1] Is it you?
[2] Yes, George, with cocoa. Do you want?
[3] Yes, come.
[4] Why wouldn't you take the cocoa from my friend?
[5] I'm not crazy. I know you. But not your friend.
[6] I was working, send my friend.
[7] Right then I drink your cocoa.
[8] Where then?
[9] In the barracks. I'll fetch it. Wait here. I'll come back.

motionless figure. As I burrowed through he whispered, "They're away! Nine altogether. I'll fix the wire. Good luck!"

It was the man with the crutches.

I reached back, impulsively wrung his hand, then dived into the coil of Dannerts. I scrambled out just in front of the stands, right on the path leading to the German bath-houses. I decided to take a chance. Instead of swinging right, keeping on the inside of the wire, I darted towards the bath-house door, then branched off between a low privet hedge and the outer fence. I ran, bent double, for perhaps fifty yards and vaulted over the privet.

There was a muttered expletive and two hands groped for my throat.

"It's me—George!" I panted. "Who is it?"

"Larry. You nearly broke my bloody——"

"Don't talk. Keep down and follow me."

On hands and knees we skirted the privet until we were back at the outer fence. We straightened up and began to run. Suddenly Larry stopped me, gripping my arm and pointing towards a stack of logs black in the gloom. My straining eyes detected a slight movement where the shadows lay thickest. I whistled invitingly and in a few seconds the rest of the party had crawled to the wire opposite us. Without a word, one of them began snipping at the inner fence, while Larry got to work with the spare cutters on the outer one. In less than a minute we were all standing together under a tree some yards from the wire.

We were out.

Dodging from tree to tree, we manoeuvred towards the grass bank running up to the Elbeuf road. There was very little moon, but I could vaguely make out a little knot of people near the railings. I coughed once.

There was no answer.

Again I gave the signal, louder this time, and began to climb towards the silent group. They're Jerries, I thought despairingly. . . . Playing with us. . . . When we're near enough, they'll blast us to hell and gone.

I heard a short dry cough above me. I hurtled madly up the slope, bobbed under the rail, and threw myself into the welcoming arms of Raymond. With him were the two girls and three other men. One of the girls draped an overcoat over my shoulders. Then the major and Larry appeared and Raymond drew the three of us to one side.

The rest of the team quickly assembled and, with the minimum of talk, were split up amongst Raymond's associates. The girls took four between them and the men one each. 'Silver' had not made it.

Raymond conducted the major, Larry and me to a piece of waste ground opposite the race-track. Telling us to wait under a tree till he returned, he hurried back to the others and set off with them towards Rouen. We pocketed our balaclavas and stood there, watching the road.

Then, without warning, two tall figures loomed through the darkness and scraps of conversation reached us. They were a couple of German officers, evidently using the waste ground as a short cut to the camp. We turned our backs on them and pretended to urinate against the tree trunk. They saw us, but passed by without challenging our presence there.

"Come on," I said when they were out of sight. "Let's lie low behind this wall. I'll keep my eyes skinned for Raymond."

We squatted behind a crumbling garden wall and from time to time I peeped over the top and scanned the roadway. At last Raymond reappeared. "Come quickly!" he said curtly. "Keep a few paces behind me until we are over the bridge."

We tumbled along on his heels without speaking. On our right twinkled the lights of the camp; ahead of us lay the town centre. We had no idea of the time, but knew we would have to move fast if we were to beat the curfew.

There were ack-ack batteries manned by German soldiers at either end of the bridge we had to cross. We slunk past, ignored by the Jerries. We had just caught up with Raymond and were congratulating ourselves on our smooth progress when suddenly the air was split by a tremulous wailing, rising and falling, rising and falling, then swelling to a terrifying crescendo of sound.

It was an air raid warning.

In immediate response searchlights probed the sky and the batteries on the bridge hammered out a fierce barrage. Twisting about like hares, we dived down a maze of narrow, deserted back streets until we reached the porch of a large shuttered block of flats. Raymond must have given a special

knock, for the door swung open at once. In we went and up to
the first floor flat. Four more of our party were there and we
were told that the other three had been taken to a different
quarter of the town. We should actually have taken refuge
elsewhere, but because of the air raid Raymond had used the
nearest safe house.

We were given wine and sandwiches and we pressed
cigarettes on all our French helpers. Then the owners of the
flat left to stay with friends, leaving us alone with Raymond.

When the 'All Clear' sounded, Raymond said he had to
go. "As a police detective," he informed us, "I may walk out
after curfew without interference. I must now go to the
Sûreté. If anyone knocks, don't answer. When I come for you
in the morning, I shall let myself in. Oh yes—it would perhaps be wise if you used no lights. So far luck has been with
us, but we must take no unnecessary risks. *Au 'voir.*"

After his departure we all settled down for the night. The
major and I had a bed each and the rest of the team slept on
chairs or rolled up in blankets on the floor.

We had to wait until mid-day before Raymond arrived.
He was laughing all over his face.

"What's amusing you?" I asked him.

"I've been to the camp," he chuckled. "The Boches
'phoned for a policeman this morning, so I went there myself,
hoping that somebody had murdered the Kommandant, but it
wasn't quite so serious as that. I saw the Kommandant himself
and what do you think, *mes amis?*[1] Eleven prisoners attempted
to escape last night! A shocking affair, *hein?*[2] Ten of them got
away, but one was picked up near the wire. The Kommandant
wants the officer and the two N.C.Os. caught as soon as
possible, especially—this will make you laugh, Georges—
especially Dunning. Apparently this criminal fellow Dunning
was in charge of the wood-cutting party and took advantage
of his position to contact civilians and make all the escape
arrangements! Oh yes, Georges, the Kommandant was very
disappointed in you! He went on to say that I must do my
best to round you up, but he does not think I shall be successful. He thinks your break-out was planned with the co-operation of the R.A.F. and that a British plane collected you last

---

[1] My friends.
[2] Eh?

night between the camp and Elbeuf. He deduces that the air raid was used as a cover. How clever these Germans are!"

We all felt sorry for poor 'Silver' whose last fatal cocoa delivery had robbed him of freedom. The rest of Raymond's droll recital cheered us considerably. If we were supposed to have been whisked away by the R.A.F., the Germans were not likely to carry out a particularly vigorous search. The very fact that the Kommandant had handed the job over to the civil police suggested that he was inclined to wash his hands of us.

Raymond stayed with us till dusk, then we were split up again. This time my companion was an Australian whom we knew as Clarry. Raymond took the two of us out of the house, along the street, to a busier part of the town. We had to pass a German canteen with dozens of Jerries milling about outside. We elbowed our way through the crowd of rowdy jostling soldiers and eventually reached a garage in a cobbled side street.

Raymond tapped out his special Morse on the door and we were promptly admitted. We crossed the garage to a door in a corner, went up a flight of metal stairs, along a landing, and came to another door through which we passed into the living quarters. The cars in the garage, I had noted with a certain amount of uneasiness, all bore swastika emblems. They were German staff cars.

Inside the room were a young man and a young girl whom we instantly recognised. They had frequently waved to us from the Elbeuf road and the Rue Madeleine during our wood-cutting sorties. They seemed delighted to see us and provided us with a really appetizing meal. Raymond took his leave while we were eating.

The young people then showed us up to an attic, comfortably furnished, with a wood fire in the grate and a pyramid of logs beside it. "You must stay here," said the girl. "Do not come down on your own. Always wait to be brought down by Raymond or by one of us. Tomorrow you will meet my parents and my sister. All your meals will be served to you here except for supper which you may eat downstairs. You will be perfectly safe as long as you obey instructions. The Boches use the garage, working there all day. They never interfere with us. Raymond will visit you each day until the next stage of your journey has been arranged. *Bonne nuit et dormez bien!*[1]

We lived in the attic for five days and were extremely well looked after by our generous hosts. We learned that we were in a neighbourhood infested with Germans. They worked below us during the day, patronized the canteen only twenty yards up the street at night, had a block of offices next door and some sort of a legal set-up behind the garage. Despite their dangerous situation the family had voluntarily accepted the responsibility of our presence and seemed genuinely reluctant to part with us at the end of our stay. I believe that after the war the garage owner received some high honour from the civic authorities for assisting two allied prisoners-of-war to escape. He certainly earned it.

To our surprise Raymond took us back to the flat where we had spent our first night of freedom. The major and the other boys were already there. We were photographed, our finger-prints were taken, and in a very short time we were all fixed up with fake identity cards and other phoney documentation. The major had removed his eye-patch, which was too conspicuous, and now wore a pair of spectacles fitted with one opaque and one plain glass. He had also tried to dye his moustache, but with most unfortunate results. It had turned an intriguing shade of green!

Before leaving us that night, Raymond told us that on the morrow we should be going by train to Dijon, the last large town before the demarcation zone. Once again we were to move off in groups. The major, Larry and I were to travel under his tutelage. There was a twinkle in his eye when he recommended the major to do something about his moustache.

Next morning our group was the last to set out for the station. Our tickets, Raymond said, were already bought. We walked in twos—Raymond and the major, now clean-shaven, in front; Larry and I a few paces to the rear. As we drew near to the imposing façade of Rouen main station, Larry nudged me and drew my attention to a resplendent military figure standing outside one of the entrances chatting to two handsome lieutenants.

It was the camp Kommandant, Oberst Martin. . . .

[1] Good night and sleep well.

XV

ESCAPE FROM A CANADIAN GAOL

from

Rap Sheet

By BLACKIE AUDETT

Blackie Audett, notorious bootlegger and bank-robber of the thirties, a pal of John Dillinger, made many daring escapes from American and Canadian prisons. Blackie started life on a farm near Calgary, ran away at the age of ten because of his father's ill-treatment, and—since he was big for his age—passed himself off as being fifteen. Although under-age, he served in the 1914-18 war and was decorated for bravery. On his return to Canada, he found that his mother had died in the 'flu epidemic. Kicking around at a loose end in bad company, he and his friend, Henry, took part in a bullion train robbery. Their shares were about 108,000 dollars each, so they cached most of it, and then set out on a spree. But the arm of the law reached out and grabbed them.

Blackie's story of their escape from this first of the many gaols in his life is taken from his autobiography Rap Sheet, *which gives a terse and terrifying account of gangster life.*

THEY tossed us in gaol in Macleod, the main town of the area, a few miles away. It was just a little gaol and we was the only prisoners. We was pretty famous prisoners, too. It was the first and maybe the last time they ever had two robbers in that gaol there who had heisted a train of half a million dollars.

The officer in charge was a provincial named Corporal Watt. Him and his wife lived downstairs. The gaol was on the second floor.

Part of Corporal Watt's duties was to bring us our meals. The rest of the time, they just left us up there in a little cell by ourselves.

The police, naturally, was more interested in the missing money right then than they was of us. They knowed where *we* was, all right. But the money and what had happened to it was something else again. We figured they had found it for sure in the alley, where Henry had throwed it. If they hadn't, somebody sure had. Two hundred grand can't just lay around in an alley for ever.

They questioned us for hours, together and separately. We denied everything, in spite of them telling each of us that the other one had spilled the works and we might as well come clean.

So pretty soon we put it together from their questions that they didn't have no more idea where the money was than we did.

Then one afternoon Helen came to the gaol to see me. When she showed up, Scotty Lawrence he come down with an attack of nose trouble. He begin sniffing around to find out why Helen was so all-fired anxious to get in touch with me.

Scotty's sniffing taken him on a quick run back to Granum to search Helen's room. Meantime, they made her wait downstairs, on one stall or another, at the Macleod gaol. In her room Scotty found two suitcases full of money. The whole works was soaking wet. Well, they brought the money back to Macleod and faced Helen with it.

They had discovered it stacked in a closet in her room, so there was nothing for her to do but tell them the truth about where she found it.

When Henry throwed them suitcases over the roof there had been a slight interception. There was a big rain barrel sitting down there in the alley, right below the eaves. Them suitcases hit spang into it, one on top of the other. Henry couldn't have done that good if he'd been trying. There was enough water in the barrel to cover the bags, and there they set.

When the police searched the alley, nobody thought of looking into that barrel of water. That evening, Helen went out to get some rain-water. There in the barrel she found them two suitcases. She hauled them out and opened them up, right there in the alley, and you can just imagine! Holy mackerel and Katy bar the door!

The police was pretty tough on Helen, but they couldn't figure what part she could have had in the train robbery. They wouldn't believe what she told them about finding it.

They questioned her for hours, but she stood with the story about the rain barrel. They told her they would put her in the pen for life if she didn't tell them the full story of the robbery. She couldn't tell them nothing, naturally.

Then they brought me and Henry downstairs and told us Helen was going to prison unless we come through with the identity of the others in the stick-up. I told them I not only knowed nothing about any others, I didn't even know nothing about no stick-up. They couldn't prove nothing on Helen just because she had the money in her room, without me and Henry squealed. We said we never seen them suitcases before in our lives. Helen stood by her story and they finally had to let her go. They put us back in our cells to wait transfer back to Lethbridge or Calgary, where we was to be charged and held for trial.

We was sitting on our bunks, there in Macleod, feeling mighty low.

I said to Henry, "If they ever get us back to Calgary or Lethbridge we are sunk. If we're ever going to get away, it's going to have to be here. And quick."

"It sure don't look any too good for getting away, here or no place else, when you get right down to it," Henry said.

"One thing in our favour here that won't happen in the next gaol is we only got one guard," I said. "If we can take care of him we're on our way."

Henry thought that one over and come up empty. He just set there glum-like. Then he said, "Sure wish we had that there steak we didn't buy in Calgary. Wonder what Watt will bring us up tonight?"

That done it. I seen our answer, plain as day.

"You got it!" I told Henry. "Corporal Watt's our man!"

Then I spilled the plan to Henry.

Corporal Watt come up alone with our supper every night. It was cooked down below and he brought it up on a tray. They had our cell fixed good and proper, so far as the door was concerned. First, it was locked with a big gaol key. Then there was a chain and padlock. Just to make sure, there was a pair of handcuffs snapped around the steel bars at the edge of the door.

Each night when Corporal Watt brought our supper, he had to set the tray down in the hall, pull a big ring of keys

out of his pocket and unfasten the three locks. Then he had
to bend back down, pick up the tray and carry it in.

I went over all this with Henry.

"That's when we take him," I said.

But it wasn't quite that simple. If we tried to take Watt
bare-handed, he would put up a yell before we could get out
the door. Our only chance was to knock him cold some way
before he could holler.

It was Henry who figured out the answer to that.

There was a sort of lean-to right outside our barred
window. It had a crumbly old brick chimney sticking up out
of it—a lot of loose bricks. We could get our arms out through
the bars, but not far enough to reach the bricks.

Well, Henry, he was right on his toes. He tore strips off
our blankets and we fixed a running loop in one end to make
a lasso. We begun to toss it at the chimney.

It taken us a couple of hours to snag one of them bricks,
but we finally got a hold of one and hauled it in through our
window. Then we tore off another piece of blanket and made
a sling for the brick. That made us a sap big enough to knock
down an elephant.

We hid it in the bed and waited for Watt to show with
our supper.

Henry wanted to be the one to let him have it, but I was
a little leery. I was afraid Henry, hot-headed like he was,
would hit him too hard and kill him. Last thing we wanted to
do was kill Watt. We was deep-up in enough troubles, way
things was. We just wanted to knock him out. Finally, Henry
agreed to let me go ahead and do the honours.

"But you better make it good," he said. "There ain't
going to be no second round."

The corporal was right on time with supper. He set down
the tray and went through the rigmarole with the locks. Then
he picked up the tray and come on in.

He never knowed what hit him. We drug him into the
cell and pulled off his shoes and coat. They had taken our
own shoes away from us and our outer clothes.

We had to have shoes if we were going to make a break. I
wear a size seven. Watt's boots was size ten, but I pulled them
on. Then we went downstairs.

Watt's wife was standing by the stove. We stood her off

with the gun we had taken off her husband. Henry held the gun on her and I rustled around for another pair of shoes, some fur caps and stuff the provincials wear as a kind of winter uniform. I also stole a couple more guns.

I wanted to find my own shoes for a very special reason. In the toe of the left one was the express claim check for the $30,000 suitcase we had sent to Fernie.

I found the shoes, but not in time to change. So I carried them with me and wore Watt's big boots. We must have put up quite a picture busting out of that gaolhouse, part in our own clothes and part in the uniform of provincial police.

Watt was still out cold when we took off. We didn't see nobody when we come out into the street.

There was a fellow run a Dodge garage that I knowed, down the street. His name was Sandy McDonald. He was not very friendly toward us and he'd given the police some information about us being up there in Granum. But I didn't hold that against him.

What I held against him that night was a gun. We walked in on him and told him we had to have a car and what we would do to him if we didn't get it. He believed us, completely.

He come up with a brand new Dodge he had in the place, and didn't put up no squawk when we made him drive. I told him to head for Granum and not get no unhealthy ideas.

My car—the McLaughlin—was in Granum. I really wanted that car. I scarcely had had a chance to drive it. So we taken this fellow McDonald and he drove us to the garage in Granum where I had stored the McLaughlin.

Well, we let the garage man and his car go on back home a little too quick.

When we located my car in the Granum garage, the police had put a long chain through the spokes of the front wheels and padlocked it. Besides that, they had taken off the whole distributor head. The McLaughlin Special was a brand new model and there was no spare parts around there that would fit it.

So there we was. No car. And we had let the Dodge man go.

Well, me and Henry went out on the street and there was an old Mitchell Six sitting there. The keys was in the lock. We got in and took off.

We didn't have a cent to our name and just a beat-up old wreck of a car. On top of that, them clothes we was wearing made us look like a couple of scarecrows coming off a bender. We sure had come down in the world fast. Only a few days before we had been running our fingers through half a million dollars!

We taken out as fast as that Mitchell would go and we come to a little town—Claresholm, or something like that. The police by that time was setting up roadblocks of one kind or another all over that district. In this little town we come to, the provincial duty had taken and put a bunch of chicken crates across the street. I guess that's all he could find in town that was big enough to reach across the road. There was ten or a dozen of them. Most of them had live chickens in them.

Well, Henry was driving. Just before we get to them chicken coops, there was a policeman standing in the middle of the street—a fellow name of Jack Swain. Henry knowed him. Swain was waving his arms, trying to flag us down.

I pulled out one of the pistols we'd grabbed at the Macleod gaol and fired a shot in the ground, right by his feet. With that, this here Jack Swain, he jumped right straight up in the air. And when he come down, he was heading the opposite direction. His feet was already going when he hit ground and he was really picking them up and putting them down.

He was running so fast he couldn't make the turn at the corner. The last we seen of him he went sprawling into a ditch. Me and Henry was laughing so hard Henry couldn't scarcely make the turn neither. When he did make it, there was them damn chicken crates right smack across the road. We was moving too fast to stop or go around. We just hit them head-on.

Them chickens went every which way. All over everything. Chickens in the windshield. Chickens in the back seat. Everywhere. But we kept going, chickens and all.

We got out of there, chewing feathers for all we was worth.

But we bogged down in the snow and sand with that old Mitchell a few miles out of town. We had to leave the car and we was sure the police was hot on our trail. So we taken off afoot into the Porcupine Hills.

Them Porcupine Hills stretch for miles along the border

between Alberta and Montana. There is a ranch every now and then, or was at that time. But mostly the hills was just open range land. One ridge looked just like the next and the only way you could tell how you was headed was by the sun.

Well, after walking so long it seemed like we must surely be almost in Mexico, we come on to this old deserted barn and there was these two horses. Anything looked better than walking, right then. But it turned out to be something of a toss-up. Them horses was the most spavined, broken-down plough team this side of a glue factory, and skinny to boot. It had been a tough winter in Alberta and the spring grass wasn't even up to one bite high. Riding them skinny horses for miles and miles couldn't of been any better than being rode out of Canada on a fence rail.

We was leery about riding in broad daylight, but we was afraid of getting lost if we tackled it at night. Henry had been raised-up there in that country, so that helped a little. He had a general idea of where people lived that he knowed. Besides, he was hungry and still complaining about having all that money and not enough to eat. I told him what was left of that money was a long way off and it would be some time before we got to it.

It was coming on dark when we rode over the top of the hill, and there was a house in the valley.

Henry looked it over careful and decided maybe he knowed the people. He didn't, it turned out. But we rode up in the barnyard and there our old plug horses practically collapsed. So did we.

The rancher come out to see what was going on and Henry told him we'd got lost on a hunting trip. The rancher sort of snickered.

"You boys hunting in disguise?" he said. "And with your bare hands to boot?"

Well, one thing led to another and we told him the truth. A little of it, that is. Much as he needed to know.

The rancher he was sympathetic. He said he'd had a little run-in with the law himself awhile before. He taken us in the house and his wife fixed us up a good hot meal. They bunked us down out in the barn.

Next morning there was two fresh young saddle horses tied to the rail outside the barn. The old plugs was gone.

The rancher just give us the wink and said, "Leave the horses at Smith's ranch on the Montana side, when you get around to it. I'll be down that way in a week or so. Now get the hell a long ways away from here, before the provincials get nosy."

His wife give us a big package of food and we taken out, feeling pretty pert. We was practically in sight of the U.S.A. We circled way up in the hills so as to come into Montana through the rough country where it wasn't likely the police would be looking for us. Besides, there was another ranch that Henry knowed about that was just a good day's ride. He figured our lunch would about last till we made this second ranch. That was Henry every time.

We got to the second ranch about sundown and Henry knowed the people this time.

When we rode up, there was a big pack of dogs come barking at us. We figured that was good, because if the police or anybody come in the night, them dogs would warn us.

These people treated us royal, but we decided we had better sleep in the barn again, just in case. The people knowed exactly who we was and what we had done. A provincial policeman had come through earlier that day and told them to be on the lookout. But they was distant kin to Henry, and besides, they didn't have much use for the law either, on account of some question there had been sometime before about their brand showing up on the wrong cattle. We was among friends.

But the police found some friends, too, that night. Man's best friend, like the feller says.

Scotty Lawrence had noodled out the general way we would have to take and had men spotting all the ranches in the district. During the night, Scotty sneaked up to the ranch with a bunch of hamburger and made friends with them dogs. He short-circuited any chance barking with them hamburgers. Then he hid his men around in the woodshed and places and laid low until daylight.

It was not until me and Henry had sat down at the breakfast table that Scotty struck. He come crashing into the kitchen from the woodshed with that same big thumb-buster gun in his fist. At the same time, another policeman busted the kitchen window with his gun barrel and covered us from there. Four others come hot-footing it in from the yard when Scotty blowed his whistle.

We didn't even have to surrender. The cuffs was on us before we could even say we wanted to.

They taken us down to where they had a couple of cars stashed out in a draw. They tied us up in enough chain and padlocks to hold an army. A few hours later we was back in Macleod, the same gaol we had busted out of two days earlier.

Corporal Watt was waiting for us, with his head bandaged up like an Arab in a turban.

XVI

ESCAPE INTO LITHUANIA

from

The Road to Liberty

By Jean Brilhac

Of the hundreds of thousands of Frenchmen taken to prison camps in Germany after the fall of France, 220 made successful escapes into Russia. Of these, 186 arrived in London on 12 September, 1941, to join the forces of General de Gaulle. The Road to Liberty is the incredible story of these 186 who fled, either singly or collectively, from the clutches of the sadistic Nazis.

Henry Claye's escape across the border into Lithuania is only one of the many thrilling episodes in this book, but it is typical of the spirit which made all of these men determined to make a bid for the freedom which was dearer to them than life. A spirit so well and simply expressed by Jean Brilhac in the following paragraph:

"At dawn on 30 August, 1941, our last day in Russia, we stood on the quayside at Archangel, lined up in threes. Then, as though the last moment needed to be marked by a symbolical gesture, Deschamps walked along the file and gave each of the 186 men a cigarette. God alone knows where these cigarettes came from or how Deschamps had managed to keep them until this moment, or rather, for this moment. How we enjoyed that last cigarette in Russia, which we smoked while we were about to become FREE FRENCHMEN again! We inhaled each puff with delight, and between each puff we filled our nostrils with the breath of freedom."

I met him for the first time in Russia. He was bending over a basin and washing his hands: he had the build of a wrestler and the huge muscles of his arms stood out beneath his rolled-up shirtsleeves. . . . When he had finished washing he put on his rings and called out to me in a husky voice, "So you are the newcomer?" (Having reached Russia four months ago he looked upon himself as an old-stager.) "Where do you come from?" "From Paris," I replied. "Paris . . . Paris. . . ." **He**

repeated this word several times as though it had a magical
significance, then turning to me confidentially, "Do you
remember," he said, "the film in which Jean Gabin says to
Mirelle Balin, 'You smell of the Métro. . .?' Well, old man, I
have had to travel 2,500 miles to find out what he meant.
What would I not give to smell that smell of the Métro again,
and on a woman."

This was Henry Claye.

Most men have two loves; Henry Claye had two prides:
first, that he was a man, secondly that he hailed from Paris,
and not just anywhere in Paris, but from Barbès. Who cares
which of the cafés of the Place Pigalle he used to frequent
before the war; or that his photograph appeared in art publications and that he 'played catch'? What matters is the fact
that this 'tough guy' accomplished great feats.

The ordinary man in the street is a character in fiction
without realizing it, but Claye must have always known that
he was just that. But he could never have guessed that
imprisonment would one day cause him to embark on more
heroic adventures than the cinema has ever depicted—
because they would have been considered too far-fetched!—
and that he would emerge with honour, bringing credit not
only to himself, to Barbès and the Place Pigalle, but to
France. His escape, like the feats he has accomplished in de
Gaulle's army, was not a triumph of cunning (which he
despises), nor of astuteness, but a triumph of energy. In Claye
prehistoric man came to life again for a week in all his native
simplicity. A hostile world surrounded him: he was confronted by monsters, hunger and thirst, and he went through
the anguish of the trapped beast. Yet, with no other weapon
than his physical strength and his extraordinary powers of
endurance, Claye fought his way to freedom.

He arrived in Germany at the beginning of August 1940
and was sent to a work camp in East Germany. He at once
made up his mind to escape to the nearest country, Lithuania.
Two of his comrades, Parisians of course, decided to throw in
their lot with his, and they all began to make preparations.

It was an enormous undertaking. They would have to
cover 100 miles on foot (the distance from the frontier as the
crow flies); not one of them knew German, they knew nothing
about the locality, they had no maps, no compass, no money

and no means of obtaining money. Their main concern was to escape before the cold weather came, and they were certain that once they had managed to get outside the camp all would be well.

It was not at all easy to get out of the camp. The Germans had turned the hut where they slept into a regular prison: the window was covered with a grille which was bolted from outside with ten huge bolts; the door was locked, and at night, reinforced with iron bars. Moreover, to prevent the prisoners from escaping, the guards used to lock up their clothes every night.

Overcoming such obstacles was child's play for the three friends. Claye, while at work, managed to get hold of a large pair of pliers, and as soon as he got the chance, he hid behind some friends and undid all the bolts down one side of the window-grille. The grille remained in position but was no longer fastened. The problem of clothes was also settled in no time, as several prisoners had, besides their uniform, a spare outfit of fatigue clothes; as for shoes, there were just enough extra pairs in the hut to enable the three plotters to keep theirs back at night. Everything seemed to be going satisfactorily, and they fixed their date of departure for 23 August.

The whole scheme almost failed, just because of one pair of shoes. On the night of their escape, when the time came to collect the shoes for the night, the hut's fifty-third pair of shoes had disappeared. Everything was turned upside down (discreetly however, so as not to arouse suspicion) to find the missing pair. At last, after a thorough search, the shoes were found; it appeared their owner had simply gone to sleep after hiding them as he always did. Claye calmly handed them to the soldier in charge of collecting shoes.

Then the hut was locked up and lights put out. Claye slipped a fatigue dress over his uniform which was far too conspicuous; he had come all the way to Germany with a pair of riding breeches and long fawn gaiters, and had also brought his field-glasses, his camera and his magnificent hunting knife. He was determined not to leave any of his precious possessions behind for the use of the Germans. His two comrades only had their private's uniform, without even a fatigue coat to camouflage them. The three men waited for a while, then shook hands with a few friends; they were just about to set off when the tragedy occurred. One of the three bumped into a man asleep near the window, who woke up and began grumbling. He happened to be the owner of the unlucky pair of shoes, and again, as luck would have it, the first thing he noticed was that his shoes had disappeared. While Claye was opening the window, twisting the grille back, and was about to slide down the outside wall, the owner of the shoes began to kick up a terrible row and the whole hut resounded with his shouts. Claye climbed back into the hut and went up to the man.

"You are making such a din you'll have the sentry here in a moment. I warn you: I have got a knife here. If the sentry comes in, I will stick my knife into his stomach." It was obvious that he meant it; the man shut up, and the three prisoners were able to climb out without any further hitch.

As the sentry was patrolling up and down on the other side of the hut, the three men went straight to the provisions hut. They had made keys to unlock the door, but alas, their keys were round when they should have been flat.

So, besides having no map and no compass, they had no food. For a moment they wondered if they were insane to start out so badly equipped. Coming from Paris was not like coming from the country and knowing where to find potatoes and beetroots and how to cook them. If they had realized what a handicap this entire lack of provisions was going to prove, they might have postponed their escape—but they were not going to let themselves be held up by such a trifling thing as food! They had made up their minds to leave and nothing was going to stop them. So they jumped over the barbed-wire network of the camp and plunged into open country with only the stars to direct them.

On the very first night of their escape they had their first alarm. While they were walking along the road, in single file, with Claye bringing up the rear, towards half-past two in the morning they heard the sound of hoofs behind them. "It must be a cow following us," said Claye. He looked round: the cow turned out to be a mounted policeman wearing a brown shirt and with a swastika on his armlet. The policeman kept up a volley of questions which none of them understood. As he persisted in pestering them, Claye, still walking, turned on him and shouted in French, "Well, what's wrong?" He looked so ferocious that the policeman turned round and galloped away. But they all three knew that within ten minutes they would have a whole company on their heels.

They decided to take cover at once. There was a little bridge over a stream just ahead of them. They examined it carefully and found that it was supported by three large beams. In a flash each of the three men had climbed along a beam and hidden under the superstructure of the bridge. Sure enough, within less than ten minutes a patrol arrived and began searching for them all over the place. They even went down into the stream to look for them. With thumping hearts, the three men could see the butt-ends of the rifles moving about below, almost at arm's length. Luckily they could not be seen in the dark, and none of the soldiers bothered to hoist themselves up under the bridge. Before long the patrol moved off and all was well.

When they had given the soldiers time to get back to the town, the three men set off again. It was getting late and they would soon have to look for somewhere to spend the daylight hours. Being quite unfamiliar with the country, they had fully expected to find a suitable shelter, a mill for example. There was not anything of the sort in sight, and it was dawn already. They could hear the church bells striking five. While they were still wondering where to find shelter, they noticed that a peasant had laid some boards across a ditch by the side of the road, for his cattle to walk over.

It seemed a good hiding-place, so they began to crawl under the boards. Claye, with his huge build, found it almost impossible to wriggle in, but at last all three of them had got inside and they decided to stay there. They lay in the ditch, one man's feet touching the next one's head, with the planks just above them, like the lid of a coffin—and there they were stuck for the whole day, without a scrap of food. Even if they had had food with them, they were so tightly packed that they would not have had elbow-room to get it to their mouths! To make matters worse a storm blew up and the rain poured down all day long, filling the ditch so that the three men felt as though they had been tied up and thrown into a sewer. It was nine o'clock at night before they dare extricate themselves from their hiding-place. Then, aching all over, they set out again.

Fortunately, the next twenty-four hours were fairly uneventful. They were inclined to quarrel because they did not agree on where the east lay; they occasionally walked in the wrong direction; they played hide and seek with the railway officials in the goods-yards at Insterburg and had to throw themselves flat on the ground and hide under a train—but such things were the common lot of prisoners trying to escape. 25 August was only marked by one alarm, and that a comic one. They were spending the day hiding under a railway bridge. While one of them was busy relieving himself beside the line, a railway worker was seen approaching, and the unfortunate Frenchman, caught in the act, had to throw himself into the nettles with no protection for his legs.

Food continued to be the worst problem. For the first forty-eight hours they had not had a morsel to eat, and when they set out on their third night's walk they felt weak from the start. Nevertheless, they kept on along the railway track until half-past four in the morning. By then they began to suffer terrible pangs of hunger. They picked up potatoes and ate them raw, but were sick immediately afterwards. They made no attempt to cook them—and perhaps they didn't know how to! By hook or by crook they must get food, so Claye, who was less likely to be recognized as an escaped prisoner because of the fatigue dress he was wearing, set off alone towards a large farm. He climbed a wall, drew near to the farm buildings and tried to get into what he thought might be a store-room. It was useless: all was securely locked up. He turned away dejected.

As he was about to climb back over the wall he saw something come panting behind him. Looking round he noticed an enormous German sheep dog about to leap on him. A door stood open only a yard or so away, but could he reach it? Claye stood still with the sweat pouring down his face, the dog watching him closely. Very slowly, hardly raising his feet from the ground, Claye slowly edged his way towards the door. Reaching the doorway and taking a deep breath he leapt through, slamming the door behind him. The dog pounced too late, barking furiously. Claye was so overwrought that he had to lean up against a tree to steady himself. Then he went back to his comrades growling, "We shall have to tighten our belts another hole!"

It was almost daylight and high time to take cover. Near the road was a field which had recently been cleared of tree stumps, leaving holes in which they could lie curled up. There they spent the 26 of August, devoured by mosquitoes and unable to move because of the passers-by on the road only thirty yards away. And still they had nothing to eat.

It rained all day long. . . .

On the fourth night they could hardly walk and their hunger was agonizing. Claye was still active, but his friends were on their last legs. Towards midnight, when they were near a group of houses, Claye, who was by now an expert in night reconnaissance, went off alone through the fields towards the church.

At the end of a field he came to a meadow, and then to a large white wall. He climbed over, let himself slide down on the other side. Somehow it seemed a long drop. On looking around he found he was at the bottom of a pit ten feet deep. He touched the sides which were dead straight and slimy with mud. He could only take a few steps in either direction: he was trapped. It was impossible to get out! He tried hoisting himself up, cutting steps with his knife: quite useless, because the mud slithered beneath his feet, and he fell back, the sweat pouring down and his throat parched.

His two friends began to grow uneasy at his absence and set out to look for him. They also walked towards the church and climbed over the white wall. Luckily when they landed on the other side they were near enough for Claye to hear them. He began to whistle and call them in hoarse whispers so as not to wake up the villagers. At last they heard him and in the dark they tried to discover his exact position. "Where are you?" they called under their breath. "Here, here," he called back in a deathly voice. It was only after an hour and a half that poor Claye was hauled out of his pit. He looked round him: there were white slabs of stone everywhere. He shivered with horror when he realized that he was in a cemetery, and that the deep black pit where he thought he was stuck for ever, was a freshly dug grave waiting for a dead man!

At dawn on 27 August the little band took shelter in a copse about seventy yards from the road. Their adventures in the cemetery had taken their minds off their hunger, but now that they had calmed down again they began to feel the pangs more acutely than ever. They could not even sleep. "My comrades," said Claye afterwards, "were so played out that although I was pretty nearly done myself, I had to spend my time trying to pump a little strength into them."

Towards the early afternoon Claye could hold out no longer. It was impossible to wait till nightfall: he set off in broad daylight towards a nearby farm. He opened the gate. The house looked dead. He looked round him: what should he see lying between double window-panes but three rows of tomatoes, which had been put there to ripen in the sun. What luck? He was just slipping his hand through the outer window when an old man's face peered at him through the inside window. He drew his hand back like lightning.

The old man opened the window, leant out, and began to speak. Claye did not lose his head: he had to do something, and so he pretended to be dumb. He began to gesticulate, pointing to his throat with a helpless look and uttering inarticulate sounds. Then he drew a piece of paper from his pocket, on which he had asked a friend at the camp to write in German 'Strasse nach Riga?' (The road to Riga?) in case of emergency. The man looked at the paper, but did not seem to understand. He gazed with growing suspicion at this haggard tramp, who had not shaved for four days, and went on making hysterical sounds. Having at last deciphered the writing, he pointed towards a road. Claye could only walk away with his tail between his legs.

When he neared the gate he found some hens in his path. Claye is not one to let this kind of opportunity slip. He was careful to leave the door ajar and the hens followed into the road. A clump of trees hid all this from the farmer and his wife. Claye let a couple of hens get ahead of him and then shooed them towards the wood where his friends were on the look-out for him. By the time he reached them they had already wrung one hen's neck, torn off its feathers and were devouring the flesh. Claye had become too primitive to be sickened by this sight and rushed towards them to get his share. He secured the two drumsticks, which he promptly stripped clean. "It tasted more or less like chicken; but it was warm, as though still alive. Ghastly!" He swallowed the raw gizzard as well as an egg which the hen had been about to lay.

Then the three men looked at one another with shining

L

eyes and smiled. For the first time since their departure they no longer felt hungry.

This savage satisfaction was, alas, short-lived: before long they were all suffering from violent diarrhoea, which left them weak and incapable of anything except sleeping.

Somehow Claye could not rest. He was too anxious. He had seen the farmer's wife set out along the road and he was afraid that she had gone to warn the police. Every time he began to fall asleep, he felt the need to get up and look around. Before long he saw in the distance the farmer's wife now accompanied by an armed platoon. He quickly shook his comrades out of their sleep and warned them that the man-hunt was on again.

The presence of danger lent them new strength. They took to their heels and fled, skirting farms, ducking behind hedges and dodging from one clump of trees to another. They must have travelled in a circle for they found themselves on the main road, behind the soldiers. They had always avoided walking along a road in broad daylight, but this time they had no alternative. They followed at a distance, walking slowly; just when they thought they were out of danger, they saw the armed platoon coming back towards them. Some peasant must have put their pursuers on their track again; they had split up into search parties and were combing the woods. It was obvious that although they had not yet been spotted they soon would be, and that if they remained on the high road they would be caught. The best thing to do was to take cover again. They went into a potato field and lay flat on the ground, not more than twenty yards from the road. The sound of tramping feet came closer. Now the soldiers were on a level with them—some scattered to search a little wood before rejoining the main body of the platoon. They were walking straight on past their hiding-place. . . . Now they had passed. . . .

Dusk fell at last on this eventful day. At 9 p.m. the three men set out again, walked all night long, and found themselves at 3.30 a.m. on 28 August at the entrance to Tilsit. Without waiting for daylight they climbed up on a railway bridge, lay down alongside the track and went fast asleep.

The next day was still one of starvation, but worse than this, it was a return to civilization. They were startled out of their sleep by the sound of cars hooting: it was already nine o'clock in the morning, and below them there were buses, cyclists and pedestrians passing under the bridge. Then they realized with horror that they had chosen a spot which was plainly visible to anyone who happened to look upward, and that if no one had spotted them already, it must be because there is a god who watches over fugitives! As soon as the road was clear for a minute, they clambered down from their pedestal and plunged into the first little wood they could find.

Towards the end of the morning, what should they see on the road only a few yards away but a band of fifty French prisoners, guarded by German soldiers, marching past on their way to work. This depressing sight reminded them of what they themselves had been only a week ago. It was better to be outcasts and starve to death than to be thrown back into that herd of slaves: this they felt so deeply that when evening came they found new strength to set out again.

But they were not through with Tilsit yet. They decided to follow the course of the river, thinking that this would be the best way to skirt the town. Alas, far from avoiding the town they landed right in the middle of one of its most popular parks. It was crowded with loving couples, soldiers arm in arm with their *Gretchen*, téte-a-téte in the arbours. It looked as though the entire garrison of Tilsit had been ordered out to learn the art of love. In the midst of this *Féte Galanté* all they could do was hide behind tree-trunks.

As the clocks were striking eleven there was a blare of trumpets in the neighbouring barracks, and one after the other, Don Juans in field-grey returned to their quarters; the park was deserted, except for a small group of officers who were talking together on a bridge. This bridge they must cross if they were ever to get out of the park and reach the frontier. They took off their forage caps and jackets and walked boldly past the officers without arousing suspicion.

Two hours later they reached the banks of the Niemen. What a strange coincidence that these three pathetic soldiers of a defeated France should have reached the river at the precise spot where, 130 years ago, Napoleon had discussed the future of the world with the Tsar Alexander of Russia! Time and time again, from Friedland to Tilsit, from Lützen to Eylau, French prisoners passed thus under the shadow of Napoleon.

Still they had to find a way to cross the Niemen. They were far too exhausted to swim across, and it seemed hopeless to try to find a boat. This only left the bridge, or rather a series of three steel bridges which stretched from one bank to the other, 1,000 feet long. But the bridges were lighted up, and most certainly guarded. Encouraged by their success in the park, they decided to take the risk. They walked steadily across the bridge, keeping as close to the railings as possible so as to be out of the rays of the lamp-posts. On each of the three bridges there were two sentries guarding the middle road. Six times the Frenchmen called out "Heil Hitler!" and six times the sentries replied "Heil Hitler!" They had crossed the Niemen!

After they had spent another day resting and still without food, they set out again on the evening of 29 August for the last lap of their journey. Already the frontier seemed quite close, probably less than fifteen miles away. Without this consoling thought they could never have endured their utter exhaustion and their ravenous hunger, and might even have abandoned the struggle. But it was now certain that this was to be their last night, and that within a few hours they would have crossed the frontier . . . or lost their lives.

This thought spurred them on, although they were deadbeat and could hardly stand or drag themselves along. They walked mechanically, stumbling at every step. Unfortunately they did not know the exact position of the frontier, and just when they needed to be most on the alert they hardly had the strength to hold their heads up. Then, to crown everything, they began to quarrel. This was the time when they should have been most united; yet at this precise moment the man whom they called 'the Engineer' said he could walk better by himself than in a gang. He crossed over to the other side of the road and stubbornly refused to join the other two. So they staggered on, two men on one side of the road and one on the other, so that Henry Claye, whose exceptionally strong constitution enabled him to stand up to the strain better than his two comrades, had to go from one man to the other to keep up their courage.

Suddenly, just as they were leaving the slumbering village, they saw three lights coming towards them on the road. In the distance it looked like bicycle lamps, and they supposed it must be workers returning home from night work. But the lights did not seem to come any closer. Though this struck them as curious, they were too worn out to be able to act with caution. Then as they approached the lights and were about to walk past them they were startled by a hoarse shout of *"Wer da?* Halt!" and three German soldiers sprang up between the lights.

"Franzosen—do not fire!" shrieked 'the Engineer' who had almost walked into the sentry-box and now saw a gun levelled at his chest. At this cry, the sentries hesitated. The other two Frenchmen seized the opportunity to leap into a little side road. Bullets were whistling all around. Claye realized that it would be fatal to stay on this road in the line of fire. Followed by his comrade he sprang across the road and dived into the fields. Within a few moments he heard the heavy thud of a body falling to the ground. There was no need for him to look round to realize that he was now alone. . . .

The sound of firing continued while Claye tore at full speed across country. Without stopping, he reflected that it would be wisest to take a bold course. When he had left the sentry-post a mile and a half behind he returned to the main road, where no one would expect to find him. He was bathed in sweat, dead-beat and desperate. He never slackened his pace, however, but for an hour or more plunged straight on, falling down time after time and picking himself up again. In his mind there was only one thought, 'I must get through.'

But what were those lights in front of him? Was it hallucination, or had he come to another sentry-post, another trap? This time he had learnt his lesson. He left the road and again took to the fields on his left. He was among wheat-sheaves and he decided to cross the field by dodging from one sheaf to another. He had not progressed very far when he saw a beam of light sweep across the ground and settle on him. His heart stood still. The beam of light was not coming from the main road but from an unexpected road on his left, running parallel to the main road. When his eyes had grown accustomed to the glare, he could make out the form of the man behind the beam. It was a soldier. The fact that he was so near his goal gave him fresh courage. He leapt forward to the next sheaf. The beam of light followed him. With his heart knocking wildly against his ribs he asked himself why the alarm had not been given, and why he was not being fired at. . . . He made another leap forward. . . . No, he had not been spotted. It was just an illusion. The beam of light left him and began sweeping the sheaves. Slowly the soldier moved away. . . .

Claye continued his advance among the wheat-sheaves. In spite of his exhaustion he had never felt more tensely on the alert.

Walking doubled up, or crawling on all fours, he at last reached a little wood surrounded by a hedge. Gingerly, he made a gap in the hedge and began to push his way through. Suddenly, just in front of him, there was a man squatting beside the hedge, probably a sentry. Whether he was there by chance or was waiting for him, Claye does not know to this day. At the time he acted instantaneously.

"The fellow was more surprised than I was," says Claye. "I seized him by the arms and gave him a kick. He fell over backwards. Without pausing I hit him in the face. Then as he was moaning, I gave him several kicks in the jaw, and in the ribs. I don't know whether I killed him or not, but at all events, he can't have many teeth left. If I had known for certain that he was a Hun, I should have knifed him."

When this job was finished Claye set out once more across country. He went through several more fields, fell into some water when he least expected to, and pushed on until the water was up to his neck. He came out on the bank on the other side of what must have been a river. Wet as he was, he continued to walk at a good speed for some time. Suddenly he was surprised to see, right before him, a soldier who was not a German. He was a Russian, wearing a peaked cap and the red star. Claye could hardly believe his eyes. When he got to the village, he saw a poster bearing the words 'Kaunas Printers'. It was only then that he knew for certain he was in Lithuania.

Claye was wet through and ravenously hungry. Now that the tension was over he felt exhausted and stupefied. A man was coming towards him. "Good morning, sir," said Claye in French. The man looked at him with amazement. "Embassy! Consulate!" implored Claye. The man understood, pulled out a piece of paper and wrote '125 miles'. That was too far. "Police!" demanded Claye—Claye, the escaped prisoner and the Free Frenchman! The time was exactly 4.40 a.m. and the date 30 August, 1940.

XVII

ESCAPE FROM THE JAPANESE

from

You'll Die in Singapore

By CHARLES MCCORMAC

Charles McCormac, D.C.M., was serving with the R.A.F. at Singapore when the Japanese swept through Malaya in January, 1942. He managed to get his wife evacuated on one of the last ships to leave the port and remained behind to join the island's military defenders. But he was caught by a Jap patrol, thrown into a prison camp at Pasir Panjang, tortured, and forced to labour with other prisoners at clearing bomb rubble at the docks. Taunted by their bestial guards that they would 'die in Singapore,' he and sixteen others made a mass break-out from the camp.

Thirteen of the escapers were killed, but McCormac and three companions managed to reach Sumatra, the first step on their contemplated journey of 2,000 miles to Australia and freedom. It was the start of a hazardous and gruelling five-months' trek through the jungles of Sumatra and Java, at the end of which only McCormac and Don were left. Eventually, little more than walking skeletons, the two were picked up by a flying-boat and taken to Darwin.

You'll Die in Singapore, the story of this amazing journey, is a monument to their courage and endurance.

BACK in camp that evening, Don and I put our heads together. We thrashed out every possible way of escape. For one or two men several alternatives presented themselves; but we, to avoid reprisals, must get the whole working-party away. It seemed a pretty hopeless task. But now we knew that we could not expect to be treated as ordinary prisoners, any desperate chance seemed to me worth seizing. And that evening we had further evidence of the urgency of our position. The guards were in good form. Amid roars of laughter they explained to us in detail and with no fine point omitted, that they had

been to watch a mass execution—the beheading of twelve
Chinese and Malays suspected (only suspected) of being anti-
Japanese. Doubling up with laughter and slapping each other
hilariously on the back, they gestured and gyrated their hands
in a downward spiral pantomiming the victims' heads as they
rolled away from the executioners' swords. Those heads might
soon be ours.

Our nerves had by now become taut and strained. In my
own case, despair for the future alternated with the deepen-
ing conviction that Pat was dead. For us in Pasir Panjang the
accepted standards of civilized life were remembered only
distantly, as though belonging to another world. The old
familiar routine of daily living had vanished; it had been
replaced by a more primitive pattern of life—the animal
instinct to survive. This new existence did not seem to us a
dream. All that was past was the dream—sleeping in bed,
shaving, baths, good food eaten with cutlery, newspapers,
pyjamas, clean underclothes, beer, having a wife, the promise
of becoming a father—all these were memories from a half-
forgotten world; misty images from a fantasy long ago experienced. Now there was only one reality—survival; a survival
that entailed sweat, hunger, filth and Japanese barbarity. We
were animals. Given the chance of freedom, we would fight
savagely and we would die fighting; with no chance of
freedom we would die miserably. Logic was reduced to very
simple terms. Don and I recognized that logic. It was—escape
or die.

"Let's sound our party again about escaping," I said.
"Now Rodriguez will help they may come in with us."

We went round the next day tackling each man individ-
ually, trying to convince him of the futility of simply waiting
to be killed. The result was better; much better; but there
were still six men who wouldn't at any price join in.

The solution came to me suddenly.

"Listen, Don. There's no roll-call in the camp. To the Japs
our working-party consists simply of seventeen Europeans and
three Asiatics. The Japs aren't interested in names. All they
worry about is numbers. Six of our men won't join in; all we
need do is go round the rest of the prisoners tonight, find six
chaps willing to come in with us and swap them for the six
who won't."

Don smiled slowly and then smacked his fist with the other palm.

"You've got it, Mac," he said.

It was as simple as that. By the cold light of the arc-lights, we crawled from one party of men to another and quickly found six who were keen to make the attempt. The actual method of the escape was left to Don and me to work out, though it was agreed that we would all stick together and, once we had got away from the camp, make for Rodriguez's boat and thence over to the mainland to join the guerrillas. None of the Asiatics could be trusted to join in so the escape was planned for the seventeen Europeans only.

The first step was to keep Rodriguez informed of our intentions. He was on duty the next day at the docks and I told him that the whole working-party, including the six new men (whom he hadn't noticed until I pointed them out) had decided to attempt an escape. We knew what our fate would be if we were recaptured, but we were, I told him, determined to go through with it.

He did not look too happy.

"How do you propose to escape?" he asked, rather fearfully.

"That will come later. But we'll definitely need your boat. You won't let us down, will you?"

His mouth took a firmer line.

"No."

"Okay then. I'll tell you when we're set."

He fidgeted uncomfortably.

"You can't do it during the day, while I am in charge of the party. I have a wife and six children to think of. You'll have to do it at night. Then suspicion won't fall on me."

"That's fair enough."

"Which night will it be?"

"Don't know yet. Probably tomorrow."

"All right. If you get away tomorrow night, come to my house at Paya Lebar and I'll take you to the boat. Do you know Paya Lebar?"

I said I did. It was a tiny village a couple of miles from Seletar airfield on the Serangoon Road, and about twelve miles from the compound at Pasir Panjang.

"How will I recognize your house?"

He gave me full details of how to find it.

That evening at Pasir Panjang Don and I studied the gate into the camp. It was only a flimsy affair—a nine-foot bamboo bar entwined with barbed wire which was lifted up by the sentries whenever we entered or marched out. A few yards outside the compound, to the left of the gate, was an atap hut used as the guard-house. To the right of the entrance was another atap hut, used, we suspected, as a power-house or control hut; here, obviously, was the main switchgear for the arc-lamps. Round the camp, which was of course patrolled by sentries, was the electric wiring that fed the arc-lamps and was connected at intervals by junction-boxes. Between us and that heavy flex lay the coils of barbed wire.

I stared at the electric flex and the junction-boxes, and a very simple plan began to take shape in my mind.

I have abnormally long arms. If only I could stretch through the barbed wire, I might be able to pull the leads out of a junction-box and so disconnect the circuit. The compound would be plunged into darkness; in the confusion the seventeen of us could charge the gate, and if we got through make a dash for it.

I explained my idea to Don. It was the sort of simple, uncomplicated scheme that at once appealed to him.

"That's it, Mac. You've got it. If only you can reach through to a junction-box."

"Let's try," I said.

We waited until the guards were out of sight then crawled slowly towards the wire. Face downward, I pressed my arm carefully through the coils, twisting and turning it to avoid the barbs. My hand was still eighteen inches from the box. I couldn't do it.

Don was crouching beside me.

"There's only one thing for it, Mac," he whispered. "Ease your head through one of the coils. I'll push the wire up, then maybe you can make it."

"Don't touch it now," I muttered. "The noise of the wire grating will bring back the guards." I quickly gauged the distance, and reckoned that with my head through the first roll of coils I would just be able to grasp the box. We slid away on our bellies.

That night the plan was passed on, in whispers, from one

to another of the seventeen. We were each of us to find any weapon we could lay our hands on—a stick would be better than nothing. The attempt would be made the next day at dusk, just after the arc-lights were switched on. We would rush the gate, force up the bar and then scatter singly for the jungle, and reassemble later at Rodriguez's house. If any one of us was wounded or left behind, there was to be no returning for him, no waiting, no help. He would be left. It was a grim prospect, and that night few of us slept.

One possibility especially terrified me. What if the officer decided to interrogate me again the next day? The prospect haunted me as I lay staring at the night sky. I thought about the wiring system too, and decided to alter the plan slightly. For it occurred to me that if I disconnected the circuit just before the lights were switched on rather than just after, the sudden release of the power load when the Japs switched on would have no escape and might, if there were no adequate fuse precautions, blow the switch-box.

Next morning the parade took place as usual. We were counted and, by the grace of God, none of us was held back for interrogation. We marched, in the coolness of early morning, down to the docks. All of us were nervously excited. Two or three set up a tuneless whistling, partly, I suppose, to relieve their tension and partly out of pure bravado.

"Shut up, you idiots," hissed Don.

The guards looked round threateningly and, with shame-faced grins, the warblers stopped their whistling.

Down at the docks, through the long, hot morning and longer and hotter afternoon, we sweated at clearing rubble. Sweated from the sun's heat, but sweated even more from nervousness at the thought of what the evening would bring. Thank God that once we were back in camp we would not have long to wait.

We told Rodriguez.

"I'll be expecting you tonight then," he quavered. And the trepidation in his voice made us more nervous still.

Every ordeal must, I suppose, end some time, and when at long last we were paraded again for the march back to Pasir Panjang each of us had managed to find and conceal some sort of weapon. I had a thick club-shaped piece of iron-wood. Don had a lump of lead and three to four feet of thin rope, which he knotted to the heavy metal, making a primitive bolo. It was a fearsome arsenal hidden that evening under our shirts and shorts, but the guards spotted nothing.

Back in camp we wasted no time; each man had his own part to play and knew exactly what to do. Alone or in couples, the seventeen of us, laughing and chattering, infiltrated towards the gate. This manoeuvring went on for over half an hour, by which time Don and I and two others had edged towards the barbed wire to where the nearest junction-box was positioned. My heart was pounding deep inside me like the beat of a ship's engine. I wiped the sweat off my forehead.

It was getting dark now. In only a few minutes the Japanese sentry would be crossing over from the guard-house to the atap hut where the switchgear and generator were.

I looked carefully around me, and saw some of our party eyeing me expectantly. Two guards passed on their routine patrol round the perimeter. It would be six and a half minutes before they completed the circuit. I took a deep breath.

"Okay, Don," I muttered. "This is it."

Taking my time, I flattened out on the earth, then, lying at full stretch, started to slither carefully towards the coils of wire. Don was watching the disappearing guards; at strategic points four other look-outs were posted. They had their backs to us and were apparently disinterested; but each at the right moment gave a prearranged signal, and Don leant towards the wire.

"Coast is clear, Mac," he muttered.

He pressed backwards on to the first coil, and I heard his hissing intake of breath as he heaved against the taut wire. I slipped my left arm over a spiral of barbs, and eased my head through the first coil. My fingers, stretched out, were still a foot from the junction-box. The barbs were digging into my left shoulder and blood trickled down my face as the sharp barbs tore through hair and skin.

"Not quite," I panted. "Press back as hard as you can."

Don grunted and I felt the wire tightening under the weight of his body. I squirmed forward with the wire, inch by inch, until I could stretch no farther. My face was almost at right-angles to my shoulders, twisted away from the lacerating spikes.

"Another two inches." The sweat was running down under my armpits. It tickled.

"Don, I can't see what I'm doing."

"Move your fingers left," he grunted.

I did—and touched the electric cables.

"Buck up, Mac, for Christ's sake!" panted Don. "The guards are coming back. They're only fifty yards off."

I gritted my teeth and jerked the cable sideways. The barbs bit deep into my shoulder and neck; but the strands, thank God, were loose in my hands.

"Okay, Don."

I slithered back towards him, wincing as, for the last time, the barbs tore into my flesh. Some two or three yards inside the wire we half rose and squatted on our haunches. The sentries ambled by, glanced at us curiously but seemed to notice nothing amiss and carried on round the perimeter.

The others were in scattered groups now on either side of the gate, silent, watching and waiting. Waiting for the Jap soldier to appear from the guard-hut and cross to the power-house.

It can only have been a couple of minutes before we saw him strutting cockily across, but to each of us the minutes seemed like hours. We tried not to look at him, but I for one, each time I tried to look away, felt my eyes slide back to the short, bespectacled little man who would, in a matter of seconds, open for us the road to freedom.

He stared at us and seemed to sense that something odd was happening; then shrugging his shoulders he disappeared into the power-house. Almost as one man, in the gathering darkness, we started to edge towards the gate. We were none of us prepared for what happened next. We heard a generator start up, then a sudden, blinding flash lit up the huts, silhouetting its broken supports, its windows and its disintegrating walls. The sharp crack of an explosion echoed across the compound. The roof caved in and burst into flames.

For perhaps a couple of seconds we stood rooted to the spot, staring in disbelief. One man swore softly, another let out a ghastly cackle of laughter.

"Now!" shouted Don, and we tore towards the gate. Men shrieked in pain as the vicious coils of wire lacerated their hands, but we lifted the bamboo bar from out of its socket and flung the gate up and over. At the same moment a handful of Japanese rushed out of the guard-hut. For a second they wavered, then came the staccato crackle of tommy-guns, ending abruptly as we threw ourselves on them. I was lucky. I got Pigface. I saw him tearing towards me, his teeth bared, his bayonet swinging back; with all my strength I smashed the lump of wood down and on to his face. As he dropped, I lashed at him again. I heard the bone splintering and his skull felt oddly soft. I dropped my club, grabbed his bayonet and sprinted for the rubber trees. Behind me, the outline of struggling men stood out sharply against the glare of the burning hut. No going back, we had said. I tore on. I passed Donaldson; he was struggling and jerking at what looked like a dead body.

"Come on, Don!" I yelled at him. Behind us machine-guns were chattering angrily. I dared not stop. I was running now through tangled undergrowth, dodging quickly from one tree to another. Then I was in the open, and felt the sharp blades of lalang grass whipping against my legs. On and on I rushed, my lungs heaving like bellows, until at last I could run no farther. I slowed down to a walk. But already someone was catching up with me. I could hear him crashing his way through the rubber plantation. I stopped in a little hollow, and crouched there, waiting. It was Don. He almost tumbled headlong over me, but at the last moment spotted me in the flickering light from the guard-hut, now some quarter of a mile behind us.

"All right, Mac?" he panted.

"Uh, uh." I squatted there gasping for breath. "My wind's gone."

"Don't wait, for Christ's sake."

We went on, zigzagging whenever we were able, sometimes running, sometimes trotting, sometimes stumbling. Behind us the sounds of fighting grew fainter and finally died away. Both of us were breathing heavily and raspingly. But we were exultant.

"Why on earth were you hanging about outside the gate?" I panted, as we slowed down to a walk.

"Fatarse had my bolo."

"Good Lord, man! Why ever did you stop for that?"

"I dunno. The ball had stuck in his head and wouldn't come out. I left it in the end and took his bayonet."

"Much the same as me," I grunted. "I got Pigface. And I took his bayonet, too."

Don laughed. "Well, that's two of them at any rate. And two of the nastiest at that. Mac, boy, we're out! Do you realize it? We're out! We're free men!"

"I wouldn't crow yet. We're not out of the wood by a long chalk."

"Worst part's over though."

"I wonder."

There was a sudden rustling among the rubber trees to our left which started us running again. We were soon out of the small plantation and came to a wide stretch of secondary jungle, where the tall lalang grass reached up to our waists and sometimes to our chests. We had, so far, been moving due north; but I reckoned that to reach Rodriguez's house we needed to head somewhere between north and north-north-east.

"We'd better turn off to the right," I told Don. "Somewhere here we ought to hit the Bukit Timor Road."

"You're the navigator, Mac. But I tell you, man, if your plotting's wrong, I'll send in a formal complaint to the Air Ministry when this lot's blown over."

Partly by luck and partly by judgement, my navigation was dead accurate. We skirted through the outlying districts of Singapore where, if we were stopped by a Jap patrol, we hoped to pass as Eurasians (the north-eastern suburbs were full of Eurasians); then we came to a road—the Bukit Timor Road—and followed it for nearly a couple of miles. Once we tumbled hurriedly into the long grass as a party of Japanese soldiers went clumping by. We thought of keeping to the lalang grass; certainly it was tall enough to hide us, but as we brushed our way through it, it rattled and the noise seemed to us loud enough to wake the dead; so we went back to the road again. It was quite dark now. There was no sign of any of the others.

After about an hour we left the Bukit Timor Road, and struck into a wide belt of rubber trees which I knew stretched and sprawled for several miles almost up to the village of Paya Lebar.

It was dark and cool among the trees, but sweat was rolling off us as we moved warily through the endless succession of symmetrically planted estates, crouching low, gripping our bayonets, turning sharply at every suspicious sound, often diving for cover and lying motionless until we were satisfied there was no cause for alarm. The sky was cloudless and the bright twinkling stars acted as guides in our diagonal north-easterly trek. Behind us, towards the town of Singapore, hung belts of low mist lying in thin layers above swamp and jungle. Our impulse was to continue running and to reach Paya Lebar in the shortest possible time; but reason prompted caution; and the journey of only about eight miles took us more than six hours.

"Wonder where the others are," I whispered to Don as we scrambled along a rough track leading through thick luxuriant foliage.

"Can't make it out," he whispered back. "We were almost last out through the gate; the others should be way ahead of us. Did you get hurt on that barbed wire?" he added.

"No—just a scratch or two. My shirt and shorts are ripped to pieces though. How about you?"

"Oh, I'm okay. My shirt's okay as well."

"Mustn't dirty your pretty silk shirt!" I gibed. Don was proud of his shirt.

It was close on midnight when I recognized the approach to Paya Lebar along the Yio Chu Kang Road. Once there had been a Naval W.T. Station here, not far from the southern perimeter of Seletar airfield. We moved cautiously through a maze of small intersecting tracks. Then out of the darkness loomed the great tree Rodriguez had said was less than fifty yards from his house; the moment we spotted it our feeling of tension increased. Squatting beside the track we discussed our next move.

"Now what?" asked Don. "Do we knock Rodriguez up or wait a bit for the others?"

"Better wait a bit," I advised. "I don't know about you, but I could do with a rest."

"Agreed," said Don. "We don't know what we may be in for."

So we lay side by side, stretched on the grass by the huge bole of the tree, both of us were trembling and perspiring.

After about twenty minutes, we heard a rustling in the trees behind us; we lay quite still, watching and listening. The noises grew more distinct—the snapping of twigs, the soft pad of running feet, then from beneath the heavy leaves emerged two crouched, bedraggled figures. Another pair had reached the rendezvous.

"Okay, boys," I whispered, "take it easy." They dropped thankfully beside us.

By the bole of the tree we waited for nearly an hour. After ten minutes three more arrived; then a chap on his own; then another couple, and another, until at last there were twelve of us.

"Still five short," observed a tall young Scot.

We held a council of war. I ought perhaps to explain that, as we were a mixed party, composed of men and N.C.Os. from all three services and also civilians, it was difficult for any one of us to assume the rôle of leader. Donaldson and I had initiated the escape and, in the short time we were together, the others probably looked to us to take important decisions. We, for our part, thought it best only to outline a general plan of campaign and leave the others to follow on or not as they thought fit.

"I reckon we've waited long enough," I said.

"Sure," agreed Don. "We'll stay under cover; you call on friend Rodriguez."

The others scattered into the bush as I slowly made my way, crouching low, towards Rodriguez's house. There was a door almost fronting on to the track, and a pale light streamed from the single open window. I knocked softly. There was no reply. I knocked again. There was a shuffling on the other side of the door, which opened a few inches. Rodriguez, his face round and shiny, his eyebrows raised, and his forehead wrinkled, peered through apprehensively.

"It's me, McCormac."

"Come in." He opened the door just wide enough to let me through, then closed it quickly.

"How many got away?"

"Seventeen broke camp, but only twelve are here so far."

He shook his head; his eyes darted furtively around the untidy room. He looked scared out of his wits. His fear was infectious.

M

"Are there Japs about?"

"I don't think so. It's quiet enough." He looked at me unhappily. "Twelve's a lot for the boats."

"We can cross in relays. Where exactly are they?"

"Kranji Point, three hundred yards west of the Causeway."

"Good God, man, that's miles away!"

Rodriguez nodded. I saw the perspiration soaking through his singlet and his crumpled, threadbare slacks. He shifted uneasily.

"Yes, I know. That's the trouble."

There was a pause—an uncomfortable pause. He seemed to make up his mind quite suddenly.

"I can't go with you. I can't risk my family. You'll have to fend for yourselves."

I couldn't find it in me to quarrel with his decision. I knew as well as he did the sort of reprisals his family might expect.

"Can we use your boats?"

"Sure you can—don't worry about that. Do you know how to get there?"

I nodded, but as an afterthought asked him for details about the last few hundred yards. Then I smiled and patted his wet, podgy shoulder. "We'll be okay and thanks for all you've done." I turned towards the door, but he stopped me and pushed into my hand a wad of paper money—a thickish roll of Japanese dollars.

"Good luck," he whispered.

The door closed softly behind me.

I walked back to the tree, and the others, materializing out of the undergrowth, crowded eagerly around me. I found that another three escapers had arrived safely. We were still two short.

"Better wait for them, Don," I said. "We can't leave 'em on their own."

"Okay."

"Anyone know what might have happened to them?" I asked.

A short, thick-set civilian muttered that he thought a couple of chaps had fallen to the Japanese tommy-guns.

"How many Japs did we get?" Don asked him.

"Dunno. There were six or seven sprawled face down

beside the guard-house. It was all over too quickly to see much."

We waited about half an hour but the last two never came. "They've had it," muttered Don. "Let's go."

We decided to make our way to the Causeway in groups of twos and threes, with about twenty yards between each group. Don and I were to lead the way, for I was in familiar territory and knew the roads and the best points at which to cross them. We were to regroup on the far side of the Naval Base Road, which led to the Causeway. The latter was the danger spot and was certain to be well patrolled and guarded.

We set off, Don and I in front, the next group some twenty-five yards behind, from which distance they could just see our shadowy figures moving cautiously from tree to tree. At first we kept to the welcome gloom of the rubber trees on the south side of the Yio Chu Kang Road. We passed the W.T. station, then a small burned-out village. There was no sign of life among the charred ruins. Then we came to a woodland area again, close to where I had joined the road-blocking party before Singapore had fallen: how many weeks ago. . . .

At last we reached the Naval Base Road, and saw at the bottom of it the twinkling lights of the Causeway over the Johore Straits. On the other side were the mainland, the hills, the jungle, the guerrillas. Our chance of freedom. Near the Causeway Don and I stopped among the twisted trunks and roots of the mangroves, waiting for the rest of the party to catch up. It was agreed that if we got across the Straits we would again split into pairs and make our way independently towards the Kuala Lipis hills.

Once assembled we made a compact group and, bent low from the hips, we edged slowly forward across the mud-flats towards the water, which we could hear lapping against the shore. The mud-flats were slippery and quite devoid of cover. But there, thank God, drawn a little above the water's edge, were the two boats.

"Good old Rodriguez!" muttered a Welshman close behind me. "So he played ball after all!"

"Shut up, you fool!" snapped Don.

Instantly all of us stiffened and froze motionless. Only ten yards away, dead in front of us, a number of dark figures were walking purposefully towards the boats. A Japanese patrol. Had we stood still and remained quiet, we might perhaps have got away with it. But from the rear of our party came a frightened yell.

"Japs!"

There were startled orders from the shadowy figures ahead, then the biting orange flashes of point-blank rifle-fire. We had only one chance. Springing forward as one man, we rushed the patrol. Clubs and bayonets wielded by desperate men are terrible weapons. In a second we were among them, and a slithering mass of bodies fought savagely beside the quietly lapping water. I saw the white gleam of a Jap's teeth and, like a maniac, slashed my bayonet at his face. Together we dropped on to the mud and I felt him squirming beneath me, his nails tearing into my thighs. I changed my grip on the bayonet and using it like a dagger, stabbed it again and again into the writhing body clawing round my legs.

As suddenly as it had started, the fight was over.

Together with seven others I scrambled over the fallen bodies and rushed towards the nearest boat. A couple of Japanese fled in silent terror into the fringe of the mangroves. And seven of our party lay dead or dying on the wet, shining mud.

"Come on," someone muttered. "In a minute the swines will be swarming out."

There was just room for the eight of us in one boat, and this we together pushed and shoved down towards the water. It slid smoothly over the slime and mud and, once it was afloat, we tumbled in. The Welshman found a paddle lying in the bottom and with it he pushed off from the shore. He heaved hard, and the rest of us dragged our hands deeply through the water. Slowly—painfully slowly—we moved into the Strait.

"How many dead?" muttered Don.

"Seven, I think."

"Only half of us left." The speaker was another Welshman: a small, dark-haired man half hanging over the gunwale. He was beating frantically at the water, using his hand as a paddle.

I looked round for oars or sail, but apart from the solitary paddle and a short stump of mast the bottom of the boat was almost empty. We tried paddling with our hands, using the paddle as a rudder, but seemed to make very little progress. In spite of our efforts we drifted eastward, parallel to the shore and towards the Causeway. Obviously we were caught in the five-knot current that comes sweeping in from the open sea towards the Causeway, only to turn northward at the last moment and again flow out to sea. As hard as we paddled to the northward we were carried towards the east, towards the Causeway, and the lights and the Japanese.

"Thank heaven it's dark," growled Don.

But it was not dark for long. Suddenly from the Causeway a searchlight flashed out brilliantly. For a few seconds it flicked on and off, then it steadied into a full broad beam, moving slowly in a golden pathway across the water. There was no escaping it. It was swinging in our direction.

"Down!" I hissed sharply.

Huddled on the floorboards below the level of the gunwale, we lay perfectly still. Suddenly the boat floated into light; light was all round us; and then it was dark again as the beam passed on.

"Don't move," muttered Don. "It'll be back."

It was. Again the pale golden light flooded over the boat; this time the beam steadied and remained trained on us. Every minute we expected to hear the rattle of machine-gun fire or the engine of an approaching launch. But after what seemed like hours, the light moved on and the boat was dark again.

Don peered over the gunwale. "Keep down, chaps," he ordered sharply.

There we lay, motionless and terrified, each of us feeling the adjacent bodies panting in and out, in and out.

"It's coming back again," he grunted. "Keep right down."

The searchlight played around us, like a cat uncertain whether the mouse is dead; then suddenly it cut off. As, with grunts and groans, we pulled ourselves up from our cramped positions, I saw that the scattered lights on the Causeway were much farther away. We must have moved round with the current, have drifted up to and parallel to the Causeway, and were now drifting away from it, westwards, out to sea.

"Not much point in trying to paddle," I said. "There's a

five-knot tide here and it's taking us just about in the right direction."

"Thank God for that!" Don began to button up his shirt, for the night wind, striking off the water, was keen and chill.

It was reassuring to see the lights of the Causeway fading farther and farther into the distance, away into the milky haze of the horizon. All the same we were heading out to sea, out into the broad Strait of Malacca. I hoped that the tide would sweep us up the Malay Peninsula, and that, once we had drifted a fair way from Singapore, we would be able to paddle ourselves ashore into the mangrove swamps along the west coast of Malaya.

XVIII.

ATTEMPTED RESCUE FROM MOUNTJOY

from

The Big Fellow

By Frank O'Connor

Many daring escapes have been made with outside help, and this poses the question: When is the result an escape and when is it a rescue?

During the troubles in Ireland, Michael Collins—the Big Fellow—one of the leaders of the Irish Republican Army, rescued Eamon de Valera from Lincoln prison by means of a carefully arranged plan. With an altar candle de Valera managed to make an impression of the chaplain's key to the side gate of the prison. A drawing of this was sent out, and Collins had a key made and smuggled in. It was a failure, but after several attempts a key of the proper size was obtained by de Valera, and on the night of 3 February, 1919, he unlocked the side gate and walked out to where Collins and others were waiting with a car to take him to freedom.

Collins's scheme to rescue his trusty lieutenant, Commandant Sean MacKeon from Mountjoy Prison, Dublin, in 1921, was on equally bold lines. MacKeon, who had been arrested in Longford, was shot while trying to escape and was taken first to a military hospital. Although Collins's own life was in constant danger, he began at once to plan a possible rescue. The attempt was a failure, as will be seen from the following pages, but it deserves attention not only as one of the incidents in the Big Fellow's wild and exciting life—a life which ended in violence—but for its place in the annals of escapology.

In April he had another close shave, one of dozens. His Intelligence Office at Mespil Road was raided. At a desk by the window the raiders found a brace of loaded revolvers. Fortunately for Collins they did not find the intelligence files, though they almost tore the house to pieces; they were hidden under the window in one of the secret cupboards built for him by Batt O'Connor; if they had, Collins or no Collins, they could have paralysed the movement within a week or two, for the files would have revealed the exact extent of his information as well as its sources.

But at least they hoped to get their man, and occupied the house, clearing away all sign of their presence. At nine sharp Collins would ride up on his bicycle, push it round to the side and stride in the back door in his usual fearless way—walking into their arms. Miss Hoey, who, with her invalid mother occupied the upstairs portion of the house, was arrested and taken to Dublin Castle. She, too, knew what was about to happen. She bluffed for all she was worth; the stakes were high. She was a journalist, and the Press of the world would hear of their treatment of a woman. Late into the night she continued her fight for Collins's life. At last they gave in, and she was brought back to the house under escort.

The position seemed as hopeless as ever, but she persuaded her mother to sham collapse. There was a long struggle with the officer before he would consent to have a doctor called, but again she bluffed her way through, and went off to find a woman doctor—escorted once more by policemen. The doctor, puzzled by Miss Hoey's statement that she had seen the old lady before, but vaguely suspecting that there was some urgent need of her, agreed to come. It was a strange party in a city of the dead, two women, one trying to tell the other of the trap, the other trying to understand and failing, while beside them walked two nervous Black and Tans who jumped at every sound.

When they reached the house Miss Hoey refused to allow her mother to be examined while the room was occupied by Black and Tans. Again there was a long argument; again she had her way. They withdrew on to the landing, and under a barrage of rattling bottles she revealed the extent of Collins's danger.

Even when the doctor had got free with the story and Collins's friends were informed, it was still questionable if he would escape the trap, as no one knew where he was staying. Scouts were finally posted at every road leading to the office, and Collins himself, Cullen, and Miss Lyons were all stopped in time. Once again he had escaped by the skin of his teeth.

MacKeon was now nearly well again, and Collins was busily planning to rescue him. It seemed an impossible task.

While he was still lying wounded in the military hospital he was visited by a priest who promptly proceeded to reproach him for his activity as an officer of the Volunteers. MacKeon, who felt he had enough to bear, considered this a bit thick. Suddenly he heard the priest's tirade interrupted by a whisper, "I'm from the Big Fellow." He cocked his ear. The room was cleared of guards. Then the priest hastily unfolded the plan. Like most of Collins's plans it was extraordinarily daring. Next evening the guard would be changed in the ordinary way, but a half-hour sooner. The guard would be Volunteers dressed in British uniform. For one reason or another the carrying out of it was postponed for a few evenings. On the evening when it was finally due to take place MacKeon was transferred to Mountjoy; an hour and a half too soon.

He was scarcely in Mountjoy before Collins was in touch again, this time with the aid of a lady doctor. She smuggled in a plan of the prison, on which two spots had been marked with red ink. No more. Later there came a hacksaw, a bottle of three-in-one oil, a cake of soap, some clothes, and a watch. The plan was that at five minutes to seven on the following evening MacKeon would get through the cell window while the sentry was detained in conversation at the other side of the gaol by a friendly warder, strike down the path towards a wicket gate and inform the sentry that he was Warder —— going for a drink. Finally he would come to another gate, and on this, at the very stroke of seven, he was to knock. It would be opened for him by men of the Squad, who would bring a bicycle on which he would ride to Batt O'Connor's house in Donnybrook.

All night MacKeon worked, his task interrupted every three minutes by the stride of the sentry on the pathway outside his window. In the early morning the bars were completely severed and the trace of the hacksaw filled with soap. But the night's labour had left him utterly exhausted. The prison doctor who visited him at noon was confounded. He turned upon the hospital orderly and abused him for having left the patient so long in a small, damp, ground-floor cell instead of having him shifted upstairs. The orderly promised

to see that the change was made without delay. MacKeon
begged to be allowed to remain for just one more day, giving
as his excuse that his mother was coming to see him and
would not be able to mount the stairs. But the doctor was
adamant; his duty was to see that MacKeon got well, and
the shadow of the gallows drew a little nearer.

Another man would have lost heart at two such unlucky
shots. Not Collins though. He went to see Mrs. MacKeon to
comfort her. "Next time I come," he promised, "I'll bring
him with me. And it won't be long either." He had got fresh
inspiration from the report of the abattoir superintendent
that an armoured car visited the abattoir each morning at an
early hour, and that it might be possible to capture it. Dalton,
whom he sent to spy out the ground, reported in similar
terms. Collins had a revolver smuggled in to MacKeon in the
prison hospital, warned him to try and reach the Governor's
office on the stroke of ten, and everything was ready for the
great attempt.

Each morning the Squad waited in a position from which
they could see a signal from Dalton, who occupied an upstairs
room in a house overlooking the spot where the car halted.
The essential thing was to get the whole crew outside, and
that was a question of time. Each morning Collins visited the
store from which the Squad departed, to see that everything
was correct, even to the dungarees of the men who were to
drive. When his hostess, an old lady, remonstrated with him
for his foolhardiness, he nodded to O'Reilly who was just
cycling off to early Mass from the house next door. "I'm in no
danger while I have that lad praying for me," he said, and
it was the new and humble Collins who was speaking.

For days Dalton watched; then one morning he saw the
whole crew emerge to smoke a cigarette in the morning sunshine. He raised the blind, and in a few moments the
armoured car and its crew was surrounded. So far so good.
The men who were to take the car pulled down the legs of
dungarees, which were hidden under their coats. A short
distance away they stopped to pick up two men in the
uniform of British officers, Emmet Dalton and Leonard.
They had duplicate keys for the prison, with which Collins,
with his amazing thoroughness, had supplied them.

At the prison gate Dalton produced Collins's demand for

the body of MacKeon. It was in an official Government
envelope. The prison gates opened and the car swept in.
There were two inner gates, and under pretence of turning,
the driver, MacCrea, manœuvred the car between them, so
that neither could be closed. Emmet Dalton and Leonard
strode into the Governor's quarters as though they owned
the prison.

The next step in the plan was that some woman with
parcels for prisoners should engage the warder at the main
gate in an argument so as to keep it open. If that failed there
were two men near with revolvers. It did fail. The warder was
in surly mood; he proceeded to shut the gate in the women's
faces, whereupon the two men drew revolvers and covered
him.

The sentry in the courtyard, where the car had stopped,
saw the drawn revolvers and fired at the two men, wounding
one. Then one of the car's crew gave him the surprise of
his life by shooting him dead. But the alarm had been given
and the machine gun on the roof began to spatter bullets
all round. MacCrea shot the car forward and jammed the
main gate.

Meanwhile the plan had failed in its most important
particular. For several mornings in succession MacKeon had
contrived with one excuse or another to be in the Governor's
office on the stroke of ten. This morning the guard was being
changed, and he was told he must wait until the change was
complete before being escorted to the office. Accordingly
Dalton and Leonard, faced by a suspicious Governor, who
wished to phone to Dublin Castle for confirmation of the
written authority they bore, tied him up in his own office. As
they rushed out to try their luck on the Chief Warder, firing
began outside, and realizing the game was up they bolted for
the car and made their escape under a hail of bullets. They
had nothing to show for their pains but a couple of machine
guns and some revolvers—these and the moral effect of their
escapade, which was considerable. But they did not atone to
Collins for the loss of MacKeon, and he took the failure
badly.

XIX.

ESCAPE FROM HOSPITAL

from

Return Ticket

By ANTHONY DEANE-DRUMMOND

*Anthony Deane-Drummond, an officer in a parachute
unit, was parachuted into Italy in February, 1941, to blow up
an aqueduct. The mission was a success, but the party was
captured and imprisoned in a P.O.W. camp at Sulmona. In
December Dean-Drummond escaped and managed to reach
Como, with a view to getting over the Swiss frontier and freedom, when he was arrested. He was put in solitary confinement in an old castle at Montalbo, and then taken to Campo
27, for dangerous prisoners, between Florence and Pisa.
In May, 1942, he escaped again, while in the Florence
Military Hospital, and this time got safely into Switzerland,
the first stage on his journey home.
In September, 1943, he returned to Italy with the 1st Air-
borne Division. A year later he took part in the Arnhem
raid, was captured, and escaped once more—after hiding for
thirteen days and nights in a cramped cupboard.
Apart from the excitement of these adventures,* Return
Ticket, *is particularly effective because of the simple force
with which it is written.*

★

IT was about a month later, at the end of April, that we first
heard a rumour that headquarters in Rome had decided that
our camp was not good enough for desperate characters like
us, and were opening a really escape-proof prison somewhere
in the south of Italy. It turned out later on that this camp
was to be the notorious Number 5, which was located even
farther north than Campo 27.

Realizing that our next camp was going to be no sinecure,
I decided that I must make an attempt before the move. But
when we were warned on 7 May that we would leave on the
15th, no time remained to plan a new way out of our camp.
My only chance seemed to be to get to a hospital while still in

the north of Italy. I had been operated on for mastoids behind my left ear when I was a boy, and so it was not difficult to pretend extreme pain and deafness. The local doctor said I must see a specialist at once, so the next day I was taken to Florence Military Hospital.

The big snag of the hospital idea was the question of the clothes that I was going to wear when I got out. I would almost certainly be searched on entering the hospital, and any but the simplest of disguises would be impossible to take in with me. As a result of my experiences on the Italian railways six months before, I finally decided that clothes did not really matter as long as they were not obviously uniform. Eventually I took with me to hospital a navy blue roll neck pullover which my mother had just sent me, battledress trousers with the outside pockets removed, and brown shoes. As a hat I had one which had been issued to me by the Italians and was in the form of one of their own field service hats dyed a dark chocolate brown colour; the peak could be pulled down and the straps going over the top of the cap cut off, to make quite a presentable peasant's cap as worn all over northern Italy. My money and maps were in the usual place between my legs and stuck to me with sticking plaster.

The train journey to Florence and the cab ride out to the hospital were uneventful, but I tried to remember the way, especially the direction of the station. The hospital was a large building facing the main Florence-Bologna road, and stood about two miles from the centre of the town. I was hustled up to the top storey and was searched quite thoroughly by a carabinieri who signed for me from my escort. I was then shown into my room, which was not unlike that in many English hospitals and contained three beds.

I was in the hospital for nearly a month and I had quite an amusing time. The food was excellent compared with prison fare, and the Italian nurses were kindness itself. The specialist came on the second day and said he did not think there was much wrong with my ear, but he understood that life in a prison camp might not be very amusing and told me I could stay as long as I liked. Apparently quite a high proportion of the hospital patients had little the matter with them, but the doctors encouraged this attitude as it gave them less to do. My treatment consisted of two injections of insulin each day and a visit from the specialist once a week. I understand that insulin is only used for diabetes and not deaf ears!

Most of the nurses were volunteers for the duration of the war and came from well-to-do Florentine families. The one who had most to do with me was called Traxler Camerana, and she brought me flowers for the room and pre-war English books and magazines for me to read. Her mother was Swiss and her father Italian and I think she hated the war and the Fascists, but never in her talks to me was she disloyal to her country. She could speak French and German as easily as Italian, and usually we talked in a mixture of the first two languages so that the carabinieri outside my door would not know what was being discussed. Her husband was in the Navy and she had two pretty children whom she brought to the hospital to see me. My German improved considerably during the month and I could speak quite fluently, if a little ungrammatically, at the end. She told me of her home, her love for peace, and the English visitors to Florence before the war and a hundred and one anecdotes about life in wartime Florence, such as her difficulties with rationing and the black market, or a description of a cocktail party or a holiday by the sea. In fact she opened the window to the outside world a little and helped me to keep my sanity. She certainly reversed some of my opinions of the Italians as a race. "I am so sorry," she said, "that I cannot help you any more, for I have my children and my home to think of." I hope that she was not penalised when I eventually escaped. She certainly did not deserve to be.

The wing where I was had rooms all about the same size, two on each side of the corridor. In addition there was a sitting-room and a balcony where I was allowed to sit in the morning. This balcony looked on to the main road outside the hospital, and this bird's-eye view of life outside was a constant attraction to me. The room next door was occupied by a Blackshirt lieutenant who had been wounded in Russia, and whom I rarely saw. On the other side of the corridor one room was empty and the second occupied by two Jugoslav generals who had been captured when their country was overrun. One had had an operation on his eye and the other on his ear, and both were at least sixty years old. We used to meet on the balcony every morning and they were cheery souls who disliked the Italians intensely. We got on quite well speaking German, and their tales were the usual hard-luck stories which every prisoner of war has and which can always be produced on demand. While I was in hospital, one of them had a letter to say that his whole family, wife and three children had been shot by the Germans because there had been sabotage on the railway near the village where they lived. Poor old soul, he grew ten years older overnight; everything that he had been living for had suddenly been cut away from under his feet.

One day I saw a sight that I shall never forget, whilst sunning myself on the balcony. I remember reading a very similar description of the Italian army by Ernest Hemingway which referred to the 1914-18 war.

I could hear shouting and singing coming from some distance away, and it was not till a ragged band of men came marching along the main road towards Florence that I realized that this was an Italian battalion on its way to the city to take part in a local feast day celebration. There were no officers to be seen at the head of the column, which was led by senior N.C.O.s on bicycles. Some of the men carried their rifles one way and some another, their uniforms were shoddy and their equipment badly-fitting. A few even fell out to talk to a passer-by, and then doubled up to take their places in the column after they had finished their chats. Their singing was confined to individuals trying to be tenors and giving their own renderings, all different, of the better-known operatic arias. The rabble, because that is its best description, was divided into four lots, presumably companies, and behind each minced three or four lieutenants in tightly-fitting jack boots but no equipment except a Sam Browne belt to which a tiny pistol was attached in its holster. The boots must have been extremely painful from the expression on some of the officers' faces as they gingerly marched along the road. Their sleek, oiled and waved hair was draped over their ears and allowed to hang over their collars at the back of their necks, while their hats were worn at the jauntiest possible angle. The climax came when a four-wheeled horse cab brought up the tail of the column, in which a fat old major and his four captains sat playing cards till the time came for them to take their place at the head of their men and march triumphantly through the main streets of Florence. It gave the Jugoslavs and me the best laugh we had for years, much to the annoyance of my carabinieri guard. The whole scene was so pathetic in some ways, and yet so reminiscent of Mussolini as the sawdust Caesar. The Italian army had not improved much, even with the help of Fascist discipline and all the shouting.

When I was in my room a carabinieri guard was on watch outside my door continuously, being relieved every eight hours. The door was kept locked. Every time I wanted to go to the lavatory I had to bang on it, when it was unlocked, and the caribinieri would walk with me to the lavatory just down the passage. When I sat on the verandah he came too, and the prospects of getting away did not seem very bright. Luckily the prison camp had not warned the hospital that I had escaped before and was considered 'dangerous' or otherwise they would have taken rather more stringent precautions. Six months later in England I heard that the wretched commandant of the prison camp was sent to the Russian Front for not having warned the hospital! The dread the average Italian has for fighting for his country always amused me. He would be prepared to go to any lengths for a job at home, and being posted to an active front was always regarded as punishment. No wonder they were never much use as soldiers.

Outside my window was a seventy-foot drop to the courtyard below and no handy drain pipe to slide down. The old device of knotted sheets for a rope could not be used because of their rottenness and the fact that the number I would require was many more than I could raise. However there was a decorative moulding about four feet below my window, which ran all the way round the outside of the building. The top of the moulding was in the form of a slightly sloping ledge about five inches wide, and I thought it might be just wide enough to use.

Gradually my plan evolved. I would get out of my window and move along the ledge, past the Italian officer's bedroom window, round the corner of the building and then in at one of the lavatory windows. I could easily make sure it was open by going to the lavatory about midnight. I would then go through the lavatory door, which I would also leave open, and then down the stairs which were in a well of their own and separated by doors from all landings. The snag was that I could not very well open the door leading down the stairs when I went to the lavatory, but I hoped that over a course of days I would be lucky one night and find that it had been left open. The carabinieri always sat in his chair facing my door and he would be most unlikely to hear me flit in stockinged feet between the already-opened lavatory and the stairway doors. Having reached the ground floor I would jump out through a window into the courtyard, and circling round the building to the right I could quite easily get on to the main road leading down into Florence.

I had been in the hospital a fortnight when my plan had crystallized. About then a Flight-Sergeant Cox came into my room for three days with tonsilitis. He was working as a batman at the Generals' Prison Camp at Fiesole, just outside Florence, having been captured when Air Vice-Marshal Boyd was landed by mistake in Sicily instead of Malta. He gave me all their news. He told me how Air Marshal Boyd spent his whole time doing carpentry, how General Gambier-Parry was a very able sketcher and artist, and how General Young-husband was a most successful gardener within the limited area which was available. General Carton de Wiart was the only one he could not understand, but "he has only one arm, one eye, and a V.C., so that must explain a lot." I agreed.

At the time I thought it was just possible that he was a stooge and so I did not tell him of my intentions. It was a welcome respite, however, to be able to talk in English again.

As soon as Cox had gone back to Campo 12 at Fiesole, I started my midnight visits to the lavatory, but it wasn't until ten days later, on the evening of 13 June, 1942, that the door leading down the stairway was left open. 13 June was St. Anthony's Day, which I felt was a good omen for my adventure.

I decided to start about 3 a.m. and aimed at being on the main road by 4 a.m. This would give me two hours to walk into Florence and get an early train to Milan. In planning for our escape from Campo 27 I had remembered that an express train for Milan was due to leave at 6 a.m., and that was the one I hoped to catch.

I dressed as silently as possible putting one shoe in each trouser pocket where they would not be in my way, and at

N

3 a.m., in my stockinged feet, I swung my legs over into the darkness and found the ledge with my toes. Holding on to the shutter outside the window with one hand I started to move sideways to the left, flattening myself against the wall as much as possible. I had not gone more than a few steps when an attack of giddiness seized me, and I quickly went back just managing to clutch on to my shutter again. My knees were shaking and teeth chattering with excitement as I climbed back into my bedroom.

Ten minutes went by while I recovered my breath and my nerve. An occasional grunt came through the door from the carabinieri or a squeak from his chair as he shifted his seat, but otherwise the night was silent. My imagination kept telling me that I might slip off the ledge, or it might crumble under my weight. But I knew I must do it. This was my chance; I might never get another one.

Once again I tiptoed to the window and without looking downwards, levered myself out and slowly slithered my feet down the wall on to the ledge. This time I was not going to get back into the room and to make sure of it, I swung the outside shutters across the window, and I heard a click from the latch on the inside.

I had always meant to do this to keep the Italians guessing how I had got out, but on my first try I had forgotten all about it in my excitement. I had bought some particularly obnoxious and sticky hair oil whilst in the hospital, and I had used this to lubricate all the hinges and catches on the shutters and on the lavatory door, to stop any squeaks.

There was no going back now. I held on to the closed shutter with my right hand and slid as far as I could along the ledge. My left hand could not reach the shutter over the next window but I forced myself on and inch by inch moved along the ledge. I wanted to press against the rough wall as tightly as possible, but if I did this it made a scraping noise which might alarm some wakeful patient.

After six feet with nothing to hang on to, I reached the next lot of shutters and using them as hand holds, quickly passed under the window. I then came to the worst part of the ledge, where it went round the corner of the building out of reach of all shutters. Again I had to leave go with my right hand and move spreadeagled to the corner. Here the finger-tips of my left hand were able to follow the wall around and give slightly more security. At the same moment the ledge under my left foot suddenly felt loose, and I had visions of the whole corner of the building breaking away. All at once my giddiness returned and I felt sweat slowly trickling down the side of my nose. My knees shook, but I held them still by pressing against the wall, while I gingerly transferred my weight to my other foot and felt around with my left toe to see what was loose. Something was very wobbly right on the corner and looking down I could just see that the cement surface was quite free and if dislodged, a three-foot length would crash into the courtyard below. The moulding underneath the surface felt solid enough. It made a gritting noise as it wobbled and felt very insecure, but I slowly worked my way round the corner and then along a short length of wall to another corner, which was an inside one and much easier. A few more yards and I was under the lavatory window.

I heaved myself up and dropped on to the lavatory floor where I stood for a minute or two to get my breath. Never have I felt so relieved as I did when I had finished that awful traverse along the face of the building in pitch darkness. Never do I want to do anything like it again. It might have been child's play to an expert mountaineer, but I was not one.

Cautiously peering round the corner of the lavatory door I saw the carabinieri awake and looking disconsolately at the ground in front of his chair. I saw that, if I crossed the passage to the other side before moving along opposite the doorway to the stairs, he could not see me if he looked up. All went well and soon I was standing opposite to the doorway leading down the stairs. There was not enough room for me to get through and I prayed and hoped that it would not squeak when I opened it a further few inches. The door opened without a murmur and, like a flash, I passed down the stairs without the carabinieri knowing what was happening. I would have a clear five hours' start till about 8 a.m. when I was called, and by that time I hoped to be well on the way to Milan. In case the carabinieri put his head inside my room during the remainder of the night, I had rolled up a greatcoat to look like me in bed, and I was confident it would pass all right for any casual look.

Creeping down the stairs I arrived at the bottom, and

dropped into the courtyard through an open window on the ground floor. I rather misjudged the height because I landed on the paving stones on all fours and severely strained my wrist in the process. I crept round the outside of the hospital and then through an allotment and so came to the wall bordering the main road where I put on my shoes. I also pulled out a brown paper parcel from my trouser seat, which I planned to carry instead of a bag to give me the necessary *raison d'être*. It was five minutes to four, and at four o'clock precisely I swung over the wall and started to walk down the main road towards Florence.

XX.

ESCAPE INTO RUSSIA

from

No Citation

By JAMES ALLAN

James Allan, a Corporal in the Military Police, was
wounded during the retreat to Dunkirk, captured, and taken
to a P.O.W. camp at Torun in German-occupied Poland.

Determined to escape, he thought at first of copying his
hero, Monte Cristo, and tunnelling his way out; later, how-
ever, he decided that a simpler plan would probably work
better. So he got put on an outside working-party and kept
his eyes open. On 17 December, 1940, his chance came while
the party was digging up bombs near a wood. He and his pal,
Harry Clark, a Canadian, had made up their minds to make
a break together, so when a German guard was photograph-
ing the prisoners, Allan hit him with his spade, and he and
Clark ran for the wood.

Allan eventually reached Russian territory alone. It was
the beginning of a long nightmare in Russian gaols, for he
was suspected of being a spy. However, after Russia entered
the war, he was finally released and brought home with the
Allied Mission that was in Moscow at the time. Back home
he wrote the story of his experiences, but was forbidden
under wartime security regulations to publish it, and for
twelve years it lay in a cupboard in his Yorkshire home.

James Allan was awarded the D.C.M., *but the award was*
published in the London Gazette *and in his unit's Part II*
Orders without a citation. Though there is no doubt that he
was decorated for his courage while in Russian hands, this
has never been officially admitted.

I HAD decided what to do and there was no time to consult
Clark. My nerve was at breaking point, and though I did not
like to do it even to a German, I gripped my spade, took one
bound forward, and felled him with a single blow from the
shovel. Not one of the men in the group had made a movement to show that they saw me coming.

In a flash Clark and I were sprinting for the long grass and the wood. Whether any of the others tried to escape I shall never know, but if they did none of them headed in our direction. Clark was just ahead of me as we pounded away. I felt elated, and despite heavy boots and tiredness due to the tension, I seemed to travel like a bird from a cage. I soon caught up with Clark, and, sticking to the trees, we ran on and on without speaking.

We ran for what seemed like hours. We had no idea of direction, all that mattered was that we should put as great a distance as we could between us and the prison camp before we were forced to stop for a rest. This was not easy without roads to guide us, but I noted the position of the sun in relation to the camp, and that enabled us to keep going without the risk of finding ourselves back at Torun.

Across fields and through plantations we went, avoiding all buildings. Finally, I pitched myself full length in a clearing among the trees and Clark dropped beside me. For about five minutes we could not speak. We lay there gasping and wheezing, taking great gulps of air. My heart raced like a trip-hammer and the stitch in my side throbbed painfully. When I got my breath back I sat up and looked round. "Well, we made it," I said, "but I don't know where the hell we are."

Clark propped himself up on his elbows. "They're sure to have a search party out by now," he said in his Canadian drawl. "Reckon we'll have to keep movin' even if we don't know where we're going."

He looked up at the tall trees around us. "I could climb one of these," he said, "and have a look over the country-side."

I thought this was a good idea, so when we had rested for a few minutes longer, I gave him a leg up to the lower branches, and soon he was scrambling upwards high above me. Once near the top I saw him looking in all directions. I waited impatiently while he came down slowly and precariously. "What did you see?" I demanded.

"Not a bloody thing," he replied. He explained that the fields and woods stretched away in every direction. The only signs of life were a few cottages and wooden shacks.

We stayed in the clearing a little longer, talking in low voices about our plans. We agreed that for the time being our main object must be simply to avoid capture. Then, in a day or two, when the hunt for us would probably have died down, we could begin to think about our ultimate destination. We set off again at a fast walking pace, then after about half an hour met an elderly Polish woman wearing a shawl over her black dress and a scarf round her head.

Her face was the colour of parchment and deeply wrinkled. She was obviously afraid as soon as she saw us, and my few German phrases and involved signs asking if she had any food upset her even more. She hurried past us as fast as she could, without saying a word.

We pushed on, through plantations and over more fields, meeting no one else until we were just on the fringe of a particularly thick forest. There I spotted a woman walking along the edge of the plantation in our direction. We were both worried as to what kind of treatment we could expect from civilians. We were in the German minority part of Poland, but it did occur to me that the true Poles would have little love for the Nazis. I decided that this time I would not speak in German.

The woman proved to be an attractive girl of about eighteen or twenty. We smiled at her so that she would not be scared, then I pointed at myself and Clark.

"English," I said. "British Army. Escaped. Free. From Torun prison." I pointed in the direction of the camp. At first she seemed baffled. I repeated the words and made gestures of breaking out of something.

I think she must have understood that we were escaped prisoners, for she beckoned and turned off into the wood. We followed warily, fearing a trick, but she led us to a secluded clearing and indicated that we were to wait there until she returned. When she had vanished into the trees Clark and I agreed that we should hide somewhere nearby in case she brought troops or the police. She seemed genuinely friendly, but we could not afford to trust anyone.

About twenty minutes later she was back, with a basket on her arm. She looked round the clearing, but we stayed in hiding for a minute or two longer to make sure that she was on her own.

No one else appeared, so we walked into the clearing again. The girl smiled when she saw us, put the basket on the ground and began to empty it. She had brought meat, bread, cigarettes, matches, sugar and eggs.

Later we realized that this must have been a considerable sacrifice because most of the Poles were very short of food. We thanked her as best we could, and I tried to ask whether she could get us any old clothes, but she did not understand. It was essential that we should get a change, and I felt horribly conspicuous in my red breeches. The girl smiled, said a few words in Polish which probably meant 'Goodbye and good luck,' picked up her basket, and left us. We had been unable to find out from her where we were or which direction we should take.

It was nearly dusk, and I suppose the most sensible thing would have been to push on as hard as we could until dark. But the sight of food was too much for us. We sat down on the grass and made a good meal of the meat and eggs. There was nothing we could do with sugar, but we did not throw it away. For the first time since the Germans took over the hospital at Boulogne, my hunger was really curbed. It was a rare feeling of contentment which followed that meal. Afterwards we lay on our backs and puffed cigarettes.

The excitement of the escape began to wear off, and as we lay there, watching the sky darken, we realized for the first time that the weather, though dry, was cold. We dare not light a fire. The huge areas of trees around us were obviously not wild forests. They were plantations, carefully graded according to size and set out in close neat order. It seemed certain that there would be forest wardens or keepers to guard against fire and pests, so even in the thickest trees we could not be completely at ease.

I had a very rough idea of where Torun lay and I knew that we could make our way south to Rumania, or head east and get into Russian-occupied Poland. Clark and I discussed the various merits and demerits of these countries, but we finally decided against Rumania because we remembered that to get there would mean crossing the Carpathian mountains.

"Russia seems to be our bet," I whispered.

"Yeah, but how do we get there when we don't know where we're starting from?" asked Clark. He had me there. "And what will the Russians do with us?"

I pointed out that Russia was a neutral country. At the

worst we could expect to be interned for the duration of the war; at the best we might be handed over to the British Ambassador and returned to England. We agreed on Russia.

That night we had to sleep in the forest. It was bitterly cold, and we divided the time into two-hour watches. In fact, we were both awake two-thirds of the time, stamping about and flinging our arms around our shoulders to keep warm.

At dawn the next day we worked out our position by the sun. We discovered that we must have been heading west from Torun, a route that would eventually take us back to Germany. Now, of course, we wanted to go east, but that would mean going back towards the camp and taking a foolish risk of running straight into the arms of any search party. The only thing to do was to go southwards until there was a safe distance between us and the camp, then turn north-east and make for Russian-occupied Poland as fast as we could.

We decided that we must keep to the fields and plantations, avoiding all towns and villages. We could not risk begging for food, so anything we ate would have to be stolen or found. Thus began a nine-day trek during which we travelled in a huge arc, covering about 120 miles and ending up on the banks of the River Vistula about fifty miles south of Torun.

For the second day of our trek Clark and I kept up a good walking pace through the seemingly endless plantations. We drank from streams—and bathed our feet in them. About mid-afternoon the effects of the meal we had eaten the previous evening had worn off, and we were both hungry. While crossing some open grassland we saw a herd of cows.

"A drink of milk would be better than nothing," said Clark, "if we had anything to drink out of."

My thoughts went back to my boyhood, when I spent a great deal of time on a farm in Yorkshire.

"Why worry about that?" I asked. "Come on, and I'll show you how it's done."

I singled out a cow that looked a bit plumper than the rest and made sure she was ready for milking. Clark looked at me in the manner of a man determined to be tolerant with someone who was obviously to be pitied.

"Lie down there on your back," I told him, pointing to a place within range of the udder.

"What the hell . . ." he began. Then he shrugged his shoulders and got down. I began to milk the cow, and soon a stream of white liquid was shooting into Clark's open mouth.

Some of it went slightly adrift, of course, and once he accused me of deliberately squirting in his eye, but he got a good drink of milk. Teaching him to do the same thing for me was more difficult. He had never milked a cow before, and the beast soon realized that she was in inexperienced hands. After a few false starts, I got a drink too. This 'straight from cow to consumer' system became one of our staple methods of feeding.

That night we found a barn to sleep in. It was remote from any farmhouse or cottage, and we removed some boards from the back of it as an escape route, in case anyone came in. There were some sacks inside, and we managed to have a fairly warm and restful night, keeping watch and sleeping alternately. We moved out as soon as it was light the next morning, hungry as usual.

On the open ground was a tantilizing sight. Mushrooms were growing in tens of thousands, like a ghostly grey carpet. But we had no idea which were edible, and there seemed to be dozens of different kinds.

By midday we were so hungry that we decided to risk asking at a cottage for food. After all, we might be lucky and strike a family who hated the Germans as much as we did. It was decided that I should knock at the door while Clark hid nearby in case of trouble.

We reached the edge of a plantation and across a field saw about five tiny cottages. An old man came out of one of them and began to walk towards us. It was safer to tackle him than knock at a door, so Clark hid in the trees while I walked slowly towards the Pole, and when I was near enough called out to him. He was an old man, round-shouldered and thick-set, with a mass of grey hair and a weather-worn face. I tried a few words of German on him, and he seemed to understand, but showed no signs of friendliness.

I hastened to explain that we were English soldiers and as soon as he realized that he grasped my hand and smiled, nodding his head and saying "Good, good," in German. It was not difficult to make him see that we needed food and a change of clothes. I asked him where we were and he said something which sounded like "Pormozy". This, I discovered later, was the Polish province of Pomorze.

He made for the cottages again at about double the speed of his approach. When he was out of sight I returned to where Clark was hiding and told him of my success.

Nevertheless, we both remained hidden until he returned. We could see he was carrying clothes and food. There was no one else in sight so we emerged from our hiding-place.

The clothes he had brought were old and decrepit, but to us they were more valuable than blue mink. He had also brought a loaf of bread and a big chunk of cheese. We thanked him as best we could, shaking his hand and clapping him on the back. Then we doubled back among the trees until we were about a mile from where we had met him.

First we made a meal of the bread and cheese. Then we stripped off our clothes and dressed in those the old man had brought. While I was standing there nearly naked, and Clark was pulling on a pair of trousers, there was a sudden scuffling noise in the trees nearby. There followed a sound like someone running. I grabbed all the clothes I could and prepared to bolt, naked into the trees; but before I could move Clark burst into a roar of laughter. A wild pig charged across the clearing, almost knocking my legs from under me, and vanished again into the trees at the other side.

I was still wearing my hospital bed-socks and pyjamas for underclothing. I picked out a brown jacket, a blue striped shirt and a pair of tattered grey trousers. The trousers fitted quite well, but the jacket was very tight across the shoulders and its sleeves far too short. Clark had a similar pair of trousers and a painter's jacket, splashed here and there with the bright traces of its former owner's trade. We took the opportunity of renewing the fight against lice, but it was as rewarding as trying to count grains of sand. We tore our former clothes to shreds and buried them; I was glad to see the last of those red breeches.

The next day, the third since we had escaped, was uneventful. The only human beings we saw were woodsmen—and women—at work in the forest, cutting and sawing trees. We also glimpsed a man we took to be a forest warden, wearing a dark-blue tunic.

On the fourth day we had two pieces of luck. Skirting the fringe of a farm, we noticed some hen-cotes, and Clark decided that he would risk taking a few eggs. His idea was to take them from the nests. But when we got near we saw a basket full of eggs on a ledge near one of the cotes.

At almost the same moment we spotted a man, presumably the owner of the farm, watching us from a distance. We stopped and looked at him. He never moved. Clark walked forward and picked up the basket. Still the man stayed where he was. So we made off with the eggs as hard as we could go. I can only think that he must have been scared of us.

Raw eggs are not the most palatable of foods, but we ate them without a pause and threw away the basket.

My feet were beginning to get very sore and blistered. Neither Clark nor I had shaved for about a week, and our hair was getting matted and straggly. Twice a day we had to have de-lousing parades, when we picked the creatures from our hair and bodies in their thousands. The weather was getting colder, especially at night, and unless we were lucky enough to find a barn, sleep was almost impossible.

Later that same day we came upon another farmhouse, bigger than any we had seen so far. A careful prowl round convinced us that there was no one in, so we knocked on the door to make sure. No one answered. I tried the door, and it opened at a touch. Clark hid outside while I went in to find food. Hanging over an old-fashioned range in the kitchen was a side of bacon. At first I was tempted to grab it whole. But the Poles had been so good to us that I felt a twinge of conscience. I found a knife on a rough kitchen table, and cut a big slice off the bacon, leaving the rest where it was.

I glanced round, but could see no other food. On the table, however, I noticed a newspaper. I opened it out and turned the pages, more out of idle curiosity than anything else. At the top of one page was a map, which I soon realized showed the very part of Poland through which we were travelling, as well as a section of Russian-occupied territory. This was just what we needed. I tore it out, stuffed it in my pocket, and rejoined Clark.

From the map we learned that Torun is on the River Vistula, and that we must get back to the river as the first stage of our journey to Russia. We agreed that after another day of heading south it would be safe to turn east towards the land where we felt we would find freedom.

That night we tried to chew the raw bacon, but it was so tough that our jaws were tired before we had reduced even a small piece to a state in which it could be swallowed. We had the matches given to us by the Polish girl, but still we dare not light a fire.

The following morning, about an hour after we had set off again carrying the bacon, we saw another shack across the fields. I suggested knocking at the door to see if it was empty and Clark agreed. We crossed several cultivated fields as we approached it, and between us collected several pounds of potatoes and a cabbage. It was arranged that Clark should hide while I went to the door. There was no answer to my knock, so I rejoined him and suggested that I should go inside and try to cook the food. He would signal any danger from outside by whistling.

It was vital to be especially careful, because this house was one of many requisitioned by the Germans. It had a notice by the door which I could translate roughly as saying: "This is a German house for a German family." Its former Polish owners had probably been taken to Germany for forced labour in mines or factories.

The house was crudely furnished and poorly decorated. I found the kitchen, which contained an old tripod stove with a fire burning under it. On top was a metal sheet with a round hole in it so that a pan or kettle could be heated from the fire inside without actual contact with the coals.

The only utensil I could find was a huge iron kettle. I poured some water into it from a pail, pushed the bacon, potatoes and cabbage inside, and put it on the stove. The water was soon boiling, and to a man as hungry as I was, the smell proved mouth-watering. Occasionally I stirred this strange stew with a spoon and listened carefully for any signal from Clark.

The whistle came before our meal was fully cooked. In my excitement as I grabbed the kettle, my foot caught a corner of the stove and overturned it. I fled from the house holding the steaming stew in front of me and ran after Clark, who was already part way up a slope crowned by a thick wood. I was exhausted by the time I reached the top and the safety of the trees. We both had a good laugh at my presence of mind in remembering the kettle. Then we looked down at the house.

A thick funnel of smoke was rising from it, and every moment or two it threw out a shower of sparks. The over-turned stove had set it alight. We could see the owner, whose return had caused Clark to raise the alarm, standing nearby. If it had been a Polish house we would have been sorry. But we had no pity to waste on Germans.

"Just a few cents off our account with the Hun," smiled Clark, as we tucked into the stew by scooping it out of the kettle with our hands.

Somehow we found the Vistula. Just how we did it has never been clear to me. Our navigation was extremely crude, we had no idea where we were most of the time, and we dare not ask anyone the way. We also had the good fortune never to meet any German troops or police, and the Poles helped us all they could.

Put it down to sheer luck if you like, but on the tenth day after our escape we found ourselves on the banks of a wide river that could only be the Vistula. We knew that we must cross the river and continue east, but the immediate problem was to find somewhere to sleep. We had left the plantations behind, and the land by the river at this point was open and flat. We followed the river northwards a little way, but by dusk we had still seen no suitable place to rest.

We sat down on the bank to discuss our next move. While we were talking we saw a man coming our way along the bank. He had already seen us, so we got up and began to walk towards him. He was a Pole of about twenty or twenty-two, slim and dark-haired, with a face full of personality. We were able to tell him that we were English and that we did not understand Polish. He tried us with French and Esperanto, but we understood neither, and he did not understand German.

He seemed friendly, but we had to treat everyone with suspicion. He gave us some cigarettes and ersatz honey, and we began to think he was a genuine friend. I learned later that his name was Zenon, and that he was a member of the Polish Underground Movement. The three of us sat down and tried for about half an hour to talk by signs and isolated Polish phrases which Clark and I had picked up.

When it was nearly dark several more Poles joined us. Their object, like ours, seemed to be to cross the river. As far as I could make out they were waiting for some signal from the opposite bank to show that it was safe to cross, but no signal came. The reason for their precautions I learned later, was that all Poles were supposed to be indoors by 7 p.m.

Eventually two Poles went away and returned with bread and milk for all of us. We sat eating and drinking in the dark. Clark and I were both convinced by now that these were genuine friends, so we had no qualms about going with them to a nearby house, where there were more men. Zenon explained to them who we were and did his best to describe our adventures. One or two of the Poles spoke a little German, and with their help Zenon was able to tell us that he knew a British agent in Warsaw. The name he gave was as British as John Brown.

All evening Clark and I watched for any signs that the Poles might betray us, but there was none. They made no attempt to tell us that they were working for the Underground, and I did not discover this until weeks later. That night we slept on the floor of a bare upstairs room in the house. Next morning Zenon indicated that if I went with him he would get me across the Vistula by boat. I assumed that he was taking us one at a time for safety's sake.

We crossed in a small rowing-boat, and at the other side he led me to a small bungalow with a big garden and there handed me over to an old man. I thought he had gone back to bring Clark, but I learned afterwards that Zenon had taken him straight to Warsaw. Why he left me behind I never found out. Perhaps it was because the two of us together would have been too conspicuous.

The bungalow where Zenon left me was in a tiny village and belonged to the old man, whose name was Tolek Zaminsky. I guessed he was about eighty, and learned that before the revolution he had been a wealthy businessman in Russia. With him lived his wife, who was about sixty, a son named Tolek, and a daughter Ilka, who was later to be killed by the Germans. The whole family made me very welcome and insisted that I should have a room to myself, though the bungalow only contained three rooms and a kitchen.

My room was really little more than a bare box with an iron bedstead, but to a man who had slept rough for so long, it seemed like a palace. I had a wash in hot water, shaved off my stubble, and started a determined drive to conquer the lice. That night, as I lay in my bed, hungry no longer and warm as I could wish, I felt that it could not be long before I was in my own bed at home.